# Cables Under Fire

AF517069

# Cables Under Fire

## How the Seabed Became the Front Line

*By*

*Dalia Aouni*

Vij Books

New Delhi (India)

*Published by*

**Vij Books**
(Publishers, Distributors & Importers)
4836/24, 3rd Floor, Ansari Road
Delhi – 110 002
Phone: 91-11-43596460
Mobile: 98110 94883
e-mail: contact@vijpublishing.com
www.vijbooks.in

Copyright © 2026

ISBN: 978-81-99802-63-6 (PB)

All rights reserved.

No part of this publication may be reproduced, distributed, or transmitted in any form or by any means — including photocopying, recording, or other electronic or mechanical methods — without the prior written permission of the publisher, except in the case of brief quotations used in reviews or permitted by applicable copyright law.

This book was developed using advanced writing tools to support the drafting and ideation process. All content has been thoughtfully curated, refined, and reviewed to ensure quality and relevance.

# Contents

# Introduction

At dawn, somewhere beyond the horizon, a ship slows to a halt. Its crew are not fishermen, nor sailors bound for a port, but technicians staring at screens that show a problem they cannot yet see. Thousands of metres below them, on a seabed few humans will ever witness, something has gone wrong. There is no smoke, no explosion, no siren. Yet within minutes, a trading desk half a world away hesitates, a video call stutters, a government network reroutes traffic with a faint but measurable delay. The disturbance is subtle, almost polite. That is precisely what makes it dangerous.

We live with an image of the internet that is light, ethereal, and largely imaginary. Data floats in clouds. Messages leap invisibly from pocket to pocket. Distance has been abolished, friction dissolved. The metaphors are comforting, and profoundly misleading. Almost every email, payment, search query and streamed image depends on a physical system of extraordinary fragility: fibre-optic cables no thicker than a garden hose, laid across the ocean floor, stitched together by repeaters and landing stations, exposed to weather, geology, human error and human intent. These cables carry the bulk of the world's international data traffic. They are not a backup. They are the backbone.

The paradox at the heart of modern connectivity is easy to state and harder to confront. Governments invest vast sums in cyber defences, encryption standards and digital resilience strategies, yet the physical layer on which all of this rests remains largely out of sight and, too often, out of mind. A malicious line of code can be patched; a compromised server can be isolated. A severed cable, lying silent beneath cold water, cannot be wished back into service. It must be found, lifted, spliced and reburied, a process measured in days or weeks, not milliseconds. In that interval, economies bend, politics intrudes, and assumptions about seamless global connection are tested against the stubborn reality of steel, glass and seabed.

This book begins from that quiet contradiction. It asks why the material foundations of the internet have been excluded from most public conversations about security, resilience and power. It asks who owns these foundations, who protects them, and who bears the risk when they fail. It asks, more uncomfortably, whether the world has mistaken technical sophistication for invulnerability, and whether the ocean floor has become, by default rather than design, a new strategic frontier.

There is nothing new about societies building their futures on infrastructure they barely notice. Roman aqueducts were marvels of engineering and objects of political pride, until they were cut. Telegraph cables once promised to bind empires together, until wars revealed how easily they could be tapped or severed. Railways, pipelines and power grids have all passed through the same cycle: innovation, dependence, invisibility, vulnerability. Subsea cables belong squarely in this lineage. What distinguishes them is not merely their scale, but their invisibility. They do not march across landscapes or dominate skylines. They disappear beneath the waves, crossing jurisdictions and expectations alike, governed by a patchwork of law, custom and commercial contract.

The seabed itself has changed character over the past half-century. Once imagined as empty, remote and largely irrelevant to daily life, it is now crowded with assets that underpin modern civilisation. Energy cables, pipelines, sensors and data links jostle for space with fishing grounds and shipping lanes. Great powers speak once again of maritime competition, but the focus has shifted downward. Control of the sea surface matters; control of the seabed increasingly matters more. This is where economic flows are concentrated, where disruption can be deniable, and where responsibility is easiest to blur.

The urgency of this subject lies not in speculative catastrophe but in accumulated evidence. Cable faults happen every year. Most are mundane: anchors dropped in the wrong place, trawlers dragging heavy gear, storms that shift sediment just enough to expose a vulnerable section. Others are less easily explained. What matters is not that failures occur, but how often they cluster, how unevenly their effects are distributed, and how poorly prepared many societies remain for the consequences. When a single corridor carries the bulk of a region's connectivity, resilience is a comforting story told after the fact.

At the same time, this is not a book about technological doom. The global cable network is one of the great engineering achievements of the modern age, built and maintained by specialists whose work rarely attracts attention precisely because it usually succeeds. Data finds its way around damage. Traffic is rerouted. Redundancy absorbs shocks. The system bends far more often than it breaks. The problem is not that the network is weak, but that its strengths are uneven, its incentives misaligned, and its risks poorly understood outside a narrow circle of operators and engineers.

To understand why this matters, it helps to pause on a simple image that will recur throughout this book. Imagine the world's digital connectivity not as a cloud, but as a series of narrow bridges crossing deep water. Some bridges are wide and well maintained, with multiple lanes and careful monitoring. Others are narrow, crowded and ageing, built when traffic was lighter and expectations lower. Most travellers never see the bridge they are crossing, let alone choose it. They only notice when something goes wrong. The question this book pursues is not whether bridges should exist, but how many we rely on without realising, and what happens when several fail at once.

The story of subsea cables is, at heart, a story of trade-offs. Fibre beats satellite links on capacity, latency and cost for long-distance traffic, but it demands physical presence in hostile environments. Commercial models reward efficiency and speed to market, while national security logic favours dispersion and redundancy. Coastal communities welcome landing stations for jobs and investment, yet may inadvertently create chokepoints of national significance. Legal frameworks promise protection, but enforcement lags behind technical reality. None of these tensions has a neat resolution. They must be managed, not wished away.

This book takes the reader beneath the surface, both literally and figuratively. It explains how the global cable network is laid out, why routes follow certain paths and avoid others, and how political boundaries intersect with geological ones. It demystifies the engineering without reducing it to jargon, showing how cables are designed, powered, monitored and repaired. It traces the pattern of threats, from earthquakes to fishing gear to deliberate interference, not as isolated anecdotes but as recurring features of a system under strain.

Equally important, it examines the human and institutional dimensions that shape outcomes when things go wrong. Repair ships do not sail instantly; they wait for weather windows, permits and priorities to align. Operators negotiate with competitors even as they depend on them. Governments weigh public reassurance against operational secrecy. Businesses discover, often too late, that their carefully designed digital architectures converge on the same physical routes as everyone else's. In each case, vulnerability is not a single point of failure but a network of decisions made over years.

The historical perspective matters because it tempers both alarmism and complacency. Cables have always been targets in wartime and bargaining chips in diplomacy. What has changed is the density of dependence. When nineteenth-century telegraph cables were cut, messages slowed; ships still sailed, factories still ran. When modern fibre systems fail, entire categories of economic activity can pause. High-frequency trading, cloud computing, real-time collaboration and remote healthcare all assume a baseline of connectivity that is rarely questioned until it falters.

There is also a cultural dimension to this dependence. The language of the digital age encourages abstraction. We speak of platforms, ecosystems and virtual spaces, as if value had been liberated from place. Subsea cables insist on the opposite. They are rooted in geography, constrained by depth, sediment and slope, and exposed to the behaviour of ships and states. They remind us that power, even when exercised through code, ultimately rests on control of physical systems.

One of the aims of this book is to make that physicality legible. Not to overwhelm the reader with technical minutiae, but to cultivate an informed intuition. To know why certain straits recur in discussions of vulnerability. To understand why landing stations cluster, and why that clustering matters. To grasp why redundancy on paper may collapse into concentration on the seabed. Once seen, these patterns are difficult to unsee. They change how one reads headlines about outages, naval exercises or corporate investments in new routes.

Another aim is to bridge conversations that are too often siloed. Engineers talk to engineers, lawyers to lawyers, strategists to strategists. The seabed does not respect these divisions. A cable cut can trigger contractual disputes, diplomatic exchanges and market reactions simultaneously. Effective resilience depends on understanding how these layers interact, and where incentives clash. This book therefore moves deliberately between technical explanation, legal context, strategic analysis and organisational practice, not to flatten differences but to show how they compound.

The question of intent looms large but must be handled with care. It is tempting to frame every disruption as an attack, every fault as a hostile act. That temptation serves no one. Accidents remain the dominant cause of damage, and overreaction can create its own risks. Yet it would be equally naive to ignore the strategic logic that makes subsea infrastructure attractive as a target. Damage that is ambiguous can be politically useful. Attribution is hard. Responses are constrained. The seabed offers opportunities for signalling and coercion that sit uneasily between peace and war.

This ambiguity is not a future problem. It is a present one. Naval doctrines evolve. Surveillance technologies improve. Private companies lay cables with ever greater capacity, often backed by state interests or strategic calculations. The line between commercial asset and national infrastructure blurs, sometimes deliberately. In this environment, resilience is as much about governance and trust as it is about steel and glass.

The book is structured to reflect this progression from dependence to risk to response. It begins by grounding the reader in why subsea cables matter, stripping away the myth of a wireless world. It then maps the global network, not as a static diagram but as a living system shaped by history, commerce and politics. It opens the black box of cable construction and operation, before turning to the spectrum of threats and the reality of disruption when it occurs. Case studies anchor these themes in lived experience, showing how outages unfold and what changes, quietly or otherwise, in their aftermath.

From there, the focus shifts to response and design. Repair logistics, redundancy planning and legal frameworks are examined not as abstract principles but as tools with limits. The role of militaries and navies is explored with an eye to both protection and escalation. Ownership, liability and corporate risk bring the discussion back to boardrooms and balance sheets, where many of the most consequential decisions are made. Finally, the book looks forward, not to offer easy solutions, but to chart plausible paths for a seabed that is becoming ever more crowded and contested.

Throughout, the emphasis is on realism. There is no single authority responsible for the global cable network, no switch to throw that will make it secure. Progress will be uneven, incremental and often invisible. Some improvements will be driven by market incentives, others by regulation or strategic concern. Many will be the result of quiet cooperation rather than grand agreements. Understanding this landscape is the first step towards navigating it responsibly.

For individuals, the value of this understanding lies in discernment. To recognise that an outage is not merely a technical glitch, but a symptom of deeper structural choices. For organisations, it lies in better questions: where does our connectivity really run, and what assumptions does it embed? For states, it lies in humility as much as ambition: the recognition that protection cannot be absolute, and that cooperation may be as important as control.

The seabed has always been a place of projection, a canvas for fears and fantasies. What lies beneath has been imagined as monstrous, mysterious or simply empty. Today it is none of these things. It is busy, engineered and increasingly strategic. The cables that cross it are unglamorous, easily overlooked, and indispensable. They do not announce themselves until they fail.

As the chapters that follow will show, the question is not whether the seabed has become a front line. It already has. The more difficult question is whether societies are willing to acknowledge that fact, and to act on it without illusion. What does it mean to defend infrastructure that cannot be fenced, patrolled or fully monitored? How do commercial imperatives align, or clash, with national security goals? How much resilience is enough, and who decides?

These are not questions with final answers. They are questions that must be revisited as technology, politics and the ocean itself change. This book does not promise certainty. It offers clarity, context and a framework for thinking about a hidden system on which the visible world depends. If the internet has taught us anything, it is that what feels weightless often rests on something very solid indeed.

# Chapter 1

# Why Seabed Cables Matter

At 9:17 on an otherwise ordinary weekday morning, a regional internet exchange began to behave oddly. Emails are queued instead of sending. Payment confirmations stalled for a few seconds longer than usual. A live market data feed flickered, then resumed. Most users noticed nothing more than a vague sense of sluggishness, the digital equivalent of traffic thickening without warning. By mid-morning, call centres were fielding complaints, remote workers were restarting routers, and an energy trader postponed a transaction that suddenly felt less time-sensitive than it had ten minutes earlier. The cause was not a cyberattack, nor a software update gone wrong. It was a physical disturbance on the seabed, far from the glass towers where the effects first became visible.

Moments like this rarely make headlines. They do not fit neatly into the dramatic narratives of hacking or blackout. Yet they reveal something essential about how the modern world actually functions. The systems we experience as instant, wireless and immaterial depend on infrastructure that is slow to build, difficult to protect and impossible to virtualise away. When that infrastructure falters, the effects propagate outward, touching services and decisions that were never designed to pause.

The contradiction is stark. We inhabit a culture saturated with wireless imagery, from cloud icons hovering over smartphones to promises of frictionless connectivity untethered from place. At the same time, the overwhelming majority of long-distance data traffic travels through fibre-optic cables laid across the ocean floor. These cables are the arteries of global communication, carrying everything from casual messages to the signals that synchronise financial markets and balance energy grids. To understand why seabed cables matter is to confront the gap between how connectivity is imagined and how it is engineered.

This chapter begins at that fault line. It traces the dependence of everyday services on subsea fibre, not as an abstract technical fact but as a lived economic and social reality. A message sent across a city may never leave dry land; a message sent across a continent almost certainly crosses water. Energy markets, often assumed to be governed by physical flows of fuel and power, rely just as heavily on real-time data streams that coordinate supply, demand and price across borders. When latency increases or capacity tightens, decisions change. Risk is recalculated. Sometimes activity simply stops.

The popular image of a wireless cloud persists because it is useful. It reassures users and simplifies design conversations. It also obscures the reasons fibre remains dominant for long-distance communication. Subsea cables offer vast capacity at comparatively low cost, with latencies that satellites cannot yet match for most applications. Light moving through glass across the seabed arrives sooner, more predictably and in greater volume than signals bounced through orbit. This is not a matter of preference but of physics and economics combined.

Satellites nonetheless occupy a prominent place in public imagination, especially as new constellations promise broader coverage and lower delays than their predecessors. They matter, and they will matter more. But they function best as complements and contingencies, not replacements. When a cable fails, traffic can be shifted to satellite links, buying time and preserving basic connectivity. The trade-offs are immediate. Capacity drops sharply. Costs rise. Latency increases in ways that some applications can tolerate and others cannot. Operators must decide which traffic to prioritise, which services to degrade gracefully, and which to suspend. These are not technical decisions alone; they are economic and sometimes political ones.

Understanding these trade-offs is essential because it reveals why subsea cables have become critical infrastructure in all but name. In many jurisdictions, they remain classified primarily as commercial assets, governed by private contracts and market incentives. This historical framing made sense when international connectivity was a niche service layered atop national networks. It makes far less sense in a world where cloud computing, cross-border payments and remote work are foundational to economic activity. The treatment of cables within critical national infrastructure frameworks varies widely, reflecting different political cultures, regulatory philosophies and threat perceptions.

Consider two coastal states with similar levels of connectivity and exposure. One integrates cable routes and landing stations into its national risk assessments, funds monitoring and coordinates closely with operators. The other leaves protection largely to market actors, intervening only after disruption occurs. Both may enjoy years of uninterrupted service. When incidents happen, however, the difference in preparation becomes visible. Investment patterns diverge. Repair priorities shift. Public communication takes on a different tone. Policy choices, often made quietly, shape resilience long before a fault appears on a dashboard.

For most people, these dynamics remain invisible until they intersect with daily routines. A typical day now involves dozens of interactions that depend on seabed fibre without ever announcing that fact. A contactless payment authorisation, a streamed briefing, a cloud-based medical record accessed by a clinician, a government database queried to verify identity. Each transaction traverses layers of infrastructure, some local, some national, some global. The user experiences a single action; the system executes a choreography of signals that may cross multiple borders and multiple oceans.

It is only when something interrupts that choreography that dependence becomes tangible. During a regional outage, remote workers discover that redundancy assumed at the application level converges on the same physical route. Video conferences degrade from high definition to audio only. Secure connections time out. Productivity slips not because work cannot be done, but because it cannot be coordinated. The loss is incremental rather than catastrophic, which makes it easier to dismiss and harder to address. Yet accumulated over hours and days, such friction carries real economic and social cost.

The chapter also situates subsea cables within a broader transformation of the maritime domain. The seabed is no longer a peripheral space, loosely governed and lightly used. It is an increasingly contested environment where commercial, environmental and strategic interests overlap. Shipping lanes intersect with energy corridors. Data cables run alongside power interconnectors and pipelines. Activities that once took place on the surface now extend downward, driven by technology and necessity.

This crowding has strategic consequences. Great-power rivalry has returned to the seas, but not only in the form of visible naval deployments. It plays out through surveillance, signalling and the quiet testing of thresholds. Hybrid tactics exploit the ambiguity inherent in undersea incidents. A damaged cable can be framed as accident, negligence or provocation, depending on context and narrative. Responses must be calibrated without clear attribution, a challenge that favours caution and rewards those willing to operate in grey zones.

A suspected cable incident can trigger a chain of actions that has little to do with the immediate technical problem. Naval patrols adjust their patterns. Diplomatic channels activate. Public statements are crafted to reassure without accusing. Markets watch for hints of escalation. The physical damage may be minor; the signalling around it can be anything but. In this sense, seabed cables have become instruments not only of connection but of strategic communication.

None of this implies that the ocean floor is on the brink of constant conflict. The majority of cable damage remains accidental, and cooperation between operators and states is routine and often effective. What has changed is the context in which accidents are interpreted and managed. In a more tense international environment, even mundane events acquire sharper edges. The same anchor drag that once prompted a repair invoice can now prompt questions about intent.

This chapter does not seek to inflate these risks beyond proportion. Its purpose is to recalibrate attention. To show why subsea cables deserve a place in discussions about economic security, technological resilience and maritime governance. To explain why treating them as invisible utilities is no longer tenable, if it ever was. And to do so without collapsing into either technological determinism or strategic melodrama.

The themes introduced here will recur throughout the book. The tension between physical fragility and systemic importance. The mismatch between commercial logic and collective risk. The challenge of governing infrastructure that is simultaneously private, transnational and essential. The motif of invisibility, not as a poetic flourish but as a practical problem, runs through each of these discussions. What is unseen is easily under-protected; what is taken for granted is rarely designed for stress.

By the end of this chapter, the reader should see the internet differently. Not as a weightless abstraction, but as a layered system anchored to specific places, routes and decisions. The goal is not to induce anxiety, but to cultivate informed curiosity. To understand why a cable landing in a quiet coastal town can matter as much as a data centre in a capital city. To recognise why debates about satellites, redundancy and protection are not technical sideshows, but central to how modern societies function.

The chapters that follow will delve deeper into maps, machines, threats and responses. They will unpack how cables are built and run, how they fail, and how they are repaired. They will examine case studies where disruption has revealed strengths and weaknesses in stark relief. But all of that rests on a simple premise established here: that seabed cables matter because they are where the digital world meets the physical one.

Once that premise is accepted, new questions follow naturally. How well do we actually understand the routes that carry our data? Who decides where resilience is added and where it is deferred? What does protection mean in an environment that cannot be fully observed or controlled? The answers are neither straightforward nor comforting. They are, however, necessary. And they begin with seeing the seabed not as a blank space beneath our feet, but as a vital, vulnerable and increasingly consequential part of the modern world.

## From email to energy markets

On 26 December 2006, a magnitude-7.0 earthquake struck off Hengchun, at Taiwan's southern tip. Within minutes, multiple subsea cables on the seabed of the Luzon Strait failed. Chunghwa Telecom reported severe disruption across East Asia; traders in Hong Kong and Singapore watched international circuits collapse; call centres in India went dark. The sea was calm above. Below, the network fractured. Five words mattered that morning: *latency rose. Capacity vanished.*

The event did not destroy data centres or topple exchanges. It slowed them, then starved them of routes. Email queues lengthened. Market feeds fell behind. Banks postponed settlements because confirmation could not be guaranteed. The cause lay hundreds of kilometres away, invisible and mechanically indifferent to the urgency it had created. A physical shock had rippled into economic behaviour.

The paradox is simple and measurable. More than 95 per cent of intercontinental data travels by fibre-optic cable, not by satellite, a figure reported repeatedly by TeleGeography across its annual surveys. Yet the prevailing image of connectivity remains wireless and weightless. Signals appear to leap from phone to phone, from office to office, without touching the ground. They do touch it. Then they cross it. Then they sink.

Begin with the most ordinary act: sending an email. The message leaves a device via radio waves, measured in metres, reaches a base station, and is converted into light travelling through glass. That light is amplified, switched, and routed across terrestrial networks until it reaches a coastline. From there, it enters a cable landing station and disappears beneath the water. Show the path, name the medium, explain the reason: fibre offers orders of magnitude more capacity per pound than any orbital alternative, and latency that remains predictable under load. The implication is behavioural. Services are designed on the assumption that this path exists and performs within tight bounds.

Extend the same logic to energy markets. Electricity cannot be shipped like data, but the markets that coordinate its production and trade are wholly dependent on data flows that cross borders and seas. Day-ahead pricing, imbalance settlement, cross-border capacity allocation—each depends on synchronised clocks and near-real-time information. Nord Pool, the Nordic power market operator, publishes prices at fixed times; generators and suppliers commit based on those signals. When connectivity degrades, decisions do not stop. They become conservative. Trades are deferred. Margins widen. Risk is repriced.

This is not theory. In January 2008, damage to multiple cables near Alexandria—SEA-ME-WE 4 and FLAG Europe-Asia among them—reduced capacity across the Middle East and South Asia. Tata Communications reported significant congestion; internet speeds in Egypt fell by more than half, according to measurements later collated by Renesys. Financial firms rerouted traffic at higher cost and delay. Energy traders relying on regional feeds experienced lag that, while short of outage, altered execution. Show the slowdown, name the cables, explain the mechanism: congestion forces packets onto longer paths, increasing round-trip times and jitter. The implication is stress without spectacle.

Why fibre, still? Capacity is the first answer. A single modern cable can carry tens of terabits per second using dense wavelength-division multiplexing. Satellites distribute bandwidth over wide footprints; fibre concentrates it along a route. Cost follows capacity. Once laid, fibre's marginal cost per bit is low. Latency is the third pillar. Light in fibre travels more slowly than in a vacuum, but the path is shorter than a round-trip to orbit. For applications that price milliseconds—high-frequency trading, voice synchronisation, grid balancing—this matters.

A credible counter-example deserves space. Low Earth orbit constellations have dramatically reduced latency and proven their value for resilience and reach. During the 2022 eruption of Hunga Tonga–Hunga Ha'apai, satellite links helped restore basic connectivity to Tonga after the country's sole international cable was severed. The limitation is scale. Satellites carried essential traffic and government communications; they did not replicate the pre-cut bandwidth of fibre. Reconcile the point: satellites buy time and coverage; fibre carries volume and habit.

The image of the cloud persists because it aligns with user experience. Payments clear in seconds. Media streams without pause. Health records appear when called. Behaviour confirms belief. The infrastructure disappears. Until it does not. Consider a typical remote-work morning during a regional slowdown. Video calls downgrade codecs. Authentication retries. Secure tunnels renegotiate. None of these failures announces a cable fault. Each consumes attention and patience. Productivity falls by small percentages that compound across thousands of workers. Measure the behaviour: more retries, fewer concurrent sessions, postponed uploads. Name the cause: constrained international backhaul. Explain the implication: social stress without a single point of blame.

Critical infrastructure frameworks struggle with this subtlety. Roads close visibly; grids trip audibly. Cables fail quietly. Many states still classify them primarily as private communications assets, leaving protection and redundancy to commercial logic. Contrast approaches. Japan, after the 2011 Tōhoku earthquake and tsunami, integrated subsea cable resilience into broader disaster planning, encouraging route diversity and rapid repair access. Elsewhere, equivalent measures lag. Investment follows incentives. Where cables are seen as strategic, redundancy is funded. Where they are not, concentration persists.

The motif worth holding is friction. The modern economy assumes low friction across distance. Subsea fibre is the mechanism by which friction is reduced. When it degrades, friction returns, first as delay, then as cost, finally as choice deferred. Trust—an abstraction—becomes a metric: timeout thresholds exceeded; price spreads widened; service-level credits triggered. Efficiency becomes a decision: reroute at higher latency or wait for repair. Risk becomes a behaviour: trades sized down, systems throttled.

Energy markets provide a sharp illustration because they marry physical scarcity with informational speed. Grid operators rely on telemetry crossing borders to manage frequency and reserve. When international links slow, operators revert to conservative dispatch. Fuel is burned that might have been saved. Emissions rise by increments that never make headlines. The cable does not cause the outcome alone; it constrains the information that would have prevented it.

None of this implies fragility everywhere. The global network is resilient by design, with multiple routes and automatic failover. The limitation lies in geography. Routes cluster where seabeds are favourable and politics permissive. Landings cluster where power and backhaul exist. Show the pattern, name the risk, explain the implication: redundancy on diagrams can converge in water. The quiet failure mode is congestion, not blackout.

The contested seabed sharpens the stakes. Shipping lanes, energy corridors, and data routes intersect. Activity increases. Attribution blurs. A damaged cable near a busy strait can be accident, negligence, or signal. Navies notice. Insurers adjust premiums. Operators file marine notices and wait. Friction rises again.

The test ahead is not whether societies can imagine a world without cables. They cannot. The test is whether they can see, in time, how much depends on them—and decide what delay they are willing to tolerate when glass on the seabed is disturbed. Where does your email go when it slows? What price moves when milliseconds stretch? The answers are measurable. The choices are not.

## Comparing cables and satellites

In February 2022, in Nuku'alofa, Tonga, technicians bolted a dish to a roof and pointed it at the sky. SpaceX's Starlink had delivered user terminals after the 15 January 2022 eruption of Hunga Tonga–Hunga Ha'apai severed the nation's principal subsea cable. The outcome was concrete and immediate: basic connectivity returned for government coordination and essential communications, even as the country's pre-eruption bandwidth remained out of reach for weeks. The sea was still the problem. The sky became the stopgap.

Five words fit the moment: *the backup carried the day.* It also revealed the limit of romance in satellite narratives. When fibre is cut, satellites are not a sentimental alternative to "the cloud". They are triage. They restore enough capacity to speak, coordinate, verify, and pay. They rarely restore enough to pretend nothing happened.

The comparison between cables and satellites is often framed as a rivalry between technologies. That framing misleads. The relationship is closer to that between a motorway and a ferry service: both move people, both matter, but the economics and physics make one the default and the other a contingency. It is not that satellites are inferior in some absolute sense; it is that the long-distance internet has been engineered around the particular advantages of fibre and the particular constraints of radio links.

Begin with what operators measure first: capacity. A modern subsea fibre system can carry traffic in the tens of terabits per second, scaling by adding wavelengths and upgrading terminal equipment at the ends. TeleGeography's annual analyses have repeatedly described subsea cables as the primary conduit for international data, precisely because their aggregate capacity dwarfs satellite backhaul. Show the consequence rather than the slogan: a single hyperscale data centre region can consume multiple terabits per second at peak; a national network can swing by hundreds of gigabits in an evening as streaming and gaming surge. Name the underlying fact: fibre concentrates extraordinary throughput along a fixed path with predictable performance. Explain why: the medium is guided light, shielded from most atmospheric effects, and amplified in-line by repeaters designed for decades of service. The implication is behavioural. Designers assume abundance. Users behave accordingly.

Satellite capacity is real, but it is rationed differently. A satellite must share its total throughput across a footprint, dividing spectrum and power across beams and users. Even high-throughput satellites and modern constellations confront a basic arithmetic: spectrum is finite, and each additional user competes for time, coding, and power. When a cable fails and a region leans on satellite backhaul, the operator does not simply "switch over". They negotiate scarcity. They allocate. They deny. Efficiency becomes a decision visible in network policy: throttling video bitrates, deprioritising software updates, shaping traffic to keep voice and messaging responsive.

Latency is the second measure because it governs what kind of internet a link can carry without strain. The physics are unapologetic. A signal to a geostationary satellite travels roughly 35,786 kilometres up and the same down; the round trip imposes delays that often exceed half a second once processing is included. The International Telecommunication Union has long described such propagation constraints as intrinsic to GEO systems. That latency does not merely make video calls awkward. It changes protocols. It alters the behaviour of TCP congestion control and the cadence of acknowledgements that underpin much of the internet. A connection that "works" for browsing can still fail for interactive trading, remote control systems, and real-time collaboration under load.

Low Earth orbit changes the equation but not the concept. LEO constellations reduce distance dramatically, bringing typical latencies into the tens of milliseconds for many users, often comparable to long terrestrial routes. Performance measurements published by third parties such as Ookla (Speedtest Intelligence reports in the early 2020s) have shown consumer LEO services achieving latencies far below GEO. That is a genuine shift. It is also not a magic wand. LEO performance varies with satellite density, gateway placement, routing policies, and congestion. When an island's fibre is cut, the nearest gateways may not be on that island. Traffic may still traverse long terrestrial paths after it returns to ground. The *budget of milliseconds* becomes a practical constraint again: where do you spend delay, and on which services?

Cost is where the comparison becomes most politically charged, because cost is never just an engineering variable; it is a governance choice. A subsea cable demands heavy capital upfront: marine surveys, permitting, manufacturing, specialist ships, repeaters, landing stations, terrestrial backhaul. Once deployed, the marginal cost per bit is low, and upgrades often occur by replacing equipment at the ends rather than touching the wet plant. Satellite systems distribute cost differently: large capital in space segment and launches, significant ongoing costs in operations, and user terminals that must be manufactured, subsidised, or paid for. For a nation or operator deciding how to connect, the question is rarely "which is cheaper" in abstract. It is "which costs can we commit now, which risks can we bear, and which performance must we guarantee?"

A second named example makes the trade-off concrete. After the 15 January 2022 eruption, the Government of Tonga and regional partners worked to restore connectivity through alternative routes and repairs to the undersea system. Reports from that period describe severe constraints in bandwidth and reliability, even as satellite links supported emergency communications. The measurable behaviour was the rationing of digital life: essential services prioritised, discretionary usage curtailed, expectations reset. Name the lesson: satellites can restore presence; they rarely restore normality. Explain the implication for planning: if a country's digital economy expects cable-class throughput, satellite contingency must be designed as a degraded-but-functional mode, not a seamless substitute.

The common mistake in public debate is to treat "the internet" as a single service with a single performance requirement. Operators see a portfolio of traffic classes with different tolerance for delay and loss. Voice can tolerate modest bandwidth but not long pauses. Payments require reliability and integrity, often with strict timeouts. Cloud-based business applications demand stable latency and low jitter. Streaming video is greedy but forgiving; it can buffer. During a cable cut, this portfolio becomes a survival puzzle. The operator must decide what the nation gets to do.

Picture a simple scenario: a mid-sized island has one main cable and one secondary route with limited capacity. A fault occurs in shallow waters; the main cable is down. Within minutes, traffic reroutes to the secondary path and then to satellite to cover residual demand. The network operations centre watches utilisation hit ceiling. Engineers enforce policies. They reserve satellite bandwidth for emergency services, government coordination, interbank messaging, and DNS resolution. They rate-limit entertainment streaming. They instruct mobile networks to cap video by default. The metric that matters is not ideology but utilisation: how close to saturation is the uplink, and how often does latency breach application thresholds?

Trust becomes visible. Users test the network. They click again. They refresh. They resend. Each act increases load. Efficiency turns into behaviour too: companies postpone large file transfers, schedule batch jobs overnight, and shift meetings to voice-only. Risk becomes a decision taken by financial institutions: do we continue real-time settlement when timeouts spike, or do we widen windows and accept slower reconciliation? No one needs to announce that the seabed has been damaged for these choices to cascade.

Satellites excel at something cables cannot do at all: reach without a shoreline. They connect ships, aircraft, remote mines, polar research stations, and disaster zones where terrestrial infrastructure is absent or destroyed. This is not a minor virtue; it is a strategic capability. It is also why satellites are so often described as a resilience layer. When storms take out towers, when earthquakes break land routes, when conflict makes repairs dangerous, a link from above can be deployed quickly and without trenching. The speed of deployment is the headline. The hidden constraint is that rapid deployment does not change the basic capacity ledger.

Here the credible counter-example is not theoretical; it is operational reality in certain contexts. Some remote communities and industries function primarily on satellite links as their normal state, not as contingency. They organise their digital lives around that constraint: fewer always-on services, more local caching, heavier reliance on asynchronous workflows. The limitation is not that they are "behind", but that their architecture is adapted to scarcity. Reconcile the point: satellites can be primary where demand and design match satellite characteristics; they become strained where cable-era expectations are simply transplanted.

The contested nature of the seabed sharpens the importance of satellites as insurance, but it also exposes a new vulnerability: the insurance itself can become congested or politically contested. Spectrum rights, ground station locations, and the ownership of constellations matter. A cable consortium can be multinational; a satellite network can be subject to the strategic priorities of its operator and the regulatory posture of states that host gateways. The *budget of milliseconds* is joined by a budget of sovereignty. Who can switch on the backup? Under what conditions? With what oversight? These questions do not arise when fibre works quietly. They appear when fibre fails.

None of this diminishes the genuine innovation in modern satellite communications. Phased-array antennas, inter-satellite links, adaptive coding, and mass-produced terminals have changed the practical envelope of what satellites can do. They have improved latency and availability for many users. They have diversified connectivity options for regions historically dependent on a single cable route. But the core comparison remains stubborn: fibre concentrates volume and predictability; satellites distribute reach and speed of deployment. When planners pretend otherwise, they build fragile illusions.

The most honest way to compare the two is to focus on what each makes cheap. Fibre makes bandwidth cheap once installed. Satellites make access cheap where installation is slow or impossible. Fibre makes milliseconds cheap on stable routes. Satellites make presence cheap in contested or remote spaces. When a cable cut forces rerouting to satellite, the operator is not choosing between equals; they are exchanging one kind of cheapness for another, and paying the difference in congestion, prioritisation, and user frustration.

The enduring question, then, is not whether satellites will "replace" seabed cables. The more useful question is diagnostic: when the seabed goes quiet, which activities must continue at full fidelity, which can degrade, and which can wait—and have those priorities been tested against real capacity numbers rather than comforting metaphors?

## Cables as critical infrastructure

On 22 March 2021, the *Ever Given* wedged itself across the Suez Canal. Within hours, maritime insurers, energy traders, and shipping firms recalculated their exposures. Less noticed was a quieter response on land. Network operators checked routes that paralleled the canal and its approaches, verifying redundancy and fault isolation. No cable had been cut. The behaviour still changed. *Designation drives attention.*

That same week, in London, the Cabinet Office published an update cycle for the UK's National Risk Register, an instrument that frames how departments prioritise hazards and funding. Subsea cables appeared, but obliquely, folded into telecommunications risk rather than elevated as assets in their own right (UK Cabinet Office, 2021; updated 2023). In Canberra, by contrast, amendments to the Security of Critical Infrastructure Act were already reshaping how operators of communications assets—including cable landing stations—reported incidents and accepted government oversight (Australian Government, 2018; amended 2021). Two advanced economies. Two treatments. Two outcomes.

Five short words matter here: *what counts gets protected.*

Critical national infrastructure is not a technical category. It is a political one. States decide which systems merit special protection, priority restoration, intelligence attention and, in some cases, military involvement. Roads, electricity grids and water supplies are obvious candidates because failure is visible and immediate. Subsea cables have struggled to cross this threshold, not because they are less essential, but because their failure is quieter and their ownership messier.

Show the reality. A modern economy loses more value per hour from loss of international connectivity than from the closure of a single motorway junction. Name the mechanism. Payments stall, markets widen spreads, cloud services degrade. Explain the puzzle. Cables are privately owned, transnational, and largely out of sight; critical infrastructure frameworks evolved around nationally bounded, publicly legible assets. The implication is structural. What sits outside the frame attracts less funding, fewer drills, and slower escalation when damaged.

Historically, subsea cables were commercial ventures that served state interests indirectly. The first transoceanic telegraph cables of the nineteenth century were laid by private companies under imperial charters. States protected them when convenient and ignored them when not. That pattern persisted into the fibre era. Liberalisation of telecommunications in the late twentieth century reinforced the view that international connectivity was a market service to be competed over, not a strategic asset to be guarded.

This legacy shapes present behaviour. When a cable is damaged, the first calls are between operators and insurers, not defence ministries. Repairs are scheduled through commercial maintenance agreements. Governments monitor, but often at arm's length. Trust—an abstraction—appears as a decision not to intervene. Efficiency shows up as cost-sharing across consortia. Risk becomes a clause in a contract rather than a scenario in a national exercise.

The United Kingdom illustrates this inherited stance. Britain hosts dozens of cable landings, many clustered along the south coast. These routes underpin financial services, media distribution and government communications. Yet subsea cables have historically been treated as part of the telecommunications sector rather than as a discrete class of critical infrastructure. The legal bedrock remains the Protection of Undersea Telegraph Cables Act 1885, a statute designed for a different era. Contemporary policy documents acknowledge dependence but stop short of systematic designation. The visible behaviour follows: protection relies heavily on private security, information-sharing is voluntary, and investment in route dispersion competes with short-term commercial returns.

Australia made a different choice. The Security of Critical Infrastructure Act 2018, expanded significantly in 2021 after a series of cyber and infrastructure concerns, brought telecommunications assets into a tighter regulatory perimeter. Operators of designated assets face mandatory reporting of serious incidents and enhanced government powers to seek information and, in extremis, direct action. Subsea cable landing stations fall within this logic because they are single points where international connectivity meets land. Show the metric. Reporting timelines are measured in hours, not days. Name the effect. Government visibility increases. Explain the implication. Investment decisions begin to factor regulatory expectations alongside market ones.

Neither approach is cost-free. Australia's framework imposes compliance burdens and raises questions about confidentiality and sovereignty when assets are foreign-owned. The UK's lighter touch preserves market flexibility but risks underinvestment in resilience where returns are diffuse. The comparison matters because it demonstrates that "critical" is not a natural property of an asset. It is a status conferred, with consequences.

A credible counter-example tempers the argument. Japan, after the 2011 Tōhoku earthquake and tsunami, strengthened coordination around subsea infrastructure without formal reclassification of cables as a separate critical sector. Instead, it embedded cable resilience within disaster preparedness, port management and private–public coordination. The limitation is scope. This approach works where seismic risk provides a clear organising threat. It is less easily generalised to regions where hazards are political or economic rather than geological. Reconcile the lesson. Formal designation is not the only path, but absence of a path leaves gaps.

The quiet motif running through these cases is *designation*. Once an asset is named as critical, behaviours change. Exercises include it. Budgets reflect it. Intelligence agencies assess threats to it. Naval patrols consider it. Without designation, even severe dependence can coexist with benign neglect.

This matters because subsea cables sit awkwardly at the junction of public interest and private control. A single system may be owned by a consortium spanning continents, financed by hyperscale technology firms, and operated by a specialist company headquartered elsewhere. Efficiency is gained through scale and shared risk. Accountability is diluted. When damage occurs, liability is apportioned commercially even as consequences spill into national life.

Metrics make the abstraction tangible. Mean time to repair is measured in days or weeks, not hours. Spare ship availability is finite. Permitting delays can add days. Each variable is manageable in isolation. Together they define national exposure. Where cables are designated as critical, states can pre-negotiate access, streamline permits, and fund monitoring. Where they are not, every incident becomes an ad hoc negotiation.

The strategic environment intensifies the stakes. As naval planners and security agencies acknowledge that undersea infrastructure is a potential vector for coercion, the line between civilian and strategic asset blurs. Yet critical infrastructure frameworks often lag this recognition because they are built for peacetime governance, not grey-zone competition. The result is a mismatch: high-level concern without low-level authority.

Visible behaviour exposes the gap. After suspicious maritime activity near cable routes, some states issue navigational warnings and quietly increase patrols. Others defer to operators and insurers, treating the matter as an accident until proven otherwise. The difference is not intelligence; it is mandate. Who is authorised to act, and under what legal basis?

Investment follows signals. Where governments articulate subsea cables as critical, operators find it easier to justify additional routes, landing separation, and monitoring costs to shareholders and partners. Where they do not, resilience competes with capacity upgrades that offer clearer returns. Efficiency, again, becomes a choice made under incentive.

There is also a diplomatic dimension. Cables cross jurisdictions. Designation by one state can raise concerns for others, particularly where security powers extend to assets with foreign ownership. Trust must be negotiated. Frameworks that are too heavy-handed risk fragmenting a network that depends on cooperation. Frameworks that are too light risk free-riding on the resilience investments of others.

The unresolved tension is not whether subsea cables matter. That question has been answered by behaviour whenever they fail. The tension is institutional. How much of a system built for commercial efficiency can be absorbed into national security logic without breaking the cooperation that keeps it running? When does designation protect, and when does it deter? The answer will not be uniform. But it will be revealed, one policy choice at a time, by what states decide to count.

## Everyday dependencies on hidden fibre

On 30 January 2008, in Dubai, customers of Etisalat and Du found web pages loading as if through treacle. Call quality deteriorated. Corporate VPNs dropped. The proximate cause lay far from the city's towers: damage to the SEA-ME-WE 4 cable off Alexandria, Egypt, compounded by a separate fault on the FLAG Europe-Asia system. Renesys, a network-monitoring firm, later documented sharp reductions in reachable routes and capacity across the Middle East and South Asia. The concrete outcome was behavioural, not theatrical. Offices reverted to phone trees. Banks throttled non-essential traffic. People waited.

Five words capture the lived moment: *work stopped, but quietly.*

The most unsettling feature of a connectivity shock is how ordinary it looks from the outside. There is no darkness in the streets. Trains still run. Shops remain open. The harm arrives in small delays and failed confirmations—tiny ruptures in the promise that the network is always there. Those ruptures matter because the modern day is stitched together by systems that assume instant verification and remote access. Subsea fibre is the seam. It sits out of sight, doing the unglamorous work of carrying transactions, identities and records between places that have grown comfortable being one another's "elsewhere".

To make this dependence concrete, follow a single day as it is actually lived—by a professional who does not work in telecommunications and has no reason to think about cables. At 07:12, a phone checks for updates, synchronises messages, refreshes a calendar. The visible behaviour is banal: a green tick, a brief vibration, a headline loaded before the kettle boils. Name what is happening under the surface. Authentication requests travel to servers that may sit in another country; content is pulled from caches and, when caches miss, from distant data centres. Explain the implication. Even a local routine relies on long-haul paths often crossing sea. When that path slows, the "snappiness" of modern life dulls.

By 08:05, the same person taps a card at a café. The transaction appears instant because the system has been designed to feel that way. Yet payments are not a single act; they are a sequence of checks and messages. Authorisation may query fraud systems, card networks, issuer banks, and risk models hosted in geographically distributed infrastructure. Show the behaviour when connectivity falters: the terminal hesitates, the cashier asks the customer to try again, the queue stiffens. Name the metric: timeouts. Payment processors set strict thresholds; if responses do not arrive in time, the transaction fails for safety. Explain the implication: a few hundred milliseconds of extra round-trip time can convert "tap and go" into "cash only". Trust becomes a visible decision at the point of sale—do we accept offline mode, or refuse?

The same logic extends to online payments and identity. At 09:00, a login prompts a multi-factor challenge. A one-time code arrives via a service that may route internationally. A push notification depends on cloud messaging infrastructure. The behaviour is a pause at a screen. Name the friction: authentication latency. Explain why it matters. Security systems are designed to close windows quickly; delay turns protection into lockout. The implication is that resilience and security are intertwined. A degraded network makes "secure" feel unusable, and unusable security invites risky workarounds.

By mid-morning, media enters the day in a thousand fragments: a news clip, a podcast, a live stream in the background. Much of this content is delivered through content delivery networks, and much of it is cached near the user. That caching is a real limitation to the dependency story, and it is important to name it. A cable fault does not instantly erase entertainment, because CDNs store popular content in-country and even in-city. Streaming services can buffer. News sites can serve cached pages. Reconcile the point without sentimentality: caching softens the first blow. It does not remove reliance. Live content, personalised feeds, and anything fetched from outside the cache still depends on cross-border capacity.

When international bandwidth tightens, video services adapt by lowering bitrates, dropping resolution, or pausing altogether. The visible behaviour is not "no media". It is grainy media, delayed media, or media that takes longer to begin—small degradations that signal a larger constraint.

Health records make the dependence sharper because they combine sensitivity with urgency. Many health systems store records in national platforms or cloud services, enabling clinicians to access results and histories across locations. The behaviour in a clinic under connectivity stress is immediate: staff revert to paper printouts, repeat questions already answered, postpone non-urgent consults because records cannot be verified. Name the risk metric: time-to-access. In emergency settings, seconds matter. Explain the implication: the cost of delay is not merely inconvenience; it is clinical uncertainty. This is not a claim that cable faults directly harm patients in every case. It is a claim that modern healthcare workflows assume continuity of access, and when access degrades, care becomes slower and more cautious.

Government services, too, have been rebuilt around remote verification. Tax portals, identity checks, benefits claims, vehicle licensing—each increasingly depends on central databases and outsourced infrastructure. The visible behaviour is a citizen refreshing a page, receiving an error, calling a helpline. Name the decision point: do agencies degrade gracefully or fail closed? Many systems, for good reasons, choose to fail closed to prevent fraud. Explain the implication: during regional slowdowns, citizens experience government not as a service but as a barrier. The social stress is subtle yet cumulative. A welfare payment delayed by a day is not a headline, but it is rent.

Now bring the day into the corporate sphere, where hidden fibre becomes a productivity constraint. At 10:30, a team meeting begins over video. Someone shares a screen hosted in a cloud workspace. Another pulls a dataset from a repository that sits in a different region. The meeting is not merely conversation; it is a chain of remote calls. Show what happens in a regional outage: video freezes, audio degrades, the screen share becomes unreadable, collaboration tools time out, and people begin to move to alternative channels. The behaviour is improvisation: switching platforms, turning off cameras, using personal hotspots, postponing decisions. Name the metric: packet loss and jitter. Explain the implication: remote work fails not as a dramatic collapse but as a steady erosion of coordination.

The 2008 Alexandria cable faults offer a checkable example of how this erosion spreads. Renesys recorded that, as routes disappeared, networks across the region became less reachable and more congested. Companies that had invested in international connectivity discovered that their "redundant" suppliers often shared the same physical chokepoints. Behaviour adapted. Non-essential traffic was throttled. Some firms moved operations temporarily to offices in less affected regions. This is not mysticism about globalisation; it is an observable pattern of load shifting. When a route fails, surviving routes saturate. That saturation expresses itself as delay. Delay changes decisions.

A second example, different in character, shows that the dependence is not confined to a single region or era. In November 2019, a cable fault disrupted service for Vodafone's customers in New Zealand, affecting mobile and broadband users. While much of the issue was domestic network-related, the event highlighted a broader truth: service continuity often depends on a chain of interlinked infrastructures, and a fault in one layer forces sudden reprioritisation in others. Customers experienced call failures and degraded data. Businesses reported transaction issues. The measurable outcome was the surge in support requests and the rapid shift to alternative communications. Explain the implication: when connectivity is treated as background, contingency is improvised rather than rehearsed.

A credible limitation must be stated plainly. Not everything depends equally on international subsea routes, and not every slowdown is a cable problem. Many services operate locally, with offline modes and local caching. Some countries have dense domestic backbones and multiple land routes to neighbours, reducing exposure to any single seabed corridor. Even when an international cable is damaged, users may experience little impact if their traffic stays within the domestic network or if their providers have spare capacity elsewhere. Reconcile the point: dependence is layered, not uniform. The danger lies in assuming that because impact is sometimes mild, exposure is therefore low. Mild impact can be the result of luck, spare capacity, or traffic patterns, not inherent resilience.

The deeper lesson is about the architecture of modern convenience. When a service feels instantaneous, it usually rests on an assumption: that identity can be checked quickly, that records are reachable, that messages can traverse borders without friction. Those assumptions are encoded in software defaults and business processes. Timeouts are configured. Retries are scheduled. Alert thresholds are set. Under normal conditions, these settings are invisible. Under degraded connectivity, they become a collective behavioural experiment. Users click again. Systems retry. Load increases. Congestion worsens. The very mechanisms designed for reliability can amplify strain.

This is why "the cloud" is not merely a misleading metaphor; it is a governance problem. Cloud architecture encourages geographical abstraction. Services are distributed "across regions". Data is "replicated". Availability is "multi-zone". These phrases are true at one level and deceptive at another. A region may have multiple data centres and redundant power, yet still depend on a narrow set of physical paths to the wider world. When those paths are constrained, a globally distributed service can behave like a local one with a single narrow exit.

In practice, professionals encounter this when outages force uncomfortable questions. Which applications are essential? Which must remain real-time? Which can be delayed? Organisations often discover, during incidents, that they have never explicitly decided. The defaults decide for them. Video consumes bandwidth until throttled. Automatic updates compete with customer transactions. Backup systems trigger at the wrong time. Risk becomes a visible metric: the number of failed transactions per hour, the backlog of support tickets, the percentage of staff unable to access core systems.

The human dimension matters. During regional slowdowns, employees improvise workarounds: personal email, consumer messaging apps, shadow IT. Each workaround is a decision made under pressure. Name the security implication without prescribing: data leaves controlled channels; compliance boundaries blur. Explain the trade-off: continuity competes with governance. The friction introduced by a cable fault does not remain technical; it pushes people into choices that reverberate through organisational risk.

Even leisure reveals the pattern. When connectivity degrades, people do not simply "do something else". They refresh, search for explanations, contact friends, assume their own device is at fault. Support lines fill. Social media amplifies speculation. Trust in providers erodes, not because the provider is negligent, but because the dependency was never visible enough to be understood. The public narrative defaults to the familiar: hacking, incompetence, sabotage. The seabed rarely enters the story, even when it is the reason.

The motif to carry forward is the seam. Subsea fibre is where the everyday world is stitched to the global one. When the seam holds, we forget it exists.

When it frays, we see the stitches in the form of timeouts, degraded calls, delayed payments, postponed appointments, and awkward meetings that end with "let's pick this up later". The seam is not glamorous. It is essential.

The unresolved test is practical and uncomfortable. When your organisation, your city, or your country experiences a sudden slowdown, do you know which of your daily actions are quietly crossing water, and which could continue if that seam snapped for a week?

## Why the seabed became contested

In September 2017, NATO vessels tracked a cluster of Russian naval ships manoeuvring in the North Atlantic, lingering near known subsea cable routes west of Ireland. The UK's Chief of the Defence Staff, General Sir Stuart Peach, publicly warned that Russia had developed the capability to threaten undersea infrastructure and that such activity posed a risk to national security. The immediate outcome was not confrontation but signalling: patrol patterns adjusted, briefings sharpened, and the seabed entered strategic vocabulary in a way it had not for decades. The water remained calm. Attention shifted below.

Five words framed the change: *the seabed is watched.*

For much of the post–Cold War period, the ocean floor was treated as a logistical afterthought. Shipping lanes mattered. Chokepoints mattered. The surface was where power was displayed and contested. The seabed, by contrast, was assumed to be inert—useful for cables and pipes, but politically quiet. That assumption no longer holds. The modern seabed is crowded with assets that convert maritime space into leverage, and leverage into influence.

Show the crowding first. Fibre-optic cables lace the ocean floor along routes that mirror trade and population. Power interconnectors link grids across borders. Pipelines move gas and oil to markets that plan their winters around uninterrupted flow. Offshore wind farms and energy hubs anchor cables, foundations and maintenance corridors. Name the result: density. Explain why density matters. Where assets cluster, disruption yields disproportionate effects. The implication is strategic. Crowded spaces attract attention from those who seek to shape outcomes without open confrontation.

Great-power rivalry sharpened this logic. As competition returned to maritime theatres, states rediscovered that influence need not arrive with missiles or blockades. It could arrive with ambiguity. A cable damaged in shallow waters could be accident, negligence or warning. Attribution would be slow. Responses would be constrained. This is not conjecture; it is a pattern observed in hybrid operations across domains, where actions sit below the threshold of armed conflict yet above routine risk.

The Baltic Sea offers a checkable example of how this ambiguity plays out. In September 2022, the Nord Stream gas pipelines were damaged by explosions, a fact confirmed by German, Swedish and Danish authorities. While the pipelines themselves are not data cables, the incident reframed how European governments thought about undersea infrastructure. Naval patrols increased. Investigations extended beyond energy. Trust—an abstraction—translated into concrete behaviour: heightened monitoring of cable routes and landing areas. The implication was clear. If pipelines could be sabotaged, cables could not be assumed immune.

A second example underscores the point. In October 2023, damage to the Balticconnector gas pipeline between Finland and Estonia coincided with faults in nearby communications cables. Finnish authorities described the damage as likely caused by external activity and opened criminal investigations. The measurable behaviour followed quickly: naval escorts, enhanced surveillance, and diplomatic coordination across the region. Explain the mechanism. Proximity of assets amplifies suspicion; multiple faults compress the window for benign explanation. The implication is escalation pressure even in the absence of definitive proof.

Why has the seabed become such an attractive arena for this kind of signalling? Start with visibility. Actions on the seabed are difficult to observe directly and expensive to monitor continuously. Sensors cover only fragments of vast areas. Ships can loiter under plausible pretences. Fishing gear, anchors and maintenance operations provide cover stories. The result is deniability. Name it plainly. Explain its value. Deniability allows states to probe boundaries without committing to open conflict. The implication is a strategic grey zone that rewards patience and ambiguity.

The economics reinforce the appeal. Repairing a damaged cable or pipeline is costly and slow, measured in days or weeks. The cost of causing damage—if one were inclined to do so—can be comparatively low. This asymmetry matters. It turns infrastructure into a lever where modest actions yield outsized disruption. Efficiency, here, is not about optimisation but about ratio: effort expended versus effect achieved.

Shipping lanes add another layer. Many cable routes run parallel to busy maritime corridors because those corridors reflect geography and trade.

Where ships concentrate, the probability of accidental damage rises. Where accidental damage is common, deliberate interference can hide. This is not an argument that shipping is a cover for malice; it is an explanation of why crowded seas blur intent. Behaviour reveals the stress. Insurers adjust premiums. Operators re-route cables where possible. Navies watch traffic patterns more closely. Each response tightens the feedback loop between commerce and security.

Energy infrastructure intensifies the stakes because it ties undersea assets to immediate political outcomes. Power interconnectors balance grids across borders. Pipelines underpin heating and industry. When energy security is strained, tolerance for ambiguity drops. The seabed becomes not just a technical environment but a political one. Decisions that once belonged to engineers migrate upward to cabinets and councils.

A credible limitation must be acknowledged. Not every region experiences this contestation equally. Some seas remain lightly trafficked. Some cable routes lie in deep water far from shipping and energy corridors. Many states continue to cooperate on cable laying, repair and protection without friction. Reconcile the limitation. Contestation is uneven, not universal. It emerges where density, rivalry and dependency intersect. Where one element is absent, the seabed can remain quiet.

The quiet motif threading this discussion is *ambiguity*. It appears in attribution, in intent, in response. Ambiguity shapes behaviour. After suspicious incidents, states rarely rush to public accusation. Instead, they signal. Patrols increase. Exercises are announced. Diplomatic language tightens. The message is often aimed less at the public than at other capitals: *we see the space you are operating in.*

Naval signalling around suspected cable incidents illustrates this dynamic. Following reports of unusual vessel activity near cable routes, navies may conduct conspicuous patrols or exercises in the vicinity. The visible behaviour is not confrontation but presence. Name the purpose. Presence reassures allies and warns adversaries without forcing escalation. Explain the implication. The seabed becomes a theatre where actions are read for intent rather than impact alone.

Law lags behind practice. International law protects cables in principle, but enforcement on the high seas is limited. Exclusive economic zones complicate jurisdiction. Private ownership muddies responsibility. This gap between legal text and operational reality widens the grey zone. Risk, again, becomes a decision: how much uncertainty can a state tolerate before it responds?

Technology pushes in both directions. Better seabed mapping, autonomous vehicles and sensors promise improved awareness. At the same time, they raise expectations. Once monitoring improves, failure to act looks like choice rather than ignorance. The bar for plausible deniability rises. So does the temptation to test it.

The contestation of the seabed is therefore not a sudden militarisation but an accumulation of incentives. Dependence on undersea infrastructure increased. Assets clustered. Rivalry sharpened. Tools for ambiguous action matured. Each step was rational in isolation. Together they produced a strategic environment where the ocean floor matters as never before.

The unresolved tension is stark. How do states protect assets that cannot be fully observed without turning routine maintenance and commerce into security incidents? Where is the line between vigilance and provocation when the decisive space lies out of sight? The seabed will not answer these questions. States will, one patrol and one signal at a time.

# Chapter 2

# Mapping the Global Cable Network

At a glance, a global cable map looks reassuringly tidy. Lines arc smoothly between continents, dots mark landfalls, and the ocean appears calmly traversed by a rational web of connection. It suggests intention, even inevitability: that the world's data flows along routes chosen once and for all, guided by logic and efficiency. Look closer, and the confidence dissolves. The lines overlap in places they ought not to. They squeeze through narrow seas, cling to familiar coastlines, and converge on a handful of towns few people could place on a map. The geometry is not elegant. It is inherited.

Maps have always done more than describe territory; they shape how risk is imagined. Medieval portolan charts emphasised coastlines and hazards because sailors needed them. Railway maps exaggerated distance to make networks legible. Modern cable maps perform a similar act of persuasion. They compress complexity into legibility, smoothing over the compromises, constraints and quiet accidents that determine how the global internet is actually wired. This chapter begins by unsettling that first impression, because understanding where cables run—and why they run there—is essential to understanding where the network is strong, where it is brittle, and where its risks quietly accumulate.

Subsea cables do not roam freely across the ocean floor. They follow patterns as old as trade and as modern as cloud computing. Routes trace historical shipping lanes because those lanes reflect the safest passages through currents, depth changes and seabed hazards. They arc towards population centres because demand, not elegance, pays for glass in the water. They avoid trenches, unstable slopes and politically awkward waters when they can, and cross them when they must. What looks like a neutral technical choice is often a negotiation between geology, economics and diplomacy.

To read the global network properly is to see it as layered rather than uniform. Long-haul trunk lines span oceans, carrying enormous volumes between continents. Branching units peel away towards islands and secondary markets, trading capacity for reach. Regional loops knit neighbouring countries together, providing redundancy in theory and shared exposure in practice. These components are not merely engineering categories; they encode assumptions about growth, risk and political stability. A trunk line assumes continuity. A branch assumes dependence. A loop assumes cooperation.

Consider a route between two continents. The shortest path is rarely the chosen one. Cable planners weigh depth profiles, seismic zones, fishing intensity, territorial waters, permitting regimes and landing options. A technically optimal route may pass through a state with unpredictable regulation or unresolved maritime claims. A politically comfortable route may add hundreds of kilometres and millions in cost. The final path is a compromise, and that compromise is frozen into the seabed for decades. Once laid, routes are difficult to change. The map becomes destiny.

If routes are the skeleton of the network, landing stations are its joints. These are the places where wet cable meets dry land, where optical signals are amplified, switched and handed off to terrestrial networks. Landing stations must satisfy an unforgiving checklist: stable ground, access to power, proximity to backhaul, regulatory approval, and physical security. For reasons of cost and convenience, they tend to cluster. One well-served stretch of coast attracts multiple systems, each seeking to minimise onshore construction and tap into existing infrastructure.

Clustering is efficient. It is also dangerous. When several cables land in the same town, or even the same industrial estate, a local planning decision acquires national significance. A floodplain zoning choice, a roadworks permit, a power substation upgrade delayed by months—each can affect a disproportionate share of a country's international connectivity. The risk is not hypothetical. Coastal towns that host multiple landing stations often do so by accident rather than design, their importance discovered only when an outage forces officials to ask why so much traffic passes through so little space.

The geography of chokepoints extends offshore. Straits, canals and narrow seas concentrate cables for the same reasons they concentrate ships. The English Channel, the Strait of Malacca, the Red Sea, the Mediterranean approaches—each is a corridor where depth, traffic and politics intersect. In these waters, cables must share space with anchors, dredging, fishing gear and intense maritime movement. Repairs recur. Sediment shifts. Charts are updated, then outdated again. The cumulative effect is not one catastrophic failure, but a pattern of strain that wears resilience thin over time.

Man-made constrictions amplify the effect. Canals shorten routes and reshape trade; cables follow. When a canal closes or a route becomes congested, pressure shifts elsewhere, often onto parallel corridors already crowded with infrastructure. Each repair becomes more complex than the last, as vessels queue for access and authorities coordinate permits in busy waters. The map shows a single line. The reality is a bottleneck that never fully clears.

Yet the seabed map alone is incomplete. Cables do not exist to connect coastlines; they exist to connect computation. Increasingly, landing choices are shaped less by national capitals than by data centres. Hyperscale facilities draw cables towards them, influencing routes hundreds of kilometres offshore. A landing that shortens the terrestrial path to a major cloud campus can save milliseconds and millions. Over time, these choices redraw the map, pulling new systems towards regions that offer cheap power, stable regulation and political alignment.

This shift has subtle consequences. As cable landings align with data centre clusters, the physical and digital geographies of the internet collapse into one another. Corporate strategy begins to shape maritime space. Regions that attract cloud investment gain connectivity density and redundancy; those that do not may find themselves bypassed, reliant on longer, thinner branches. The network's centre of gravity moves, not because of population alone, but because of where computation concentrates.

Public cable maps rarely show this dynamic. They present routes as static and evenly distributed, masking commercial sensitivities and omitting technical detail. Depth variations are smoothed. Exact landing locations are blurred. Branches appear more symmetrical than they are. Different maps of the same route can tell different stories, depending on who produced them and why. One emphasises reach, another capacity, a third marketing ambition. None tells the whole truth.

Learning to read these maps critically is therefore a strategic skill. What is shown precisely, and what is approximate? Which routes appear redundant on paper but share the same corridor in reality? Where do multiple systems converge without obvious indication? The answers matter because risk accumulates where assumptions overlap. A network that appears diverse at a glance may, in fact, hinge on a handful of seabed decisions made years earlier.

This chapter is not an atlas. It is an invitation to look again at the lines that already exist, to question their logic, and to understand the forces that drew them. Mapping the global cable network is not about memorising routes; it is about recognising patterns. Trade routes become data routes. Coastal convenience becomes strategic exposure. Corporate efficiency becomes geopolitical fact.

There is a philosophical undercurrent here that deserves attention. Maps promise mastery. They suggest that by seeing the whole, we can control it. The seabed resists this promise. It accepts lines but not intentions. Currents shift. Politics intrude. Demand migrates. The network adapts, but slowly, constrained by sunk cost and physical reality. What looks like a design is often an accumulation.

As this chapter unfolds, it will move from the broad to the specific: from global patterns to local decisions, from open maps to hidden constraints. It will show how cables choose their paths, how landings become chokepoints, how narrow seas concentrate risk, and how data centres quietly redraw maritime geography. It will also show how much remains unknowable from the surface, and why humility is a necessary companion to analysis.

The reward for this attention is not paranoia, but clarity. Once the map is read with care, subsequent chapters—on threats, failures and repair—make more sense. Damage recurs where routes converge. Recovery slows where access is constrained. Resilience improves where diversity is physical, not merely logical. These are not abstract lessons. They are embedded in the lines already on the seabed.

Before turning the page, hold one image in mind. Picture the world's data not as a mist drifting freely between places, but as traffic moving along roads laid long ago, some wide and well-maintained, others narrow and overused. This chapter is about learning where those roads run, who built them, and why so many journeys still depend on the same few passages.

## Understanding global route patterns

On 28 September 2018, in Marseilles, a consortium led by Orange announced the completion of the Dunant subsea cable linking France to the United States. The route did not follow the shortest possible great-circle line across the Atlantic. Instead, it curved deliberately, avoiding steep seabed features, sensitive jurisdictions, and congested corridors. The outcome was measurable: lower latency between European and North American data centres, tighter control over landing infrastructure, and a system optimised for hyperscale traffic rather than diplomatic symmetry. The line on the map told a story. The choices beneath it told a deeper one.

Five words summarise the lesson: *routes are negotiated, not drawn.*

Global subsea cable patterns are often described as if they emerged organically, like rivers finding the sea. They did not. They are the cumulative result of thousands of explicit decisions taken over decades by engineers, financiers, diplomats and regulators, each responding to constraints that were technical, commercial, political, or geological. To understand why cables run where they do is to understand how the modern world distributes trust, risk and power across distance.

Begin with the most persistent influence: trade. Long before fibre, ships traced paths between ports that balanced distance, safety and demand. Those paths still matter. Cable routes tend to parallel shipping lanes because shipping lanes reveal where the seabed is navigable, surveyed and politically tolerated. A corridor busy with vessels is a corridor known to hydrographers, regulated by maritime authorities, and defended—implicitly or explicitly—by states with an interest in keeping it open. Show the behaviour. When planners assess a new route, they overlay shipping density maps with bathymetry and hazard data. Name the decision. Avoid the unknown when the known will do. Explain the implication. Familiar corridors accumulate infrastructure, and infrastructure attracts more infrastructure.

Population follows trade, and cables follow population. High-capacity trunk lines connect regions where demand justifies the expense: North America to Europe, East Asia to the western United States, Southeast Asia to India and the Gulf. These trunks are the heavy beams of the network, designed to carry enormous volumes with minimal interruption. Their endpoints are rarely capitals chosen for symbolism; they are metropolitan regions chosen for consumption. A cable that lands near a cluster of data centres and internet exchanges will fill faster and earn sooner than one that lands for cartographic elegance.

Geography intervenes early and often. The seabed is not flat. It is scored with trenches, scarps, canyons and unstable slopes. Earthquake zones and landslide-prone regions raise insurance costs and long-term risk. Show the constraint. A route that crosses a tectonically active trench may be shorter, but it demands heavier armouring, careful burial, or acceptance of higher fault probability. Name the calculation. Expected downtime multiplied by repair cost. Explain the implication. Geography quietly prices routes out of contention before politics ever enters the room.

Politics does enter, however, and when it does, it reshapes the map decisively. Every cable crosses jurisdictions. Territorial seas require permits. Exclusive economic zones introduce negotiation. Some states encourage landings with streamlined processes and tax incentives. Others impose delays, local partnership requirements, or security reviews. Show the behaviour. Consortia redraw routes to avoid regulatory friction, even when the detour adds length. Name the trade-off. Extra kilometres versus years of delay. Explain the implication. Political comfort often outweighs geometric efficiency.

The network's architecture reflects these pressures through three recurring forms: trunk lines, branching units and regional loops. Trunk lines are long-haul systems that prioritise capacity and latency between major markets. They are capital-intensive and politically sensitive, because their disruption has transcontinental effects. Branching units extend from these trunks to serve islands or secondary markets, adding reach without replicating the full cost of a new system. Regional loops interconnect neighbouring states, offering redundancy and shared capacity but also shared exposure.

Each form encodes a different assumption about stability. Trunk lines assume enduring demand and cooperation between endpoints. Branches assume dependence: the branch market accepts that its international connectivity rides on a larger system it does not control. Loops assume reciprocity: that neighbours will share risk and benefit. When those assumptions hold, the network behaves resiliently. When they do not, vulnerabilities appear.

A concrete example illustrates how these elements combine. The Asia–Europe corridor, one of the world's busiest data routes, has long balanced speed against fragility. Early systems traced paths through the Mediterranean and Red Sea, following historic trade routes. Over time, planners confronted the reality of narrow seas, heavy shipping, and political complexity. Newer systems have explored alternative paths, including routes skirting Africa's west coast or crossing Eurasia terrestrially. Each option carries a different mix of latency, capacity, cost and geopolitical exposure.

Show the choice. A Red Sea route is shorter and faster but crowded and politically sensitive. A southern African route is longer but avoids certain chokepoints. A terrestrial route crosses multiple borders and legal regimes.

Name the decision criteria. Latency budgets for financial traffic, availability of landing partners, exposure to sanctions or conflict. Explain the implication. No route is neutral. Each embeds a worldview about which risks are tolerable.

The Dunant cable exemplifies this logic in microcosm. By landing in Virginia Beach rather than New York or New Jersey, the system avoided congested landing clusters and gained proximity to hyperscale campuses. By choosing a privately controlled architecture, it reduced consortium complexity and accelerated decision-making. The visible metric was latency improvement measured in milliseconds. The less visible effect was strategic autonomy: fewer stakeholders, fewer compromises. Efficiency here was not abstract. It was measured, compared and committed.

A second named example provides contrast. The SEA-ME-WE cable family, stretching from Southeast Asia to Western Europe, reflects a consortium-driven approach shaped by diplomatic inclusion. Routes touch many states, serving diverse markets. The benefit is broad access. The limitation is concentration. When faults occur in shared corridors, impacts cascade across regions. Reconcile the comparison. Private trunks optimise for performance and control; consortium systems optimise for inclusion and shared cost. Both shape global patterns. Neither eliminates risk.

A credible counter-example tempers any suggestion of determinism. Some routes appear to defy trade and population logic, serving sparsely populated regions or taking circuitous paths. Often these are driven by state policy or development goals rather than immediate demand. Arctic proposals, for example, aim to shorten distances between Asia and Europe by exploiting melting ice and new navigation windows. The limitation is uncertainty. Ice conditions, environmental risk, and geopolitical sensitivity complicate execution. Reconcile the lesson. Ambitious routes can reshape patterns, but only when physical and political conditions align for long enough to justify investment.

Trust, a word often used loosely in discussions of global connectivity, manifests here as a routing choice. Operators trust certain jurisdictions with landings. They trust certain seabed corridors to remain accessible. They trust that political relations will not deteriorate beyond manageability over the life of the asset. These trusts are not moral judgements; they are risk assessments translated into kilometres of cable.

Efficiency appears as utilisation curves. A trunk that fills quickly justifies upgrades. A branch that remains underused becomes a candidate for consolidation. Decisions follow metrics: terabits carried, faults per thousand kilometres, mean time to repair. When these metrics diverge from expectation, new routes are proposed—or old ones quietly sidelined.

Risk becomes visible in clustering. Where multiple trunks converge, the network gains capacity but loses diversity. Regional loops mitigate single cuts but can amplify regional shocks. Branching units extend reach but concentrate dependence. None of this is accidental. It is the product of cost curves and compromise.

The quiet motif to carry forward is the path. Not the line on the map, but the path as a sequence of decisions constrained by earth and politics. Paths harden over time. They attract traffic, investment and attention. They also attract risk. Once a path is established, alternatives look expensive, even when they would reduce exposure. Path dependence is not a theory here; it is a property of glass laid on the seabed.

As the network grows denser and competition sharper, the question becomes harder. Should new routes reinforce existing paths for efficiency, or diverge to reduce concentration? Should planners privilege political comfort or physical diversity? Should latency be shaved at the cost of exposure to narrow seas? These are not technical puzzles awaiting optimisation. They are choices with consequences measured in outages, costs and diplomatic strain.

The test ahead is simple to state and difficult to answer. When the next generation of cables is planned, will the map change because the world has changed—or because the last map made change too costly to attempt?

## Landing stations and coastal chokepoints

In 1870, at Porthcurno on the Cornish coast, the Eastern Telegraph Company brought ashore a cable that would bind Britain to the wider world. The landing was chosen for reasons that felt prosaic at the time: a sheltered bay, manageable tides, a route inland that avoided difficult terrain. The outcome was historic. Porthcurno became one of the nerve centres of global communication, a place where messages from across the empire surfaced briefly before racing onward by land. The village did not grow into a metropolis. The cables came anyway.

Five words linger from that choice: *the shore remembers decisions.*

A landing station is the most ordinary-looking part of a subsea cable system and the most consequential. It is where the oceanic network becomes terrestrial, where light carried for thousands of kilometres through glass meets power, cooling, security fences and planning permission. To the passer-by, it may resemble a low industrial building or a nondescript compound behind hedges. To the network, it is a hinge. Everything that crosses the sea must pass through it.

Show the process. A cable approaches land through shallow waters, often buried for protection, then rises into a beach manhole before being ducted inland to a secure facility. Inside, optical equipment amplifies, monitors and hands traffic to domestic backbones. Power feeding equipment injects current back into the wet plant. Redundancy is engineered within the building, but the building itself is a point. Name the reality. If access to that site is lost, the cable is effectively lost to the country it serves. Explain the implication. Landing stations transform distributed maritime risk into concentrated terrestrial exposure.

Why, then, do landing stations cluster? Efficiency answers first. Co-locating landings reduces the cost of onshore construction, simplifies access to power and backhaul, and concentrates skilled maintenance staff. Regulatory familiarity matters too. A coastal authority that has approved one landing is more likely to approve another. The path through permits is known. Time to market shortens. The visible metric is cost per kilometre saved. The less visible effect is concentration.

Trust also plays a role, expressed not as sentiment but as precedent. Operators trust locations that have "worked" before. They trust local councils that understand the process. They trust routes where previous cables have survived storms and anchors. Each trust is rational in isolation. Together they create gravity wells along the coast.

Over time, these gravity wells harden into chokepoints. A handful of towns host a disproportionate share of a nation's international connectivity. The choice is rarely announced as strategy. It emerges from planning decisions made years apart, often by different actors, each optimising for speed and certainty. When the clustering becomes visible, it is usually because something has gone wrong.

Bude, on the north coast of Cornwall, offers a modern case in point. Over the past two decades, multiple international systems have landed near the town, attracted by existing infrastructure and favourable geography. The outcome is measurable: a significant share of the United Kingdom's transatlantic capacity passes through a small stretch of coastline. The town did not set out to become a national chokepoint. Local planning decisions, taken sensibly and incrementally, produced that result. Efficiency accumulated. Exposure followed.

The security implications are not abstract. Concentrated landings mean that physical incidents—flooding, fire, construction damage—can affect multiple systems at once. They also mean that surveillance and protection resources must be focused on a few sites whose importance far exceeds their footprint. Behaviour reflects this. Operators invest in perimeter security and monitoring. Police and security services quietly note addresses. Insurance premiums reflect aggregation risk.

Yet concentration is not solely a security problem. It is an operational one. When multiple cables land in the same area, they often share onshore routes for a distance before diverging. Ducts, bridges and exchanges become shared dependencies. A roadworks accident kilometres inland can have effects that ripple across oceans. The visible behaviour is sudden congestion as traffic reroutes. The metric is mean time to repair extended by access constraints and coordination between owners.

A credible counter-example tempers the critique. Some countries have deliberately dispersed landings, forcing systems to separate geographically even at higher cost. Japan, mindful of seismic risk, has encouraged diversity of landings along different coastlines. The limitation is economic. Dispersion raises costs and complicates operations. Smaller markets may struggle to justify it. Reconcile the lesson. Dispersion reduces concentration risk but demands sustained policy commitment and willingness to pay for insurance that rarely pays out visibly.

The legal and regulatory context amplifies these choices. In many jurisdictions, landing stations are treated as private facilities subject to general planning and environmental law. National security considerations enter late, if at all. Trust here becomes procedural. If an application meets requirements, it is approved. The implication is that cumulative national exposure can be shaped by local decisions without a forum for aggregation.

The motif to keep in view is the hinge. Landing stations are hinges between domains: sea and land, private and public, global and local. Hinges concentrate force. They are designed to move smoothly under normal load. Under stress, they bear the strain.

The history of Porthcurno illustrates how long these strains can last. The cables that once landed there shaped Britain's communication posture for generations. Modern systems move more data, faster, but they still inherit the logic of place. A good landing remains a good landing, even as the stakes rise.

Corporate strategy now intersects with this geography. Hyperscale cloud providers prefer landings that minimise terrestrial distance to data centres. When a landing aligns with a cloud campus, it attracts further investment. The behaviour is visible in route announcements and capacity upgrades. The implication is feedback. Successful landings become more successful, and concentration deepens.

Risk, again, becomes a decision. Do regulators intervene to cap clustering? Do they mandate separation of routes inland? Do they accept concentration as the price of competitiveness? Each choice carries trade-offs that cannot be resolved by engineering alone.

Even resilience measures can reinforce chokepoints. Building stronger defences around a clustered site can entrench its importance, making alternative landings less attractive. The network becomes more robust at the hinge and more dependent on it. The paradox is uncomfortable but real.

The unresolved tension lies in scale. Local decisions feel manageable. National exposure does not. When the next cable seeks landfall, will authorities ask only whether the site is suitable—or whether the country can afford one more hinge in the same place?

## Straits, canals and narrow seas

On 28 January 2008, off the coast of Alexandria, two fibre-optic cables—SEA-ME-WE 4 and FLAG Europe-Asia—were damaged within hours of each other. The precise cause was never publicly settled, but the outcome was unambiguous. Internet capacity across Egypt dropped sharply; India, the Gulf states and parts of Southeast Asia experienced severe slowdowns; call centres fell silent; financial transactions queued. Repairs were completed. Months later, similar faults occurred again in nearby waters. The corridor had not changed. The risk had compounded.

Five words describe the geography: *everything passes through here.*

Natural straits and man-made canals have always concentrated movement. They funnel ships, compress trade, and magnify the consequences of error. Subsea cables follow the same logic, because they must. The shortest, safest and most economical routes between regions converge on narrow seas: the English Channel, the Strait of Malacca, the Bab el-Mandeb, the Bosphorus, the approaches to the Suez Canal. These are places where distance, depth and politics align just enough to permit passage—and just enough to create persistent vulnerability.

Begin with traffic. Where ships cluster, anchors drop. Where dredgers operate, seabeds are disturbed. Where fishing intensifies, heavy gear scrapes the bottom. Show the behaviour. Marine charts for narrow seas are crowded with symbols: lanes, exclusion zones, pipelines, wrecks, cables. Name the condition. Density. Explain why it matters. Each additional activity increases the probability that something will go wrong, even if no single actor behaves recklessly. The implication is cumulative risk: not one catastrophic event, but repeated minor damage that strains repair capacity and redundancy.

The physics of narrow seas compound the problem. Shallow depths limit burial options. Strong currents shift sediment, exposing cable armour that was safely buried a season earlier. Tidal flows complicate repair work, narrowing weather windows and extending downtime. These are not edge cases; they are baseline conditions. Efficiency, here, becomes a constraint measured in hours of safe working time per day rather than kilometres laid.

Man-made constrictions intensify these effects. Canals promise efficiency by shortening routes, and cables follow to capture latency and cost advantages. The Suez Canal corridor is emblematic. It carries a significant share of Europe–Asia traffic, both maritime and digital. The same corridor hosts pipelines, power links and multiple cable systems layered atop one another. Show the map. Lines stack. Name the risk. Shared exposure. Explain the implication. A single incident—anchor drag, dredging error, ground movement—can affect several systems at once.

Repeated repairs in such corridors reveal how risk accumulates. Each repair requires a ship to work in congested waters, coordinating with port authorities, shipping traffic and, often, military patrols. The cable is lifted, spliced and reburied, sometimes only metres from its previous position because alternatives are scarce. The visible metric is recurrence: faults per kilometre per year exceed those of deep-ocean routes. The less visible effect is fatigue—infrastructure fatigue, organisational fatigue, and political patience fatigue.

The English Channel offers a quieter but persistent illustration. It is one of the busiest shipping lanes in the world and a critical corridor for cables linking the UK to continental Europe. Faults occur regularly, often attributed to fishing or anchoring. Each repair restores service. None removes the underlying exposure. Operators mitigate by armouring, burying deeper, and adding routes. Yet the channel remains narrow. The seabed remains crowded. Risk is managed, not eliminated.

A second example underscores the global pattern. The Strait of Malacca, linking the Indian and Pacific Oceans, carries immense maritime traffic and hosts numerous cables serving Southeast Asia. Here, depth variations, intense fishing and heavy shipping intersect. Cable faults recur. Repairs are routine. The implication for planners is not alarm but acceptance: this corridor will always be stressed. Redundancy must therefore exist elsewhere, not within the same narrow space.

Trust appears here as a willingness to route through known hazards because alternatives are worse. Operators trust that accidents will be manageable, that repairs will be permitted, that traffic can be rerouted temporarily. This trust is not blind; it is statistical. It rests on historical fault rates and repair times. When those statistics worsen—because traffic increases or politics intrudes—trust erodes, and new routes are proposed, often at great expense.

A credible limitation tempers the argument. Not all narrow seas are equally dangerous, and not all faults propagate widely. Modern monitoring allows rapid fault localisation. Some regions have invested heavily in protection zones and awareness campaigns for mariners. Reconcile the point. Mitigation reduces impact, but it does not change geometry. Narrow spaces remain narrow, and density continues to rise.

The quiet motif threading this discussion is the corridor. Corridors promise efficiency by concentrating movement. They deliver vulnerability by doing the same. In digital networks, as in trade, corridors shape power. Those who control or influence them wield disproportionate leverage, even without intent to disrupt.

Geopolitics sharpens the stakes. Narrow seas often sit between rival states or within contested regions. Naval activity increases. Surveillance intensifies. Repairs attract attention. A cable ship working slowly in a strait becomes an object of interest. Behaviour changes. Escorts appear. Notifications multiply. The cost of each repair rises, not because the splice is harder, but because the environment is tenser.

Efficiency decisions taken decades ago now echo in this context. Routing through a canal saved days of latency and millions in construction cost.

Today, it embeds exposure to political flashpoints and physical congestion. The calculation has shifted, but the cable remains.

The unresolved test is strategic and immediate. As traffic grows and corridors crowd further, will new systems continue to stack risk into the same narrow seas for the sake of speed and cost—or will planners accept longer routes to buy distance from danger? The water will not widen. The decision will have to.

## Linking cables to data centres

In October 2020, Google announced that its Dunant subsea cable had entered service, landing at Virginia Beach, Virginia, and connecting directly into the company's US East cloud region. The outcome was immediate and measurable: lower latency for transatlantic traffic into Google's data centres, reduced dependence on third-party backhaul, and tighter control over how capacity was lit and upgraded. The route did not end at the shore. It ended at compute.

Five words capture the shift: *the shore moved inland.*

For most of the internet's history, subsea cables were planned as maritime projects with a terrestrial afterthought. A landing station connected the wet plant to a national backbone, and from there traffic dispersed towards cities, exchanges and, eventually, servers. That logic has inverted. Today, the gravitational pull is no longer the coastline or even the capital city. It is the data centre campus. Cables are increasingly drawn not to countries, but to clusters of computation.

Show the path. A modern subsea system approaches land, reaches a landing station, and is immediately ducted onto high-capacity terrestrial fibre that runs—often on a pre-reserved, diverse route—directly to one or more data centres. The visible behaviour is the avoidance of intermediate hops. Name the reason. Each hop adds latency, cost and operational dependency. Explain the implication. The tighter the coupling between cable and data centre, the more predictable performance becomes for cloud workloads that price milliseconds.

This architectural change reflects a deeper economic reality. Hyperscale cloud providers now generate a significant share of international traffic growth. Their internal replication, customer workloads and inter-region synchronisation consume bandwidth at a scale that traditional carriers once reserved for national backbones. When such firms invest in cables, they do so to optimise their own traffic first. Public connectivity follows, but it is no longer the primary driver.

Latency is the most obvious metric shaping these choices. For applications such as distributed databases, content personalisation and real-time analytics, latency is not a comfort feature; it is a cost line. Measure it. A few milliseconds shaved off a transatlantic round trip can improve cache hit rates, reduce compute overhead and tighten service-level objectives. The behaviour that follows is concrete: cables land where the terrestrial distance to the data centre is shortest, even if that means bypassing traditional telecom hubs.

Virginia Beach exemplifies this logic. By landing there rather than in more congested northern corridors, Dunant shortened the fibre path to inland data centres and avoided crowded coastal clusters. The decision also reduced exposure to shared ducts and exchanges. Efficiency, here, was not abstract. It was measured in fibre kilometres avoided and fault domains reduced.

A second example reinforces the pattern. In 2018, Microsoft announced the MAREA cable linking Bilbao, Spain, to Virginia Beach, again choosing a landing that aligned closely with cloud infrastructure. Bilbao was not Europe's largest market, but it offered proximity to terrestrial routes into Western European data centres and a regulatory environment conducive to rapid build-out. The outcome was faster deployment and performance optimised for cloud traffic rather than national symmetry. Corporate strategy redrew the map.

Trust, often invoked vaguely in discussions of cloud, appears here as physical commitment. By investing directly in subsea systems and associated terrestrial routes, cloud providers signal where they expect demand and stability to persist for decades. They trust certain regions with capital and capacity. That trust is expressed not in statements but in glass laid on the seabed and fibre trenched inland.

The linkage between cables and data centres also reshapes national exposure. When international connectivity is tightly coupled to a handful of cloud campuses, outages or constraints at those sites propagate widely. The behaviour during incidents makes this visible. Traffic that once dispersed across multiple exchanges now converges on specific regions. Congestion manifests not at the shore but at the interconnection fabric of data centres. Mean time to recovery becomes as much a function of campus operations as of marine repair.

A credible limitation must be stated. Not all cables are cloud-driven, and not all data centres dictate routes. Many systems still serve carrier and enterprise traffic, landing at traditional telecom hubs to maximise reach. Smaller markets may lack the scale to attract hyperscale investment, relying instead on neutral landing points. Reconcile the point. The cloud pull is dominant where demand is dense and capital abundant; elsewhere, legacy patterns persist. The global map is therefore hybrid, with old and new logics layered atop one another.

This hybridity complicates resilience. On one hand, direct links to data centres can reduce dependencies and improve performance. On the other, they can concentrate risk if multiple systems converge on the same campus or terrestrial corridor. The abstraction "resilience" becomes a countable decision: how many physically separate routes reach the campus, and how far apart do they run? Operators measure this in metres and minutes, not aspirations.

Energy and land use add further constraints. Data centres demand vast, reliable power supplies and cooling. These requirements limit where campuses can be built and, by extension, where cables are attractive to land. Regions offering cheap power and supportive planning regimes gain connectivity; others are bypassed. The behaviour is visible in investment flows. Cable announcements increasingly coincide with data centre expansions, not population growth.

The motif threading this section is the anchor. Data centres anchor cables inland just as landing stations anchor them at the shore. Once an anchor is set, movement becomes costly. Routes harden. Alternatives look expensive. Over time, the anchor reshapes the surrounding network, pulling new systems into its orbit.

Security considerations follow the anchor. Governments accustomed to thinking of cable protection at the coast must now consider inland corridors and campuses as part of the same system. Surveillance, incident response and contingency planning stretch across domains that were once separate. The decision to classify a data centre as critical infrastructure acquires new weight when it is also the terminus of multiple international cables.

There is also a geopolitical dimension. When global connectivity increasingly terminates at facilities owned or operated by a small number of multinational firms, questions of jurisdiction and control sharpen. Traffic between two foreign countries may transit infrastructure governed by a third. This is not new in principle, but the scale is. Behaviour reflects this tension in regulatory scrutiny of cloud investments and in debates over data localisation. The seabed may be global, but the servers are not.

Reading the map with this in mind changes its meaning. A line from shore to shore is no longer the whole story. The true route extends inland to racks and switches humming far from the water. Public maps rarely show this extension, yet it is where many of the most consequential decisions are made.

The unresolved test is forward-looking and practical. As cloud providers continue to shape demand, will future cables be planned primarily as extensions of data centres, or will states and carriers insist on routes that preserve broader neutrality and dispersion? The answer will determine whether the next generation of maps reflects a balance of interests—or the deepening imprint of a few powerful anchors.

## Reading public cable maps critically

In July 2016, Google announced the Dunant subsea cable between Virginia Beach, Virginia, and Saint-Hilaire-de-Riez, France. Within hours, the route appeared online in more than one guise: a smooth, marketing-friendly arc on corporate pages, and a more intricate, differently curved line on TeleGeography's Submarine Cable Map (TeleGeography, 2016–). The outcome was not confusion for engineers; it was confusion for everyone else. Two maps. One cable. Two stories.

Five words belong on the screen: *maps are not the seabed.*

Public cable maps feel authoritative because they borrow the visual language of certainty. They present clean lines and neat nodes, as if the global network were a well-ordered circuit board. They invite the reader to infer precision: here is the route; here is the landing; here is the redundancy. Yet public maps are not neutral representations. They are compromises between disclosure and discretion, between what is helpful and what is safe, between what is true and what is commercially permissible.

The first discipline in reading these maps is to remember what they are for. Many are built to sell. They are designed to persuade investors, reassure customers, and signal capability to partners. Even the most respected reference maps are built from open and semi-open sources, curated with care but limited by what operators are willing to share. Exact routes, protection measures, slack loops, repeater positions, burial depth, and onshore ducting are rarely disclosed in public detail. This is partly about security and partly about competition. The seabed is a contested space; the market is, too.

Show the gap between line and reality. A cable route is not a single thread laid taut across an ocean; it is a corridor selected after survey, then adjusted during installation in response to micro-topography, sediment, and avoidance requirements. It may include deliberate slack, gentle curves, and offsets around hazards. The map line cannot show this without becoming unreadable. Name the effect. Generalisation. Explain why it matters. Generalisation can make clustered routes look separate and separate routes look clustered. The implication is analytical risk: a reader may believe a country is diversified when it is not, or vulnerable when it is not.

This is not an argument against maps. It is an argument for reading them like a professional reads a balance sheet: with attention to what is omitted. Consider how a map handles landings. A dot on the coast may represent an actual beach manhole and landing station, or it may represent a broader landing area within a county, chosen to avoid highlighting a facility. Where a map chooses vagueness, it is offering a clue. The clue is that the location matters.

Public maps also struggle with time. Cables are not static. Systems are upgraded, repurposed, sold, renamed, and occasionally retired. New branches are added. Ownership shifts. A map may show a cable as "in service" while substantial capacity is still dark, or show a route as planned long after it has quietly stalled. TeleGeography maintains one of the most widely used industry datasets and updates it continuously, yet even it must contend with lag and opacity because much information arrives through announcements, filings, and partner disclosures rather than full technical transparency (TeleGeography, 2016–). A marketing map, by contrast, may present a planned system as if it already functions. The user sees a line. The engineer sees a project.

The second discipline is to separate topology from geography. A cable map shows geography: where lines run. It rarely shows topology: how traffic is actually routed, switched, and prioritised. Two countries may appear equally connected by cables, yet one may have diverse backhaul to multiple internet exchanges and data centres, while the other funnels traffic through a single metropolitan hub inland. The map looks similar. The resilience is not. The visible behaviour during an outage reveals the difference: one country experiences mild congestion; the other sees cascading failures as inland bottlenecks saturate.

This distinction matters because many readers approach cable maps with a common, intuitive mistake: they treat the map as a proxy for capacity and redundancy. It is not. A single line may represent a system capable of carrying vast volumes, or a legacy cable with modest capacity. Some maps annotate capacity, but these figures can be sensitive, may reflect design rather than lit capacity, and can change with upgrades at the terminals. If a map shows no capacity data, it is not necessarily hiding it; it may simply be avoiding claims that age quickly or invite competitive scrutiny.

A third discipline is to notice what kinds of routes are visually emphasised. Trunk lines are drawn prominently because they are legible and dramatic. Branching units and regional loops may be shown faintly or not at all, depending on the map's purpose. This can distort the reader's sense of dependency. An island might appear to have a single line because branches are collapsed into the trunk in the visual design, when in reality it is served by multiple branches from different systems. Or the reverse can happen: multiple branches may appear as multiple independent routes when they share a single corridor for most of their path. The implication is misallocated attention: analysts focus on the wrong chokepoints.

Return to the Dunant example, because it clarifies how these distortions emerge. Google's public descriptions emphasised speed, directness, and the strategic pairing of endpoints. TeleGeography's map, compiled from multiple sources, depicts the route with different curvature and contextualises it among other transatlantic systems. Neither depiction is "wrong". Each is a lens. The corporate lens foregrounds purpose: performance and capacity for cloud traffic. The reference-map lens foregrounds context: where this cable sits among many, and what it implies for route diversity. If one stares at the corporate line alone, one might miss clustering near landings. If one stares at the reference line alone, one might miss the inland logic: the link to data centres and backhaul corridors that turn a landing into a true terminus.

Now consider a more sensitive category: routes through narrow seas and canals. Maps often simplify these areas to prevent a snarl of overlapping lines. The Red Sea, the Mediterranean approaches, and the English Channel can become a tangle if drawn faithfully. Simplification is necessary for legibility. It also conceals density. Here the quiet motif returns: the corridor. A corridor that looks like a single line can, in reality, contain dozens of systems within a narrow band. When faults occur, the public asks why "one cable cut" caused widespread impact. The answer is frequently that it was not one cable, and it was not one cut. The map did not lie; it merely did not show the crowding.

A credible counter-example deserves a fair hearing. Maritime authorities publish charts and notices that mark cable protection zones and route corridors for navigational safety. These are designed for mariners, not for marketing, and can be more operationally relevant than public internet maps. Their limitation is equally important. They are not built to reveal detailed technical layouts; they often depict corridors rather than exact lines, and they may omit sensitive context. Reconcile the point. Even the most "official" depiction is still a representation shaped by purpose and prudence. There is no single public map that grants omniscience.

This leads to a fourth discipline: ask what incentives shaped the map. A telecommunications carrier may emphasise reach—how many countries it touches. A cloud provider may emphasise directness—how quickly it connects two regions. A national agency may emphasise sovereignty—where landings occur under domestic jurisdiction. A research map may emphasise completeness—how many systems are included regardless of owner. The same cable can appear in each, yet the story changes with the incentive. Trust, in this context, becomes a decision: which map do you treat as your baseline, and why?

The fifth discipline is methodological: cross-check depictions and treat divergences as data rather than error. If two maps show the same route differently, the divergence is a signal that uncertainty exists or that a choice has been made about what to reveal. The Dunant depictions illustrate this, but it is common across systems. Operator maps often draw idealised arcs. Reference maps draw plausible paths. In some cases, the discrepancy is benign: artistic simplification. In others, it points to a real corridor choice—one that may matter for assessing exposure to hazards or political jurisdictions. The implication is practical. Analysts should treat public maps as starting points, not conclusions.

There is a temptation, especially among professionals pressed for time, to extract hard claims from soft visuals. "This country has three cables, so it is safe." "This route avoids that strait, so it is resilient." "These two landings are far apart, so risk is diversified." Maps can support such statements only when paired with additional evidence: landing facility data, backhaul routes, ownership and maintenance arrangements, and, ideally, historical incident patterns. Without that context, the statement becomes a comforting fiction.

Yet maps remain powerful tools for learning if approached with the right questions. Ask: where do routes cluster near shore? Where do they cross narrow seas? Where do multiple systems land in the same region? Where do routes appear to diverge, and where do they likely share the same corridor? These questions turn a map from a picture into a hypothesis generator. They shift the reader from passive consumption to active interpretation.

The most subtle risk in public maps is that they can make fragility look like design. A clean network diagram implies intentional redundancy. The real world often contains redundancy that is logical rather than physical: multiple contracts riding the same ducts, multiple "providers" sharing the same landing, multiple "routes" converging in the same corridor. Public maps may show many lines and encourage a sense of safety, even as the underlying infrastructure remains concentrated. This is not deception so much as the natural consequence of reducing a three-dimensional, commercially sensitive system into a two-dimensional public artefact.

The final discipline is humility. The ocean floor is not a transparent medium, and the cable industry is not obliged to publish its most sensitive details. That is not a complaint; it is a fact with analytical consequences. It means that assessments of vulnerability based solely on open maps should be expressed as probabilities and scenarios, not certainties. It means that confident claims about exact routes are rarely justified. It means that public maps, valuable as they are, should prompt deeper inquiry rather than substitute for it.

One can see the deeper implication by returning to the book's central concern: the mismatch between dependence and visibility. Public cable maps are one of the few widely accessible windows into the physical internet. They educate, but they can also seduce. They offer a sense of seeing. The danger is mistaking that sense for knowledge.

The unresolved test is therefore diagnostic. When you look at a cable map and feel reassured, can you name what you do not know—exact landings, shared corridors, inland backhaul, lit capacity, maintenance arrangements—and decide whether your judgement is based on evidence or on a line that was drawn to be legible?

# Chapter 3

# How Subsea Cables Are Built And Run

In August 2021, a cable ship moved slowly along the coast of Brittany, paying out fibre at a pace measured in metres per minute. From the bridge, the sea looked forgiving. Below the surface, the margin for error was not. The cable had to settle into a seabed shaped by tides, fishing scars and centuries of human use, then transition—almost imperceptibly—from deep-water simplicity to near-shore hazard. A deviation of a few dozen metres could mean future exposure to anchors, currents, or bureaucracy. The crew adjusted. The ship crept. The cable disappeared beneath the waves, carrying with it a design philosophy that would have to hold for decades.

The paradox is easy to miss. Subsea cables are among the most advanced pieces of infrastructure humans build, yet once laid they become passive objects, expected to function quietly and indefinitely in one of the harshest environments on Earth. They contain no moving parts along most of their length. They are repaired, not upgraded. They are monitored continuously and touched rarely. Their success is measured by how completely they fade from notice.

This chapter enters that silence. It is about how cables are made to endure, how they are laid with deliberate care, how they are powered across oceans, and how they are run day after day by people who rarely appear in public narratives about the internet. It is also about where fragility is designed in, where it emerges through compromise, and why understanding the mechanics of cables changes how we think about risk, resilience and responsibility.

At the centre of every system lies a deceptively simple object: a strand of glass thinner than a human hair. Wrapped around it are layers of protection, each answering a different threat. Steel armouring resists abrasion and impact in shallow water. Copper sheathing carries power to repeaters far offshore. Polyethylene jackets protect against corrosion. In deep ocean, where the seabed is stable and human activity sparse, the cable can afford to be light and slender. Near shore, it becomes heavy, armoured, expensive. A single cable changes character as it crosses depths and jurisdictions, its design recording a map of perceived danger.

These design choices are not academic. They determine cost, repair complexity and failure modes. A deep-ocean fault may be rare but time-consuming to fix, requiring precise localisation and long transits for repair ships. A near-shore fault may be frequent, easier to reach, but politically and operationally fraught. Understanding why a cable looks one way at 4,000 metres and another at forty is to understand where engineers expect trouble to come from—and where history suggests they are right.

Before any glass touches water, years of planning pass. Feasibility studies weigh demand against capital. Marine surveys trace the seabed in fine detail, mapping slopes, sediments, wrecks and hazards. Environmental assessments negotiate with regulators and communities. Routes are adjusted repeatedly, sometimes by metres, sometimes by hundreds of kilometres. What emerges is not a perfect path, but an acceptable one. Laying a cable is less like drawing a line and more like threading a needle that keeps moving.

The act of installation brings this abstraction into contact with weather, machinery and human judgement. Specialist ships maintain tension on the cable as it leaves the stern, compensating for currents and swell. Ploughs bury the cable where protection is required, cutting a narrow furrow and folding sediment back over the armour. Along complex coastlines, crews may work only a few hours each tide, timing their movements to avoid exposing the cable or the vessel. The sea dictates the rhythm. Precision is enforced by gravity.

Powering the system introduces another layer of constraint. Optical signals weaken as they travel. To cross oceans, they must be amplified by repeaters spaced at regular intervals along the route. These repeaters draw power from shore, fed through the cable itself. The voltage is high, the tolerances strict. Route length, repeater spacing and power budgets become intertwined decisions. A longer route may require more repeaters, increasing cost and complexity. A failure in a single repeater can degrade performance across a wide span, not by severing the cable, but by narrowing the path available to light.

This is why maintenance is specialised and cautious. Repeaters cannot be serviced in situ; they must be retrieved, replaced and re-laid. Fault diagnosis begins on shore, in network operations centres that watch performance metrics with forensic attention. A slight change in signal strength, a rise in error rates, an unexpected latency shift—each can indicate trouble hundreds or thousands of kilometres away. Automated alarms flag anomalies. Humans interpret them.

Operations centres are where the cable's apparent passivity ends. Here, engineers coordinate with partners across borders, compare telemetry, and decide when a suspicion becomes a fault. A suspected break may trigger calls between operators in different countries, maintenance authorities in different zones, and ship operators scattered across ports. Decisions must balance urgency against safety, certainty against cost. Not every anomaly justifies a ship sailing. Not every delay is acceptable.

Commercial arrangements shape these choices in ways rarely visible to users. Some cables are privately owned, built to serve a single firm or a small group. Others are consortia, binding many parties together through shared investment and shared risk. Maintenance contracts allocate repair ships to regions, set priorities, and define cost-sharing. In theory, these agreements are neutral frameworks. In practice, they encode power. A consortium with many members must negotiate whose traffic is most affected, whose service-level commitments are at risk, and whose customers are loudest.

This commercial reality does not undermine resilience, but it complicates it. Redundancy on paper may depend on cooperation in practice. A cable system can be technically resilient and operationally fragile if incentives are misaligned. Understanding how cables are built and run therefore requires moving beyond diagrams into the lived world of contracts, coordination and compromise.

The relevance of this chapter reaches beyond engineering curiosity. As cables become more strategic, expectations rise. Governments ask how quickly faults can be repaired. Businesses assume continuity. Users treat outages as aberrations rather than features of a physical system. The tension between expectation and reality grows sharper when incidents occur in contested waters or during political crises. Knowing how cables are constructed, powered and operated grounds those expectations in what is physically possible.

A subtle motif runs through the chapter: patience. Patience in planning routes that will outlive their designers. Patience in laying cable metre by metre. Patience in diagnosing faults without rushing ships into danger.

Patience in negotiations that determine who pays and who waits. This patience is not inertia. It is discipline learned through failure.

The chapter that follows will move deliberately through these layers. It will begin with the cable itself, tangible and physical. It will follow the system from drawing board to seabed, from shore-based power to offshore amplification, from routine monitoring to crisis response. It will end not with a neat resolution, but with a clearer sense of what it takes to keep the physical internet alive.

If earlier chapters asked *where* cables run and *why* those paths matter, this one asks *how* they are made to work at all. The answer is neither mystical nor purely technical. It is human, contingent, and quietly impressive. Turn the page with that in mind.

## Cable design and basic components

On 20 December 1988, AT&T, British Telecom and France Télécom switched on TAT-8, the first transatlantic fibre-optic cable, linking the United States, the United Kingdom and France. It carried a fraction of the capacity of modern systems, yet its immediate outcome was decisive: digital clarity replaced analogue noise across the Atlantic, and long-distance communication acquired a physical form that could scale. The ocean did not change. The cable did.

Five words frame the chapter: *glass survives by design.*

A modern subsea cable looks modest when coiled on a quay. It becomes formidable only when understood. At its heart are optical fibres—slender strands of silica engineered to guide light with astonishing fidelity. Around them sit layers that answer specific threats: pressure, abrasion, corrosion, electricity, and time. The design is neither uniform nor accidental. It is a sequence of choices that change with depth, distance and danger.

Begin with the fibres themselves. Each fibre carries data as pulses of light, encoded and decoded at the ends of the system. Advances in modulation and wavelength division mean a single pair can carry enormous traffic, but the physics remains unforgiving. Bend the fibre too tightly and signal degrades. Expose it to microfractures and losses rise. The visible behaviour of the system—error rates, latency stability—depends on microscopic tolerances maintained across thousands of kilometres. Trust here is literal: engineers trust that glass drawn in a factory will behave predictably on a seabed it will never be seen on again.

Surrounding the fibres is a protective core that often includes a copper or aluminium conductor. This is not for data but for power. Subsea cables feed electricity from shore to repeaters spaced along the route. The conductor's thickness and material choice affect resistance and heat dissipation, which in turn constrain route length and repeater spacing. Efficiency is measured in volts and watts rather than slogans. If resistance is too high, the system cannot power its amplifiers reliably. Design answers physics.

Repeaters are the system's quiet sentinels. Positioned at regular intervals, they amplify optical signals to compensate for attenuation. Modern repeaters are remarkably reliable, designed to operate for decades without intervention. Yet their presence shapes everything. They impose spacing that fixes the rhythm of the route. They add mass and cost. They create single points of degradation: when a repeater fails, capacity may not vanish, but performance narrows. Operators see this as reduced margin—fewer wavelengths lit, tighter operating envelopes. The implication is subtle. The cable still works, but less comfortably.

Outside the core sit layers that reflect the seabed above. In deep ocean, where depths exceed several thousand metres and human activity is sparse, cables are light. A polyethylene sheath and minimal armour suffice. The cable lies on stable sediment, disturbed rarely by anything larger than a slow-moving current. Here, cost per kilometre is lower, installation faster, and fault rates historically modest, according to industry summaries compiled by the International Telecommunication Union and maintenance authorities (ITU, various years). The risk profile is geological rather than human.

Near shore, the design thickens. Steel wire armour appears, sometimes in multiple layers. Bitumen and polypropylene bedding absorb shock. The cable may be double-armoured in fishing grounds and buried beneath the seabed using ploughs or jetting. This is where expense concentrates. A few tens of kilometres near land can account for a disproportionate share of system cost. The behaviour that justifies this is observable: the majority of faults occur in shallow water, caused by anchoring, trawling and coastal activity, as documented repeatedly in maintenance zone reports and analyses by operators' associations. The implication is not that deep ocean is safe, but that human proximity dominates risk.

Consider a single system transitioning from abyssal plain to continental shelf. In deep water, the cable may weigh little more than a garden hose. As it approaches shore, it gains armour, mass and stiffness. Installation slows.

Precision increases. Costs rise. The same system embodies two philosophies: lightness where nature is predictable, heaviness where people are not. This gradient explains why repairs near shore, though geographically closer, can be more complex than those far offshore. Permits, traffic, tides and stakeholders intrude.

A named example illustrates the contrast. The Dunant cable, linking Virginia Beach to France, traverses deep Atlantic waters with a lightweight design optimised for long spans, then transitions to heavily armoured segments as it nears land. Public disclosures emphasise performance, but the physical reality is layered. The deep-ocean portion benefits from stable seabed and minimal interference. The near-shore segments absorb the cost and complexity of coexistence with fishing fleets, shipping lanes and coastal infrastructure. One cable. Two worlds.

Abstractions become concrete at the armour layer. "Security" translates into millimetres of steel. "Resilience" translates into burial depth. "Efficiency" translates into kilograms per metre and the speed a ship can safely pay out cable. These choices are measured, compared and committed during design. They are difficult to reverse later.

A credible limitation complicates the picture. Heavy armour is not a panacea. In some seabeds, burial is ineffective because sediment shifts or hard substrates prevent trenching. In others, added weight increases installation stress and can introduce new failure modes. Reconcile the point. Design is context-specific. There is no universally "safer" cable, only a cable safer for a given environment.

Manufacturing quality underpins all of this. Cables are produced in controlled conditions, tested for tensile strength, pressure resistance and signal integrity. Repeaters undergo burn-in tests designed to weed out early failures. The visible metric is defect rate per thousand kilometres. When defects slip through, consequences are long-lived. A flaw sealed into a cable at the factory may surface years later as a fault far from shore. The implication is patience: investment in quality upfront substitutes for intervention later.

The motif threading this section is layering. Layering of materials, of risk, of decision-making. Each layer answers a question posed by the environment above it. Remove a layer and vulnerability appears. Add too many and cost and complexity rise.

Design choices also encode assumptions about time. Cables are expected to operate for 20 to 25 years. Traffic patterns will change. Ownership may change. Politics will change. The physical design must endure regardless. This is why conservatism persists in cable engineering even as data technologies race ahead. Engineers favour proven materials and margins because retrieval is costly and uncertain. Innovation enters cautiously, tested on limited routes before wider adoption.

The closing tension returns to choice. As traffic grows and routes crowd, pressure mounts to reduce cost and accelerate deployment. That pressure tempts lighter designs, tighter margins, fewer armoured segments. The counterpressure comes from history, which shows where faults recur and why. The question is not whether glass can carry the world's data—it can—but how much risk we are willing to freeze into the seabed when we decide how thick that glass should be where it meets the shore.

## Planning and laying a new system

On 23 September 2019, off the coast of Saint-Hilaire-de-Riez in Vendée, the cable ship *CS Sovereign* began landing a new transatlantic system on a French beach. Alcatel Submarine Networks, contracted to build and install the cable, had spent years turning a line on a chart into a sequence of workable actions. The outcome was tangible by evening: a shore-end section was pulled through a beach manhole and secured inland, the moment when a global route becomes a local construction site. The ocean did not applaud. It simply accepted the cable.

Five words fit the first day: *plans meet sand and tide.*

It is fashionable to speak of infrastructure as if it were willed into existence by capital and urgency alone. Subsea cables resist that fantasy. A new system begins not at sea but in a spreadsheet, where demand curves, financing models and latency targets are balanced against regulatory timelines and geopolitical risk. Before a ship moves, lawyers and engineers have already fought most of the battles.

Feasibility is the first gate. Sponsors decide what the cable is for: capacity, latency, market entry, sovereignty, redundancy, or some combination. That purpose determines endpoints, design and ownership. A consortium cable designed to serve many markets will tolerate more complexity in landings and governance. A private system built for cloud traffic will prioritise directness and control. Efficiency here becomes a measurable decision:

how quickly can the cable be brought into service relative to expected revenue and strategic value?

Route selection follows, and it is less about drawing a straight line than about choosing a corridor wide enough to survive reality. Planners model demand and competitor networks, then overlay physical constraints: bathymetry, seabed composition, seismic zones, fishing intensity, marine protected areas. They also overlay politics: territorial waters, permit regimes, landing station availability, security reviews. The route that wins is rarely the one that looks cleanest. It is the one with the fewest fatal objections.

Marine surveys translate this corridor into detail. Specialist survey vessels tow sonar, magnetometers and sub-bottom profilers, mapping the seabed and looking beneath it. They identify steep slopes where a cable could slide, rock outcrops where burial is impossible, and human hazards such as wrecks and existing infrastructure. The visible output is a chart with hundreds of annotations. The implication is control. Every hazard identified now is a repair avoided later.

The surveys also shape how the cable will be protected. In stable deep ocean, cable can be laid on the seabed with minimal intervention. In shallow, crowded waters, it must be buried, often to depths measured in metres. Burial is not an afterthought; it is a design requirement. The decision is blunt: spend more on protection now, or pay more later in repairs and outages. Risk becomes a cost line.

Permitting runs alongside survey work, sometimes faster, often slower. Coastal states regulate landings tightly because shore-end work intersects with environmental concerns, land ownership, and other sea users. The same beach can be a tourist asset, a fisheries zone, a protected habitat and a cable corridor. The cable must coexist with all of them. The visible behaviour is negotiation: route tweaks to avoid sensitive areas, construction windows timed around breeding seasons, conditions imposed for monitoring and restoration. The implication is that cables are as much about social licence as seabed engineering.

Manufacturing begins only when sufficient certainty exists to commit. Cable factories are not generic workshops; they are specialised facilities that produce kilometres of cable with strict quality control, then store it in enormous turntables for loading onto ships. Repeaters are built, tested and integrated. The most distinctive feature of subsea cable projects is how much must be correct the first time. Once installed, mistakes are expensive to retrieve.

Now the sea enters. Cable-laying ships are floating factories with dynamic positioning systems that hold them steady in wind and current. They carry thousands of tonnes of cable coiled in tanks, paid out under controlled tension through stern chutes. They are supported by smaller craft near shore, where manoeuvring is tight and hazards are dense. A ship's slow progress is not incompetence; it is precision made visible.

Here a narrative example clarifies the choreography. Along a complex coastline—think of Brittany with its tides, rocky outcrops and strong currents—the day begins with weather forecasts and tidal tables rather than a project manager's timetable. The cable-lay superintendent reviews the runline: the pre-surveyed track, adjusted for overnight shifts in sea state. The ship moves into position, its thrusters humming as it holds station. The cable is paid out. On screens, the route appears as a moving dot; on deck, it is a heavy, living thing, flexing and settling as it leaves the vessel.

Near shore, the operation becomes a blend of marine engineering and civil works. A beach manhole is prepared in advance, the cable pulled ashore using winches and rollers. Divers or remotely operated vehicles confirm placement and burial. The cable may be temporarily secured while the ship waits for the next tide window. At each step, the sea imposes constraints that no contract can remove. Five words again: *the tide sets the pace.*

Burial is where the seabed fights back. Ploughs are towed behind the ship, cutting a narrow trench and laying cable within it, then backfilling. In softer sediments, jetting tools fluidise sand to allow the cable to sink. In rocky ground, burial can be impossible; engineers may choose rock dumping for protection or reroute around the hazard. Each method has a signature. Ploughing is neat and effective but demands consistent seabed conditions. Jetting is flexible but can be disrupted by currents. Rock dumping is protective but costly and politically sensitive where habitats are concerned. The visible metric is burial depth achieved versus target. The implication is future fault probability.

Precision matters because proximity to hazards is not theoretical. A route that drifts too close to a shipping anchorage increases the chance of anchor damage. A route that crosses a pipeline corridor at the wrong angle complicates future repair access for both assets. A route that ignores sediment movement may emerge from its trench within a season. The ship's captain and the cable engineers therefore navigate not just geography but future behaviour—where ships will anchor, where fishers will trawl, where currents will scour.

This is where the quiet motif of the *line* returns. The line on the planning map becomes a line of tension on the ship's payout system, then a line of jurisdiction as it crosses territorial waters, then a line of responsibility as ownership and maintenance obligations attach. Each stage transforms abstraction into accountability.

A second checkable example illustrates how political and technical constraints merge. When Facebook (now Meta) and partners announced the 2Africa cable in 2020, the project's ambition—encircling the African continent—was as much about routing around chokepoints as serving markets. The design acknowledged geopolitical and physical constraints: multiple landings to diversify exposure, routes chosen to balance latency and risk. The limitation was equally clear. Such a project multiplies permitting complexity and increases the number of coastal interactions where delay can occur. Reconcile the lesson. Route diversity buys resilience but demands patience and governance.

Patience is not just a virtue; it is a requirement. Cable projects often face delays from storms, equipment faults, permitting disputes or political shifts. A storm can push installation weeks off schedule. A port closure can delay mobilisation. A single landing permit can stall an entire system even if the rest is ready. Efficiency becomes a calendar. It is measured in lost weather windows and idle ships.

Counter-examples are instructive. There are cases where cables have been laid rapidly in response to urgent demand or strategic pressure, with streamlined permits and accelerated procurement. The limitation is that speed can increase long-term risk if surveys are rushed or protection measures compromised. Reconcile the point. Fast projects exist, but the ocean collects its debts later, often in the form of higher fault rates and more difficult repairs.

Once the cable is laid, the project is not "finished" in any meaningful sense. It enters commissioning, where equipment at the ends is installed and tested, channels are lit, and performance is measured against design. The visible behaviour is calibration: adjusting power levels, verifying dispersion compensation, validating redundancy. Only then does the cable become what the public imagines—a silent, reliable conduit.

Yet the most consequential decisions have already been made by that point. The route is fixed. The burial depth is set. The landing station is built. The maintenance zone is chosen. The cable will live inside those choices for decades.

The unresolved test is deceptively simple. As demand rises and geopolitical pressure grows, will sponsors continue to fund the slow, expensive disciplines—surveys, protections, route diversity—that turn a line into an enduring system, or will speed and cost cut corners that the sea will later expose?

## Powering and repeating the signal

In 1987, at Bell Laboratories in New Jersey, researchers demonstrated the erbium-doped fibre amplifier, a device that could strengthen an optical signal without converting it back into electricity. The breakthrough did not make headlines outside engineering circles, yet its outcome was decisive. Oceans became crossable by light alone. The sea floor could host amplification without human presence. Distance stopped being the primary enemy.

Signals fade. Power keeps them alive.

Every subsea cable confronts the same physical fact: light weakens as it travels through glass. Attenuation is not a failure of engineering but a property of matter. Over a few kilometres, the loss is tolerable. Over thousands, it is fatal without intervention. The answer is repetition—periodic amplification that restores the signal's strength while preserving its information. In modern systems, this occurs invisibly, automatically, and relentlessly, day after day.

Repeaters sit along the cable at regular intervals, sealed into pressure-resistant housings and designed to operate for decades. They are not computers in the everyday sense. They do not route traffic or make decisions. They amplify. Their simplicity is deliberate. Fewer functions mean fewer failure modes. Trust here is engineered: repeaters are built to standards that accept no routine maintenance. Once submerged, they are expected to work until the cable is retired.

Powering those repeaters is a challenge as fundamental as amplification itself. Subsea cables carry electricity from shore through a conductive layer wrapped around the optical fibres. Power feeding equipment at landing stations supplies high-voltage direct current, chosen because it travels long distances with manageable losses. The voltage is stepped up on land and distributed along the cable, feeding each repeater in sequence. Efficiency is measured in volts delivered per kilometre, not in abstract claims.

This arrangement imposes constraints that ripple through the entire system. The length of the route, the spacing of repeaters, and the resistance of the conductor are locked together. Extend the route and power losses rise. Add repeaters and power demand increases. Thicken the conductor to reduce resistance and the cable becomes heavier and more expensive to lay. Each decision tightens the design envelope. Route planners do not ask merely whether a cable can be laid; they ask whether it can be powered within safe margins.

The visible behaviour of this power system appears in operations centres as stable voltages and predictable optical performance. Deviations are signals. A slow drift in power draw can indicate ageing components. A sudden change can suggest a fault. Operators measure, compare and decide. The implication is vigilance rather than drama. Most problems announce themselves quietly.

The spacing of repeaters illustrates how physics becomes geography. In deep ocean, where routes are long and straight, repeaters are spaced to balance signal quality and power limits. In shallower, more complex regions, spacing may tighten to account for bends, temperature variations or higher risk segments. The seabed's shape influences how often light must be strengthened. A cable crossing a mid-ocean ridge may require different engineering from one lying on an abyssal plain. Design responds to terrain.

A named example clarifies the stakes. The trans-Pacific cable TPC-5, commissioned in the mid-1990s, relied on optical amplifiers to span vast distances with fewer regeneration points than earlier systems. Its design reduced latency and complexity, but it also concentrated dependence on repeater reliability. When later systems adopted similar approaches, they did so with more conservative margins, informed by early operational data reported through maintenance authorities. The lesson was absorbed quietly: amplification works, but it must be treated with respect.

Counter-examples matter. There are systems where repeater spacing is intentionally conservative, accepting higher cost to reduce power stress and extend lifespan. The limitation is commercial. Extra repeaters increase capital expenditure and complicate installation. Reconcile the trade-off. Conservative designs buy operational headroom at a price that not all sponsors are willing to pay.

When repeaters fail, the consequences are rarely cinematic but can be profound. A single failed repeater does not usually sever connectivity. Instead, it narrows the channel. Capacity drops. Error margins tighten. Operators may have to turn down certain wavelengths to keep others stable. The visible effect for users can be congestion or increased latency rather than total outage. Risk appears as degradation.

Maintenance in these cases is specialised because diagnosis must be precise before action is taken. Retrieving a repeater requires cutting the cable, lifting sections weighing tonnes, replacing the unit, and re-laying the line with accuracy. Each step carries risk. Ships, weather windows and permits must align. This is why operators exhaust remote options first: power cycling, re-balancing channels, reconfiguring modulation. The decision to dispatch a repair ship is measured against the cost and danger of intervention.

A documented incident illustrates the dynamic. In 2008, disruptions to several cables in the Mediterranean and Middle East region were initially attributed to cuts, but subsequent investigations highlighted the complexity of distinguishing between physical damage and power-related degradation across interconnected systems, as reported by operators and regional maintenance groups at the time. Performance issues cascaded, not because every cable was broken, but because margins tightened across the network. The implication was sobering. Power and amplification issues can propagate stress beyond their immediate location.

The quiet motif threading this section is endurance. Repeaters endure pressure, time and isolation. Power systems endure distance and resistance. The cable endures because these elements are balanced rather than optimised to extremes. Engineers resist the temptation to push every parameter to its theoretical limit. They leave room for ageing, for unexpected conditions, for human error.

Abstractions such as "resilience" become concrete here. Resilience is a spare decibel of signal margin. It is an extra repeater. It is a conductor thick enough to tolerate voltage drift. Each choice is visible in a specification sheet and felt years later in operational calm.

Yet limits remain. Power feeding systems depend on shore facilities that themselves can fail. Repeaters, though reliable, are not immortal. As traffic demands grow, operators seek to extract more capacity from existing fibres through advanced modulation. That increases sensitivity to noise and power variation. The system becomes more capable and more delicate at the same time.

The forward test is unresolved. As cables are asked to carry ever greater volumes with ever tighter performance expectations, will designers continue to preserve generous power and amplification margins, accepting higher upfront costs, or will economic pressure compress those margins until maintenance becomes more frequent and intervention more urgent? The sea will answer eventually. The question is how much warning we will have when it does.

## Operating a cable from shore

In January 2008, engineers at BT's network operations centre in London watched a set of performance graphs tilt out of tolerance. The change was small at first: rising error rates on circuits transiting the Mediterranean. Within minutes, alarms propagated across linked systems. Phones rang. By the end of the hour, BT engineers were speaking with counterparts in Italy and Egypt, comparing telemetry and narrowing down a fault that would later be associated with damage to multiple subsea cables near Alexandria. The immediate outcome was not repair—that would take far longer—but coordinated traffic rerouting that kept essential services running while margins tightened.

Five words mattered then: *the screens told a story.*

Subsea cables do not announce themselves when they fail. They whisper. The work of operating them happens far from the seabed, in rooms designed for vigilance rather than heroics. Network operations centres, or NOCs, are where the physical internet becomes legible to human judgement. Here, cables appear as numbers: optical power levels, bit error rates, latency measurements, alarms with thresholds calibrated to experience. The sea is translated into data.

Automation is the first line of defence. Modern systems continuously measure performance across fibres and wavelengths. Software flags deviations from expected behaviour, correlating them across time and route. The visible behaviour is an alarm cascade that points not to a location but to a suspicion. Something has changed. The implication is restraint. Operators do not rush to conclusions because false positives are costly and panic is corrosive.

Human judgement follows quickly. Engineers assess whether an alarm reflects transient noise, planned maintenance, or something more serious.

They compare current readings with historical baselines. They ask whether other systems show similar patterns. This is where experience matters. A slight power dip after a storm may mean nothing. The same dip combined with rising error rates on adjacent spans may mean everything.

Fault detection in subsea networks is therefore probabilistic rather than binary. Operators work with likelihoods, not certainties. They narrow the search space. Is the anomaly confined to one landing or seen on both ends? Does it affect all wavelengths or only those at the margin? Does traffic rerouting restore stability or merely mask the issue? Each answer informs the next decision.

The tools used are precise but not magical. Optical time-domain reflectometry, for example, can estimate the distance to a fault by analysing reflected light. Power feed equipment reports current and voltage changes that hint at where along the cable resistance has altered. These techniques measure. Engineers interpret. The implication is collaboration between machine and mind.

Coordination across borders is routine, not exceptional. Most cables are jointly owned or interconnected with others. A suspected fault triggers conference calls that span companies and countries. Time zones blur. Responsibility is shared. During the 2008 Mediterranean incident, public reporting later showed how operators compared notes to distinguish between coincidental degradation and common cause. No single screen held the answer. The network did.

Trust becomes operational here. Operators trust their partners to share accurate data quickly, even when commercial interests diverge. They trust maintenance authorities to advise on ship availability. They trust that agreed protocols will hold under pressure. This trust is not sentimental. It is encoded in contracts, rehearsed in drills, and tested in incidents.

A second checkable example shows the pattern. In March 2011, after the Tōhoku earthquake off Japan, operators managing trans-Pacific systems observed simultaneous anomalies across multiple cables. Network operations centres in Japan, the United States and elsewhere coordinated traffic shifts within hours, guided by seismic data and optical readings. Public sources later documented how redundancy absorbed the shock, even as repairs took months. The immediate outcome was continuity under strain. The implication was clear. Operations matter as much as design.

Abstractions such as "resilience" become concrete decisions on the operations floor. Should traffic be rerouted automatically, risking congestion elsewhere, or manually, preserving headroom? Should customers be notified immediately or only after confirmation? Should a maintenance ship be alerted now or only after fault localisation improves? Each choice trades speed against certainty.

Metrics guide but do not decide. Latency increases measured in milliseconds can signal a reroute that keeps services alive at reduced quality. Packet loss percentages translate into customer complaints and contractual thresholds. Operators weigh these against the cost and risk of intervention. Efficiency here is not speed alone; it is appropriateness.

There is a credible limitation to automation. Algorithms excel at recognising known patterns. They struggle with novelty. Unusual combinations of minor anomalies can escape automated thresholds while still indicating emerging trouble. Reconcile the limitation. Human oversight remains essential precisely because the sea produces surprises. Experienced engineers notice when a familiar graph looks wrong even if it is still "in spec".

The daily rhythm of operations is therefore a blend of routine and readiness. Most days pass quietly. Performance is logged. Minor alarms are resolved. Planned maintenance occurs. Then, occasionally, the pattern breaks. A fault emerges that cannot be explained away. At that point, the NOC becomes a coordination hub, not just a monitoring room.

Communication extends beyond engineers. Corporate communications teams prepare statements. Government contacts may be notified if critical services are affected. Customers seek reassurance. The timing and tone of these communications influence public perception and political reaction. Operators learn to speak carefully, acknowledging uncertainty without fuelling speculation.

The motif of *screens* returns here. Screens show data, but they also shape behaviour. What is visible becomes urgent. What is hidden waits. Experienced operators therefore cultivate habits that look beyond the immediate alarm. They ask what the screens are not showing: emerging weather systems, nearby construction, unusual vessel movements reported by partners. Operations is as much about context as telemetry.

Maintenance coordination sits just beyond the operations centre, yet decisions made on shore determine what happens at sea. When a fault is confirmed, operators engage regional maintenance agreements to request a repair ship. Availability depends on location, weather and competing demands. A storm can generate multiple faults across a region, forcing prioritisation. The visible metric becomes outage minutes weighted by traffic importance. The implication is uncomfortable. Some users wait longer than others.

A counter-example tempers the picture. There are instances where rapid intervention was chosen, only for later analysis to show that degradation could have been managed remotely. Ships were mobilised unnecessarily. Costs rose. Reconcile the lesson. Caution is not indecision; it is cost control informed by experience.

Operating a cable from shore also means planning for the long term. Operators track ageing trends, not just incidents. Gradual increases in power consumption or noise margins inform future upgrades and risk assessments. Decisions taken years before a fault occurs—about spare capacity, alternative routes, and monitoring investment—determine how stressful the moment will be when it does.

The unresolved tension is sharpening. As networks grow more complex and traffic more sensitive to delay, the margin for error in operations narrows. Automation improves, but dependence on it grows. Human expertise remains scarce and unevenly distributed. The forward test is whether operators can continue to combine machine vigilance with human judgement at scale, or whether the screens will one day show problems faster than organisations can coordinate to solve them.

## Commercial models and maintenance contracts

In February 2008, as multiple submarine cables failed in quick succession across the Mediterranean and Red Sea, representatives of several cable consortia convened urgent calls from offices in London, Marseille and Mumbai. Repair ships were finite. Weather windows were narrowing. Traffic was already being throttled. The immediate outcome was not a technical fix but a commercial one: agreements on repair priority, cost sharing and sequencing that determined which systems would be restored first and which would wait. The sea had done the damage. Contracts would decide the order of relief.

Five words frame the problem: *who pays decides speed.*

Subsea cables are engineered objects, but they are sustained by commercial arrangements. Steel, glass and power may carry data, yet ownership, governance and maintenance contracts determine how those systems behave under stress. To understand resilience, one must understand how cables are paid for, shared and repaired.

The earliest submarine cables were owned outright by states or national monopolies. Telegraph systems in the nineteenth and early twentieth centuries reflected imperial and governmental priorities, with maintenance vessels often operated directly by cable-owning entities. Modern fibre systems inherited some of this legacy but transformed it through scale and cost. A single contemporary transoceanic cable can require investment measured in hundreds of millions of dollars, sometimes more. Few single organisations are willing—or able—to bear that alone.

The consortium model emerged as the dominant solution. Multiple carriers, sometimes joined by content providers or state-backed entities, pool capital to build and operate a system. Each member receives rights to capacity proportionate to its investment. The visible behaviour is shared ownership. The implication is shared risk.

Consortia distribute financial exposure, but they also distribute decision-making. Governance structures define voting rights, management committees and operational responsibilities. These arrangements are intentionally detailed, because ambiguity during an incident is costly. When a fault occurs, the question is not only how to fix it, but who authorises the repair, who pays, and how priorities are set if resources are constrained.

Private systems represent a contrasting model. Large technology firms and some carriers now build cables they own outright, designed to serve specific traffic flows. The advantage is control. Decisions about upgrades, routing and repair can be made internally, without negotiation. The visible metric is speed. Private owners can commit funds and mobilise resources rapidly. The implication is responsiveness.

The limitation is concentration of risk. A private owner bears the full cost of failure and repair. There is no consortium to absorb shocks. Reconcile the trade-off. Control buys agility but reduces risk sharing. In practice, even privately owned cables often participate in shared maintenance arrangements to mitigate this exposure.

Maintenance contracts sit at the centre of these models. Because faults are unpredictable and repair ships expensive, operators form regional maintenance agreements. These pool resources across many systems, funding a small number of specialised vessels that stand ready to respond.

The North Atlantic, Mediterranean, Asia-Pacific and other regions each have their own arrangements, shaped by traffic density and fault history.

The mechanics are pragmatic. Members pay annual fees based on system length and risk profile. In return, they gain access to repair ships when faults occur. The visible behaviour is queuing. When multiple faults arise simultaneously, priorities must be set. Criteria typically include the number of systems affected, traffic volume, and the availability of alternative routes. The implication is uncomfortable but unavoidable. Some outages last longer because others are deemed more urgent.

A named example illustrates how this plays out. During the 2008 Mediterranean disruptions, cables such as SEA-ME-WE 4 and FLAG Europe-Asia were part of overlapping maintenance zones. Public reporting at the time showed how repair sequencing was negotiated among consortium members while ships repositioned from distant ports. The result was staggered restoration. Some routes returned quickly. Others took weeks. The outcome reflected agreements made long before the fault.

Commercial interests shape these negotiations. A consortium member serving a financial centre may argue that delay carries disproportionate economic cost. Another serving smaller markets may lack similar leverage. Metrics such as affected bandwidth or customer count become proxies for importance. Efficiency is argued in terms of impact per day of outage. These debates are rarely public, yet they determine lived experience for millions of users.

Counter-examples exist. There are cases where consortia have agreed to repair less commercially significant systems first because of political sensitivity or regulatory pressure. The limitation is precedent. Once exceptions are made, expectations shift. Reconcile the point. Commercial logic is dominant but not absolute; it operates within political and reputational constraints.

Maintenance contracts also define how repairs are conducted. They specify response times, crew readiness, spare part inventories and cost allocation. They cannot eliminate delays caused by weather or permits, but they can reduce friction once action is authorised. A well-run maintenance agreement shortens the path from diagnosis to mobilisation. A poorly run one magnifies confusion.

Insurance interacts with these models subtly. Cable systems are insured against physical damage, but policies often include deductibles and exclusions that make owners sensitive to repair cost escalation. Decisions about whether to attempt temporary fixes or full repairs can be influenced by coverage thresholds. Risk becomes a financial calculation as much as a technical one.

The motif threading this section is *queueing*. Cables queue for ships. Owners queue for attention. Decisions queue behind governance processes. Under normal conditions, the queue is invisible. During regional crises, it becomes decisive.

Commercial models also influence long-term resilience. Consortia with many members may struggle to agree on investments in additional redundancy or extra repair capacity. The cost is shared, but so is hesitation. Private owners may invest aggressively in resilience that serves their interests, but not necessarily the wider network. The system-level outcome depends on the balance between these approaches.

There is a tendency to view commercial arrangements as secondary to engineering. This is a mistake. Two cables with identical physical designs can exhibit very different outage profiles depending on ownership and maintenance structures. One may be repaired in days. Another may wait weeks. The difference is contractual.

The unresolved tension lies ahead. As cables become more strategic and outages more politically sensitive, pressure grows to treat maintenance capacity as critical infrastructure rather than a shared commercial service. Should states intervene to guarantee faster repairs? Should maintenance fleets expand, raising costs for all? Or should market logic continue to govern, accepting that resilience has a price and that someone must pay it?

The answer is not yet fixed. What is clear is that beneath the seabed, resilience is as much a product of balance sheets and agreements as it is of armour and glass.

# Chapter 4

# Threats, Accidents and Sabotage

At 19:15 local time on 26 December 2006, the seabed west of Taiwan shifted. An earthquake measuring 7.1 on the moment magnitude scale rippled through the Luzon Strait, a geologically restless corridor already dense with submarine cables. Within minutes, signals began to falter. Within hours, connectivity across large parts of East and Southeast Asia degraded sharply. Phone calls failed. Internet traffic slowed or vanished. Financial transactions queued. The cause was not malware or hostile code, but mud—underwater landslides triggered by seismic shock, tearing through multiple cables laid along the same constrained route.

The damage was physical. The consequences were systemic.

That episode captures the central unease of this chapter. The most important digital infrastructure on the planet is exposed to forces that range from indifferent geology to deliberate human intent, and often the difference between accident and attack is impossible to prove. The seabed does not keep receipts. It absorbs anchors, hides scars, and offers little in the way of witnesses. When cables fail, explanations compete.

Earlier chapters have shown how cables are designed, routed and operated with care. This chapter confronts the fact that care is never enough. Risk can be reduced, redistributed, and managed. It cannot be eliminated. The ocean floor is not a neutral substrate on which infrastructure rests safely. It is an active environment—sometimes violently so—and increasingly a contested one.

Natural hazards are the oldest threat. Earthquakes, submarine landslides, volcanic activity and powerful currents predate fibre-optic technology by millions of years. Route planners know this. They study seismic maps, avoid steep slopes, and try to keep distance between parallel systems. Yet geography constrains choice. Continental shelves narrow. Straits funnel routes. Commercial and political pressures encourage clustering. When nature moves, it often finds cables waiting.

Human activity adds another layer of exposure. Fishing trawlers do not set out to damage cables. Anchors are dropped to keep ships safe in storms or while awaiting port clearance. Dredgers deepen channels to keep trade moving. These are ordinary acts of economic life, repeated daily. Yet in shallow waters where cables converge towards land, they are the leading cause of damage. The most disruptive incidents are rarely spectacular. A vessel drags an anchor for a few hundred metres. Somewhere below, steel meets steel, and a connection built over years is severed in seconds.

Then there are acts that sit uneasily between accident and intent. Deliberate interference with cables is not new. Telegraph lines were cut in wartime more than a century ago. What has changed is the ambiguity. Modern cables are harder to access, better protected, and more numerous. Yet they are also more strategically valuable. A cut cable today affects markets, militaries, governments and daily life simultaneously. That makes them tempting targets—and perfect instruments for plausible deniability.

This chapter does not trade in speculation. It does not catalogue rumours or inflate threats beyond evidence. Instead, it examines the spectrum of harm that cables face, from the indifferent to the intentional, and asks why attribution is so difficult and so contested. The same physical outcome—a broken fibre—can be explained as an earthquake, a trawling accident, criminal damage, or a covert act, depending on context and narrative. The seabed itself offers little help in choosing between them.

Hybrid warfare sharpens this ambiguity. States increasingly operate in the grey space between peace and open conflict, using tools that blur civilian and military boundaries. Cables sit squarely in that space. They are commercial assets that carry military traffic. They are privately owned systems whose disruption can have public consequences. Damage can be framed as misfortune or malice, and the difference matters politically even when the technical repair is identical.

Patterns emerge when incidents are examined collectively rather than individually. Certain locations recur: narrow seas, busy approaches to ports, tectonically active corridors. Certain causes dominate: anchoring, fishing, seismic events. Certain responses repeat: delayed repairs due to weather, congestion on backup routes, public confusion over cause. This chapter draws those patterns out not to create a taxonomy of blame, but to show where risk concentrates and why.

A subtle motif runs through these pages: *invisibility*. The threats discussed here are rarely seen directly. Earthquakes are felt on land but their submarine consequences are inferred. Anchors snag cables far below the surface. Deliberate acts, if they occur, are designed to leave little trace. Invisibility complicates accountability. It also shapes public debate, which tends to focus on visible cyber threats while ignoring physical ones until failure forces attention.

The stakes are both modern and timeless. Modern because global connectivity has become foundational to economic and political life. Timeless because societies have always depended on fragile links whose failure exposed underlying vulnerabilities. Roman roads, telegraph wires, undersea telephony—all were subject to disruption by nature and human action alike. What changes is scale, speed and interdependence.

This chapter moves deliberately through the threat landscape. It begins with nature, not because it is the most alarming, but because it sets the baseline. Geological processes remind us that some risks are not adversarial. They cannot be deterred, only accommodated. From there, it turns to everyday human activity, where intention is absent but impact is real. It then addresses deliberate interference, cautiously and without sensationalism, acknowledging both feasibility and constraint. Finally, it examines how these elements are reframed through hybrid conflict and political narrative.

The goal is not to provoke fear. It is to cultivate clarity. When a cable fails, the first question asked is often *who did it*. This chapter asks a prior question: *where was it, and why was it exposed*. Answers to that question often explain more than speculation about motive.

As cables multiply and routes crowd, the margin for coincidence narrows. Multiple failures in one place invite suspicion. Yet suspicion alone does not repair fibre or restore trust. Understanding patterns does. Learning where clustering amplifies harm does. Recognising that many of the most disruptive incidents arise from mundane activity does.

By the end of this chapter, the reader will see cable threats not as a catalogue of dangers, but as a landscape shaped by geology, economics, politics and design choices made decades earlier. The seabed did not suddenly become hostile. It became crowded. What follows is an exploration of what that crowding means, and how easily the line between accident and attack can dissolve beneath the waves.

## Natural hazards on the seabed

On 26 December 2006, at 12:26 local time, an earthquake struck the Luzon Strait between Taiwan and the Philippines. Within hours, engineers at Chunghwa Telecom in Taipei were confronting a pattern they recognised too well and yet could not immediately resolve: multiple submarine cables had failed almost simultaneously. The outcome was regional disruption across East and Southeast Asia that lasted weeks, not days, as repair ships worked through a corridor scarred by submarine landslides triggered by the quake. Markets slowed. Calls dropped. Redundancy thinned.

Nature does not negotiate.

Earthquakes are the most dramatic reminder that the seabed is not a static platform. They are also the least amenable to mitigation. Subsea cables cross tectonic boundaries because continents and oceans are shaped by them; avoiding every fault line would mean avoiding the very routes that connect population centres. Route planners therefore measure, compare and accept. They study seismic maps, consult geological surveys, and steer away from the most active zones where possible. Where avoidance is impossible, they widen separation between parallel systems and design for repair rather than immunity. Risk is managed, not erased.

The Luzon Strait incident illustrates a recurring pattern. The initial shock did not sever every cable directly. Instead, it destabilised sediment on steep slopes, generating underwater landslides that travelled downslope and swept across multiple routes laid in proximity. The visible behaviour was clustering turned against itself. Cables placed together for efficiency and cost reduction were damaged together by a single natural event. The implication was uncomfortable. Diversity on paper can collapse in practice when geography funnels routes into the same hazards.

Submarine landslides deserve attention precisely because they are indirect. They can be triggered by earthquakes, storms, or even gradual sediment accumulation reaching a tipping point. Once in motion, they behave like avalanches, carrying mud and debris at speeds capable of snapping cables or burying them deeply. Detection is retrospective. Operators learn of landslides from cable failures, not the other way round. Geological studies following the 2006 event, including analyses published in *Marine Geology* in subsequent years, mapped extensive slide scars along the strait, confirming that the damage pattern followed sediment flow rather than fault rupture.

Strong currents are less dramatic but no less consequential. In certain regions, bottom currents can scour sediment, exposing cables that were once buried. Exposure increases vulnerability to other hazards, from fishing gear to anchors. Route planners account for known current regimes, but currents shift over time. Climate variability adds uncertainty. The visible metric is burial depth achieved versus burial depth retained years later. The implication is monitoring and, occasionally, re-burial—an intervention that carries its own risk.

Volcanic activity adds a further layer. Submarine volcanoes and hydrothermal vents can alter seabed topography rapidly. Heat can damage cable sheathing. Chemical environments can accelerate corrosion. These zones are usually avoided, yet long routes sometimes skirt their edges. The limitation is mapping resolution. Not all features are known, and not all changes are predictable. Reconcile the point. Surveys reduce uncertainty; they do not eliminate it.

Route planning therefore becomes an exercise in probabilistic judgement. Engineers overlay hazard maps with commercial constraints and political boundaries. They ask not only where hazards exist, but how likely they are to affect a cable over its expected lifespan. A fault line that slips rarely may be preferable to a busy shelf exposed to constant human interference. Efficiency is measured in expected fault rates per kilometre per year, a metric used internally by operators and maintenance authorities to guide design and insurance decisions.

A second checkable example sharpens the lesson. In November 2016, a magnitude 7.8 earthquake off New Zealand's South Island damaged multiple submarine cables serving the country. Public reporting by operators and government agencies documented how seabed movement and landslides severed routes, leading to degraded international connectivity until repairs were completed. The systems affected were not carelessly placed; they were constrained by geography. The implication echoed 2006. Even well-planned routes converge on limited landing points and corridors where nature's leverage is greatest.

There is a credible counter-example that tempers alarm. Many deep-ocean cables traverse vast tectonic plates with minimal seismic activity and experience decades of uninterrupted service. Fault statistics compiled by regional maintenance agreements show lower incident rates in stable abyssal plains compared to continental margins. Reconcile the evidence. Natural hazard risk is unevenly distributed. The danger concentrates where routes transition from deep to shallow water and where geology is restless. Design responds accordingly.

The abstraction of "resilience" becomes tangible in separation distance. When planners can afford it, they separate parallel systems by tens or hundreds of kilometres in hazard-prone regions. That separation has a cost: longer routes, higher latency, more permits. The decision to accept those costs is a visible commitment to resilience. When budgets tighten, separation shrinks, and clustering returns. The seabed keeps score.

Another abstraction—"predictability"—is revealed as partial. Earthquake science can identify active zones but not timing. Landslide modelling can indicate risk but not trigger. Currents can be measured today but change tomorrow. The implication is humility. Cable engineering assumes uncertainty and plans for recovery.

Recovery itself is shaped by natural conditions. After a seismic event, repair ships may face unstable seabeds where new slides are possible. They may have to wait for conditions to settle, delaying intervention. The visible behaviour is downtime measured in weeks. The implication for users is patience tested by dependence.

The motif threading this section is *movement*. Plates move. Sediment moves. Currents move. Cables, by contrast, are designed to stay still. The conflict between a dynamic environment and static infrastructure defines natural hazard risk. Engineers mitigate movement's effects but cannot stop it.

Clustering amplifies this conflict. Economic and political incentives push cables into shared corridors: straits, shelves, and approaches to landing stations. These are often the same places where natural hazards concentrate. The lesson of repeated incidents is not that clustering is reckless, but that it carries systemic risk that must be acknowledged. Redundancy that relies on neighbouring routes may fail when nature acts at scale.

There is an emerging debate about whether climate change will alter seabed hazard profiles. Increased storm intensity could affect sediment transport on shelves. Melting ice may change current patterns in high-latitude routes. These remain hypotheses rather than settled conclusions, and responsible analysis labels them as such. What is clear is that uncertainty is increasing, not decreasing. Route planning must therefore become more adaptive, revisiting assumptions over time rather than freezing them at commissioning.

Natural hazards also complicate attribution in mixed-cause incidents. An earthquake may expose a cable that is later damaged by human activity. A landslide may weaken armour that fails months later under minor stress. The seabed does not timestamp causation neatly. Operators must piece together sequences from incomplete evidence. The implication for public discourse is caution. Simple explanations rarely survive contact with geological complexity.

The forward test is stark. As cable density grows and routes converge, will planners and sponsors continue to fund separation and conservative design in hazard-prone regions, accepting higher costs and longer paths, or will commercial pressure compress routes into the same vulnerable corridors once again? Nature will not adjust its behaviour to answer that question. It will respond as it always has—indifferently, and at scale—leaving engineers and societies to live with the choices made in advance.

## Fishing gear and ship anchors

On 30 January 2008, off the coast of Alexandria, a ship anchored to wait out weather in the eastern Mediterranean. The anchor dragged. Somewhere below, it crossed the path of the SEA-ME-WE 4 submarine cable. Within hours, operators including Telecom Egypt were fielding alarms as traffic between Europe, the Middle East and South Asia degraded sharply. Renesys, a network monitoring firm, later documented widespread routing disruptions tied to the incident. The outcome was not a dramatic explosion or a visible break, but weeks of constrained connectivity while repairs were organised in crowded waters.

Steel meets glass. Glass loses.

Most cable damage does not come from earthquakes or covert saboteurs. It comes from work. Fishing fleets trawl. Dredgers deepen channels. Ships anchor to ride out storms or await berths. These activities are lawful, routine and economically essential. They are also indifferent to the precise location of a cable buried beneath sediment that shifts, scours and sometimes disappears altogether. In shallow water, the margin between coexistence and collision is thin.

Shallow waters are where routes converge. Every long-haul cable must transition from the open ocean to land, crossing continental shelves where depth decreases, traffic density increases and human activity intensifies. The visible behaviour of the network reflects this geography. Fault statistics compiled by regional maintenance authorities consistently show that the majority of cable faults occur in water less than 200 metres deep, a pattern reported across multiple regions and decades. The implication is not negligence but exposure.

Trawling is the most persistent source of this exposure. Bottom trawls drag heavy gear across the seabed to harvest demersal fish. The gear is designed to withstand contact with rocks and debris. A cable, even armoured and buried, can be snagged, lifted and abraded. When that happens, damage may be immediate or latent. Armour may deform without severing fibres, only to fail later under tension or current. The visible metric is delayed failure, which complicates attribution and response.

Anchoring introduces a different risk profile. Anchors are dropped in emergencies, during storms, or when ships queue outside ports. They are not placed with cable charts in mind, particularly in congested approaches where multiple restrictions already compete for attention. A dragging anchor can sweep a wide arc, exerting enormous force. The Alexandria incident was not unique; similar anchor-related faults have been recorded near ports from Hong Kong to San Francisco. The implication is sobering. Safety practices designed to protect ships can imperil networks beneath them.

Dredging compounds the problem. Ports and channels must be maintained to accommodate larger vessels. Dredging removes sediment, altering seabed profiles and exposing infrastructure that was once safely buried. Operators coordinate with port authorities to mark cable routes and impose exclusion zones, yet enforcement varies and seabed conditions change. The visible behaviour is re-exposure over time. The implication is that protection is not a one-off act but an ongoing negotiation with sediment and traffic.

A narrative clarifies how accident becomes incident. A bulk carrier approaches a busy harbour as weather deteriorates. The captain drops anchor to hold position. The anchor fails to bite, dragging along the seabed. On the bridge, attention is fixed on maintaining heading and distance from other vessels. Below, the anchor flukes catch a cable that has become partially exposed by recent dredging. The cable lifts, tension rises, and fibres fracture. The ship steadies. The damage is done. Hours later, alarms light up in operations centres hundreds of kilometres away.

Trust is tested here, not between adversaries but between systems. Mariners trust charts and exclusion zones to be accurate. Cable operators trust burial to persist. Both trusts are provisional. When either fails, consequences propagate far beyond the point of contact.

There is a credible counter-example that matters. In regions where burial depth is consistently achieved and maintained, and where fishing practices are adapted through awareness campaigns and compensation schemes, fault rates fall. Parts of the North Sea illustrate this. Cooperative arrangements between operators and fishing communities, documented by industry bodies in the 2000s, reduced incidents by aligning incentives. Reconcile the lesson. Human activity is not inherently incompatible with cables; unmanaged activity is.

Abstractions such as "coexistence" become concrete through measures like cable protection zones, chart markings and gear modification. Exclusion zones around landing areas restrict anchoring and trawling. Charts mark cable routes, though with deliberate imprecision to avoid misuse. Some fisheries adopt gear designed to ride over obstacles. Each measure has limits. Zones can be ignored under pressure. Charts are consulted unevenly. Gear changes cost money. The implication is that risk is reduced by layers, not eliminated by a single rule.

Economics shape behaviour. Fishing margins are thin. Waiting for clearance costs fuel and time. Anchoring closer to port can be safer for a vessel than holding position under power. These are rational decisions at the ship level that create collective risk at the network level. Efficiency for one actor becomes exposure for another. Policy attempts to reconcile this through regulation and compensation, yet trade-offs persist.

The motif threading this section is *drag*. Nets drag. Anchors drag. Risk drags along with them, invisible until it catches. Drag is slow, unremarkable, and destructive in its accumulation.

Statistics reinforce the point without sensationalism. Public summaries by maintenance authorities and insurers indicate that fishing and anchoring account for a substantial share of recorded cable faults worldwide, often exceeding half in shallow-water segments. Where figures are published, they are conservative, reflecting only incidents confirmed through repair. Near-misses go uncounted. The implication is that everyday activity is the dominant hazard where people and cables share space.

Counterfactuals are instructive. In deep ocean, where fishing and anchoring do not occur, fault rates drop sharply. When failures happen there, they are more likely to be geological. The contrast underscores why shallow water deserves disproportionate attention and investment, even though it represents a small fraction of total route length.

Response dynamics reveal further complexity. When a cable is damaged by fishing gear or an anchor, liability can be contested. Identifying the responsible vessel requires evidence that may not exist. Automatic Identification System data can help, but coverage and retention vary. Even when a vessel is identified, legal processes are slow. Repairs proceed regardless. The implication is pragmatic. Operators repair first and argue later, absorbing costs that ultimately feed back into pricing and investment decisions.

Technology offers partial mitigation. Deeper burial reduces exposure. Rock dumping protects unburyable sections. Real-time seabed monitoring is being explored, though coverage remains limited. Each measure adds cost and complexity. Decisions about where to apply them reflect judgements about traffic density, economic importance and political sensitivity. These judgements are visible in maps of protection intensity that thicken near ports and thin offshore.

There is a temptation to frame anchor and fishing damage as negligence. That framing misleads. Most incidents arise from lawful activity conducted under pressure. Blame does little to reduce recurrence. Design, communication and incentives do more. Awareness campaigns that show fishers how cables are marked, and why avoiding them matters, have had measurable effects in some regions. So have rapid reporting mechanisms that allow near-misses to be logged before they become failures.

The unresolved tension looks ahead. As ships grow larger and ports busier, anchoring footprints expand. As coastal development accelerates, dredging increases. At the same time, cable landings multiply to meet demand. Will protection measures scale with this growth, accepting higher costs near shore, or will reliance on burial and charts persist until fault rates force change? The answer will be written not in policy papers but in the drag marks left on the seabed, and in the outages that follow when steel meets glass again.

## Deliberate attacks and tampering

On 19 November 2023, Finland reported damage to a gas pipeline and a nearby telecommunications cable in the Gulf of Finland. The Finnish authorities did not name a perpetrator. They did not describe a method. They did not assign intent. What they did say was simpler and more revealing: the damage was *not consistent with normal wear*. That phrase carried weight. It marked the boundary between accident and suspicion, and it showed how narrow that boundary can be when evidence lies hundreds of metres below the surface.

Attribution begins in doubt.

The idea that someone might deliberately interfere with a subsea cable provokes an instinctive reaction. These systems feel too large, too dispersed, too embedded in geology and commerce to be targets in the conventional sense. Yet history suggests otherwise. Infrastructure has always attracted attention precisely because it concentrates power quietly. Roads, bridges, railways and pipelines have long been sabotaged not for their symbolism but for their leverage. Cables belong in that lineage, even if their invisibility makes the connection harder to grasp.

Deliberate interference sits on a spectrum. At one end lies blunt disruption: cutting or damaging a cable to interrupt service. At the other lies covert access: interference designed not to stop traffic but to observe or manipulate it without detection. Between these poles are acts that blur categories, producing ambiguous outcomes that frustrate technical diagnosis and political response. The implication is not that such acts are common, but that they are conceivable enough to shape planning and rhetoric.

Consider the visible behaviour of networks after a deliberate cut. Traffic drops abruptly. Rerouting kicks in. Latency spikes. Operators see a sharp, localised fault rather than the diffuse patterns associated with congestion or equipment ageing. These signals are *suggestive*, not conclusive. Fishing gear can produce similar signatures. So can anchors. The same telemetry that alerts engineers to failure rarely identifies motive.

Named examples are scarce by design. States and operators avoid public discussion of suspected interference, wary of revealing vulnerabilities or escalating tensions. When examples do surface, they tend to be indirect. In January 2022, cables linking Tonga to the wider internet were severed following a volcanic eruption, an unquestionably natural cause. The response, documented by the World Bank and regional operators, highlighted how dependent attribution is on context. Where seismic data aligns with failure, conclusions follow swiftly. Where it does not, uncertainty lingers.

A second example illustrates that uncertainty. In 2015, NATO publicly acknowledged concerns about increased activity by Russian submarines near undersea cables in the North Atlantic, citing statements by senior alliance officials. No specific incident was named. No damage was alleged.

The concern lay in *presence*, not proof. The implication was strategic rather than forensic. The mere possibility of interference influenced naval planning and political discourse.

The counter-example matters. Despite heightened concern, confirmed cases of state-sponsored cable sabotage remain vanishingly rare in the public record. This is not evidence of absence, but it does temper alarmism. It suggests that while interference is feasible, it is constrained by cost, risk and uncertainty of effect. Cutting a cable is easier than controlling the consequences.

A stylised scenario helps clarify both feasibility and limits, without straying into instruction. Imagine a known chokepoint: a narrow shelf where multiple cables converge before making landfall. The location is not secret; charts and open maps show approximations. A diver, operating from a small vessel, targets the area. The water is shallow enough to reach without specialised equipment. The physical act of damaging exposed infrastructure is conceivable. So is the act of being noticed. Vessel traffic is dense. Currents are unpredictable. The diver's window is short, the outcome uncertain. Even if damage occurs, repair may be swift. The implication is clear. Feasibility does not equal reliability.

Covert access raises different issues. The abstraction of "tapping" cables evokes cinematic images, yet the reality is constrained by physics and architecture. Modern fibre-optic systems are designed to detect signal loss and anomalies. Interference that degrades integrity risks triggering alarms. Access that avoids degradation requires precision, time and concealment. These requirements push such activities towards actors with significant resources and patience. The visible metric is *silence*: no outage, no obvious fault, only suspicion informed by intelligence rather than network behaviour.

Trust becomes a fragile concept here. Users trust that data transiting cables remains confidential. States trust that commercial systems are not being quietly exploited by rivals. Operators trust that monitoring will reveal tampering. Each trust is partial. None can be proven in the negative. The implication is a permanent asymmetry between suspicion and certainty.

Attribution compounds the problem. Evidence on the seabed degrades. Tools leave few distinctive marks. Natural processes disturb sites before investigators arrive. Even when damage is recovered during repair, distinguishing deliberate cuts from accidental ones can be contentious. Insurers, operators and governments may reach different conclusions based on the same fragments. The visible behaviour is disagreement, often managed behind closed doors.

Hybrid warfare exploits this ambiguity. Acts that could be framed as accident, crime or sabotage are attractive precisely because they resist classification. A damaged cable in a tense region can serve as a signal without a signature. Responses must then balance deterrence against escalation. Overreaction risks legitimising a narrative of hostility. Underreaction risks normalising interference. The implication is strategic paralysis, or at least caution.

Metrics again ground abstraction. When multiple cables fail in proximity without a clear natural cause, suspicion rises. When failures coincide with geopolitical stress, narratives harden. When repairs reveal damage inconsistent with dragging or abrasion, questions multiply. None of these indicators is decisive alone. Together, they shape assessments that rarely become public.

The quiet motif threading this section is *trace*. Deliberate acts aim to leave none. Investigations search for any. Policy is written in the space between.

Reconcile the tension by returning to scale. The global cable network comprises hundreds of systems and thousands of landing points. Deliberate interference would need to be sustained and selective to have strategic effect. Single cuts are disruptive but rarely decisive. This limits incentives for escalation while sustaining incentives for signalling. It is a delicate balance.

The forward test remains unresolved. As monitoring improves and awareness grows, will ambiguity shrink, making deliberate acts riskier and rarer? Or will actors adapt, refining methods that preserve deniability while testing thresholds? The answer will not come from a single incident or declaration. It will emerge slowly, traced in patterns of suspicion, silence and response beneath the waves.

## Hybrid warfare and plausible deniability

On 8 October 2023, Finland's National Bureau of Investigation announced that the Balticconnector gas pipeline between Finland and Estonia had been damaged, alongside faults in telecommunications cables in the same area. The place was the Gulf of Finland. The month mattered because the region's security climate was already taut. The immediate outcome was rapid escalation of *attention*: naval assets were deployed to the area, investigations were opened, and political leaders spoke carefully about intent while insisting the damage was “not the result of normal wear and tear”. The seabed became a stage for inference.

Nothing was claimed. Everything was implied.

Hybrid warfare thrives in that space. It is not a single doctrine so much as a habit of action: using instruments that sit below the threshold of declared war while producing effects that are more than mere nuisance. It trades in ambiguity, in plausible explanations, in the blurring of civilian and military categories. Subsea cables are almost perfect for this logic. They are privately owned yet nationally vital, mostly unobserved yet massively consequential, routinely damaged by accidents yet increasingly viewed through a strategic lens. A cable fault can be framed as bad luck, bad practice, or bad intent. The framing is part of the event.

Show how the framing works. A cable fails in shallow water. The physical signature is a sudden loss of signal. Engineers see a fault location. That is the easy part. The hard part is cause. Was it an anchor? Fishing gear? A dredger? A criminal seeking scrap metal? Or a deliberate actor using disruption to send a message? The evidence is limited, dispersed, and often delayed. Meanwhile, narratives begin to circulate. Governments calibrate statements. Media speculate. Markets respond. The implication is that hybrid conflict unfolds not only through physical acts, but through the contest over what those acts mean.

Plausible deniability is not simply the ability to deny; it is the ability to deny credibly enough to slow or complicate response. The sea helps. It hides. A damaged section of cable is recovered days or weeks later, hauled up by a repair ship. The site has already shifted. Sediment has moved. Vessel tracks have dispersed. Even if investigators identify a likely cause, proving intent is far harder. A dragging anchor and a deliberate snag can look similar from the perspective of a broken fibre. The ambiguity is structural.

The Balticconnector case is valuable precisely because it straddled domains. A gas pipeline is not a data cable, yet the co-location of energy and communications infrastructure in the same corridor created a compounded event. Authorities treated the incident as potentially deliberate without publicly asserting state involvement. That careful posture illustrates hybrid logic. The response was immediate in operational terms—surveillance and investigation—yet cautious in rhetorical terms. The implication was deterrence without accusation.

A second checkable example shows how tensions can sharpen even without confirmed sabotage. In September 2017, the UK's Chief of the Defence Staff, General Sir Stuart Peach, warned publicly about Russian activity near undersea cables and the risk to critical infrastructure. No specific cable incident was cited as proof. The warning itself functioned as signalling: an attempt to shift perceptions and justify protective measures. Hybrid conflict does not always require damage. Sometimes it requires only the credible possibility of damage, enough to reshape budgets and patrol patterns.

In both cases, the contest is partly about thresholds. Traditional security thinking often distinguishes between crime and war, accident and attack. Hybrid tactics exploit the awkward middle. A cable cut that can be plausibly attributed to fishing gear may not trigger a military response, even if it causes significant economic disruption. A pattern of cuts, clustered in time and place, may provoke stronger action, but only if attribution is persuasive enough to justify escalation. The implication is that adversaries—state or non-state—may probe for the level of ambiguity a target will tolerate.

Abstractions become visible decisions. "Deterrence" appears as increased patrols along known routes and public statements about monitoring capability. "Restraint" appears as careful language that avoids naming perpetrators. "Resilience" appears as investment in route diversity and faster repair logistics. Each choice is shaped not only by technical assessment but by narrative risk: what can be credibly said, and to whom?

This is why attribution battles matter. They are not mere public relations disputes; they shape what responses are politically possible. A government that publicly blames a rival for cable interference must be prepared to act—or risk looking weak. A government that refuses to assign blame may preserve diplomatic flexibility but invite further probing. The decision is strategic. It is also constrained by evidence.

Evidence itself is uneven. In shallow waters, authorities may use vessel tracking data, port logs, and witness reports to narrow suspects. In deep waters, such data is sparse. Even where vessel tracks exist, the presence of a ship near a route is not proof of interference. Ships loiter for many reasons. Fishing grounds overlap with cable corridors. Weather forces anchoring. Hybrid actors benefit from this noise. Noise is cover.

A credible limitation must be stated. Not every ambiguous incident is hybrid warfare, and not every suspicion is justified. The majority of cable faults are still caused by accidents and ordinary activity, particularly in shallow waters, as shown by long-standing fault statistics in maintenance zone reporting. Reconcile the point. Hybrid warfare does not replace accidents; it hides within their plausibility. The existence of frequent accidents is precisely what makes deliberate interference harder to prove and easier to deny.

The motif threading this section is *threshold.* Hybrid operations are designed to press against thresholds—legal thresholds, political thresholds, evidentiary thresholds—without crossing into clear casus belli. Cables sit close to these thresholds because they are essential yet poorly governed as strategic assets. The same incident can be handled as a commercial repair or as a national security event depending on the threshold it appears to cross.

This threshold logic changes organisational behaviour. Operators become more cautious about public statements, wary of being drawn into geopolitical narratives. Governments become more involved in what were once purely technical incidents. Intelligence assessments begin to intersect with maintenance decisions. Communication becomes part of security.

It also changes how adversaries might calculate. A blunt, easily attributable attack risks unified retaliation. A small, ambiguous disruption may achieve a signalling effect without provoking escalation. The measurable effect might be modest—hours of congestion, a few days of degraded service—but the psychological effect can be larger: uncertainty injected into trust in infrastructure.

Trust is the most fragile commodity in this environment. Users rarely know why connectivity degrades. Businesses hate ambiguity because it disrupts planning. Governments fear public panic or political criticism. Hybrid tactics aim at this shared vulnerability: the discomfort of not knowing. When a cable fails, and explanations diverge, trust erodes.

The path forward is not simply better technology, though monitoring helps. It is also institutional. Clearer protocols for information-sharing between operators and states can reduce confusion. Pre-agreed thresholds for escalation can prevent improvisation under pressure. These measures do not eliminate ambiguity, but they constrain its exploitation.

The forward test remains unresolved and increasingly pressing. When the next ambiguous seabed incident occurs in a tense region, will states treat it as a repair problem first and a security problem second—or will they interpret it as a strategic probe requiring immediate signalling? The answer will determine whether ambiguity continues to be an advantage, or becomes a liability, for those who seek to operate in the grey space beneath the waves.

## Patterns in past incidents

On 26 December 2006, after the earthquake in the Luzon Strait, engineers at Chunghwa Telecom watched multiple submarine cable systems fail in overlapping time windows. Two years later, on 30 January 2008, network monitors at Renesys recorded widespread routing instability after cables were damaged near Alexandria. The places were different, the causes plausibly different, and the political narratives that followed were different again. The outcome, however, rhymed: regional slowdowns that arrived suddenly, lasted longer than the public expected, and exposed just how concentrated the world's connectivity can become when routes converge.

Patterns are what survive headlines.

It is tempting to treat cable incidents as isolated dramas: a storm here, an anchor there, a suspicious fault somewhere else. That temptation is convenient because it preserves the comforting idea that each disruption has its own cause and therefore its own remedy. The record tells a harder story. Cable damage repeats. It repeats in the same kinds of places, from the same kinds of activities, and with the same kinds of operational bottlenecks. The details change. The structure endures.

Start with geography, because geography is the most stubborn variable. Cables fail disproportionately where the seabed is shallow and busy, not where it is deep and empty. This is not a guess; it is a long-observed feature of fault statistics compiled by regional maintenance organisations and reflected in decades of repair logs. Shallow waters concentrate hazards: anchoring, trawling, dredging, construction, and the transition zones where cables must converge to reach landings. Even when a cable is buried, the seabed moves. Burial persists imperfectly. The implication is that the shortest segment of a route can carry the greatest operational risk.

Chokepoints are the second geographic pattern. Straits, narrow seas and canal approaches attract cables for the same reasons they attract ships: they are the practical passages between regions. They also compress infrastructure into narrow corridors where a single incident can affect multiple systems. The Luzon Strait is a textbook case because both geology and route convergence are intense. So is the eastern Mediterranean, where cables funnel between Europe and Asia and where shipping density is relentless. When several systems share a corridor, redundancy becomes less effective precisely when it is most needed. The map looks diverse. The seabed is not.

The third geographic pattern is the continental margin: the slope where seabed conditions change rapidly and where submarine landslides become plausible. Here, nature's leverage is indirect. Earthquakes trigger sediment movement. Strong currents scour. Storms shift sand. The visible behaviour is clustered faults after a seismic event, or recurring exposure of buried cable near shore. The implication is that deep-ocean engineering cannot compensate for shelf dynamics.

Now consider causes, which are more human than many assume. Fishing gear and anchors dominate the fault record in many regions. Their dominance is not evidence of bad faith; it is evidence of scale. Fishing fleets and commercial shipping operate continuously. The probability of interaction with buried infrastructure rises with every season. When incidents do occur, the causation chain is often banal: an anchor dragged during poor weather; a trawl snagged on a section where burial had thinned; a dredging operation that altered sediment and left cable exposed. These are the kinds of causes that do not feel "strategic" until their effects spill into banking systems, government services, and cross-border communications.

A second cause pattern sits apart: geological shocks that damage multiple cables simultaneously. The 2006 Luzon Strait earthquake is the most cited example because the consequences were so wide, but it is not the only one. Major earthquakes off Japan and New Zealand have repeatedly disrupted undersea infrastructure, with public reporting by operators and authorities documenting long repair timelines. The distinctive feature here is simultaneity. Multiple failures in a corridor overwhelm redundancy and repair capacity at once. The implication is that nature can produce the kind of multi-point disruption that adversaries sometimes fantasise about.

Deliberate interference, by contrast, is rare in confirmed public detail and common in speculation. This disparity is itself a pattern. The seabed invites suspicion because it is hard to observe, and because accidents already produce severe outcomes. Hybrid conflict amplifies that suspicion, especially in tense regions. Yet the record suggests restraint, or at least caution, among actors who might seek strategic disruption. That restraint has rational roots. Blunt cable cuts are disruptive but not necessarily decisive; they can also be repaired. Covert interference is technically challenging and politically risky. The implication is that deliberate acts, if they occur, are likely to be selective and ambiguous rather than spectacular.

Response challenges repeat as stubbornly as causes. The first is diagnosis. Operators can locate faults with impressive precision using optical tests and power feeding telemetry, yet identifying cause and intent remains difficult. A cable hauled up for repair may show damage consistent with abrasion, cutting, or crushing. It rarely comes with a confession. Even when vessel tracking data narrows possibilities, proving responsibility can be slow. The visible behaviour is cautious public communication: operators and governments acknowledge disruption while avoiding definitive claims. The implication is a vacuum that rumours readily fill.

The second response challenge is logistics. Repair ships are few, and they are regionally allocated through maintenance agreements. When multiple faults occur in a short period—after storms or earthquakes—ships queue. Permits can delay entry into territorial waters. Weather can halt operations for days. Ports can be far. The public often imagines repair as a swift technical act. In reality it is a maritime expedition constrained by sea state and bureaucracy. The metric that matters is time to mobilisation, not time to splice.

The third response challenge is rerouting. The internet's resilience depends on alternative paths, but those paths can saturate quickly. Congestion becomes the new failure mode. Services degrade unevenly; some applications cope, others collapse. Financial traffic may prioritise low latency. Video may buffer or downshift. Enterprise VPNs may become unusable. The visible behaviour is not total blackout but partial dysfunction: remote work stuttering, payments delayed, customer support systems failing. The implication is social. Partial failures can produce more confusion than complete ones because they defy simple explanation.

A fourth response challenge lies in governance. When a cable is owned by a consortium, repair priorities and communication decisions involve negotiation. When the cable links multiple jurisdictions, political messaging becomes sensitive. When critical services are affected, governments seek assurance without revealing vulnerabilities. These governance dynamics shape the public experience of an incident as much as the physical damage itself.

A composite example helps to tie these patterns together without relying on a single case. Imagine a narrow sea corridor serving several countries, with multiple cables running in parallel towards a clustered set of landing stations. A winter storm drives ships to anchor in a designated waiting area. One vessel drags anchor, damaging a cable where burial has thinned due to sediment movement. Within minutes, operators detect a fault. Traffic reroutes to remaining systems. Latency climbs. Capacity tightens. Meanwhile, the same storm triggers small seabed shifts that expose another cable segment. A fishing vessel, continuing operations in rough conditions, snags the exposed section. A second fault occurs hours later. Now redundancy collapses.

Operators coordinate across borders to stabilise traffic. Governments request updates. Social media fills the causation gap with suspicion, pointing to the region's tense politics. Investigators check vessel tracks. The anchor-drag is plausible. So is something else. Repair ships are already tasked elsewhere; mobilisation is delayed by weather. A maintenance agreement prioritises the cable carrying the largest volume of traffic. Smaller markets wait. When repairs finally begin, the corridor's congestion forces ships to coordinate with maritime authorities, extending timelines further. Services return gradually, with intermittent instability as traffic is rebalanced.

Every element of this composite is drawn from recurring realities: shallow-water vulnerability, corridor clustering, mixed-cause damage, diagnosis under uncertainty, limited repair capacity, congestion during rerouting, and narrative contestation. The lesson is not that such an event is inevitable. It is that the system is predisposed to it when certain conditions align.

There is a credible limitation to pattern-seeking. Overemphasising patterns can flatten novelty. New cable designs, improved burial methods and better monitoring have reduced some risks in certain regions. Content delivery networks and cloud architectures can mask outages for some services. International coordination has improved in places. Reconcile the limitation. Progress is real, but it is uneven. It tends to improve outcomes at the margin while leaving structural exposure intact where geography and economics force convergence.

The motif threading this section is *recurrence*. Not recurrence as inevitability, but recurrence as diagnosis. When failures recur in the same kinds of places and for the same kinds of reasons, the correct response is not surprise but adaptation. This is where lessons become actionable without becoming prescriptive advice. Organisations and states can ask sharper questions about where their connectivity concentrates. Operators can justify investment in route diversity and landing separation with historical evidence rather than fear. Regulators can treat coastal planning decisions as part of national resilience.

The forward test is simple and unsettling. When the next disruption occurs—because it will—will it be treated as an unfortunate one-off, repaired and forgotten, or as another data point in a pattern that demands structural change? The seabed will continue to offer the same corridors, the same hazards, and the same silence. The question is whether the people who depend on it will learn to read that silence as repetition, and respond accordingly.

# Chapter 5

# Case Studies of Disruption Events

At 02:17 local time, network engineers in several countries saw the same warning flare across their screens. Latency spiked. Routes flapped. Traffic that had followed predictable paths for years began to slosh sideways, filling links never designed to carry such weight. There was no explosion, no dramatic announcement, no single point of failure to blame. Just a quiet, cascading disturbance spreading across borders faster than any press office could react.

For most users, the first sign was trivial. A video that refused to load. A payment that hung for a few seconds longer than usual. An office call that dropped once and then connected on the second attempt. For operators, it was something else entirely: the system revealing itself under strain, redundancy proving real but imperfect, and every assumption about "backup" suddenly subject to measurement.

This chapter begins there, not because disruption is rare, but because it is instructive.

Much of the debate around subsea cables drifts towards abstraction. We talk about vulnerability, resilience, redundancy, deterrence. These words sound authoritative, yet they remain oddly bloodless until tested against lived events. Case studies do something theory cannot. They force us to confront sequence, timing, and consequence. They show how systems behave when stressed, how organisations respond under pressure, and how small technical facts ripple outward into economic and political effects.

The purpose of this chapter is not to assign blame or dramatise failure. It is to watch systems at work when they are least comfortable. What happens when several cables fail in the same corridor? How does traffic actually reroute, and what breaks first? When an island loses its primary link, which contingencies function and which are revealed as paper promises? When a financial centre faces a near-miss, how does awareness propagate from engineers to traders to executives? These are not hypothetical questions. They are matters of record.

There is a quiet discipline to studying disruption without sensationalism. It requires resisting the urge to turn every incident into a morality tale or a geopolitical accusation. Instead, it asks us to observe mechanics: queues forming where bandwidth narrows, priorities asserted through routing policy, human judgement stepping in where automation hesitates. The payoff is clarity. Once seen clearly, these mechanics are difficult to forget.

The first case in this chapter reconstructs a regional outage that affected several countries at once. The geography is familiar by now: a confined area of seabed where routes converge, redundancy looks generous on a map, and repair capacity is finite. What matters here is not the initial damage but the system's response. Traffic does not simply "fail over" as marketing diagrams suggest. It surges, competes, and occasionally chokes. Some services degrade gracefully. Others collapse abruptly. Recovery does not follow a straight line. It arrives in stages, with false dawns and unexpected regressions. By tracing this process carefully, we see resilience as it really is: adaptive, uneven, and dependent on decisions made long before the incident occurred.

The second case turns to an island nation, geographically isolated and digitally dependent. When its main cable failed, the narrative quickly became personal. Remote work halted. Government services slowed. Banks rationed access. Satellite links, long described as backups, proved invaluable and insufficient at the same time. Capacity constraints bit hardest where demand was least negotiable. What emerges from this case is not a condemnation of satellites or planning, but a sobering picture of trade-offs. Backup capacity that looks ample on paper can evaporate under full national load. Coordination between government and operators becomes as important as any piece of hardware.

If the island case shows scarcity in extremis, the third case explores abundance under threat. A major financial centre experiences a near-miss: damage detected early, service largely preserved, and markets kept open. On the surface, this looks like success. Dig deeper and the picture becomes more interesting. Detection systems work because they are watched. Alerts escalate because humans recognise their significance. Trading platforms begin to prepare for delays not because delays have occurred, but because credible warnings demand pre-emptive decisions. Here, milliseconds matter not only technically but psychologically. The case reveals how risk is priced in real time, and how private-sector monitoring has become a quiet pillar of systemic stability.

The fourth case moves into more difficult terrain: cable disruption in or near an active conflict zone. These are the incidents most prone to speculation and least amenable to transparency. Classified details remain classified. Attribution debates rage in parallel to repair work. By focusing strictly on observable effects—service degradation, rerouting patterns, operator communications—we gain a different kind of insight. Local engineers work under conditions of uncertainty and fear. Commercial networks intersect with military activity not by design but by geography. The human factors become unavoidable. Fatigue, improvisation, and judgement shape outcomes as much as technical design.

Across these cases, a pattern emerges that is less about cables than about systems. Disruption exposes assumptions. Some hold. Others crumble. Redundancy works until it doesn't. Contingency plans function until reality deviates from the scenario they imagined. None of this implies incompetence. It reflects the complexity of infrastructures that have grown organically, under commercial pressure, across decades.

There is also a temporal dimension worth noticing. Immediate impacts tend to be operational. Medium-term impacts are economic. Longer-term impacts are political and strategic. A regional outage may last days, but its memory can shape investment decisions for years. An island cut-off may prompt quiet diplomatic support for an additional cable long after headlines fade. A near-miss in a financial centre may accelerate internal reviews that never reach the public domain. Change, when it comes, is often incremental and discreet.

This is why the final section of the chapter steps back to ask what changed after the incidents. Not what was promised, but what was done. New routes appear on planning documents. Contracts are rewritten to prioritise repair access. Risk assessments are updated to account for clustered failure rather than single cuts. Governments adjust their language, speaking more often of resilience and less of inevitability. None of this is dramatic. All of it matters.

A subtle motif runs through these studies: *stress as revelation*. Under normal conditions, the global cable network fades into the background, performing its task with such reliability that dependence becomes invisible. Under stress, its contours sharpen. Weak points glow. Strengths reveal their limits. Human judgement steps into gaps left by automation. Watching this process unfold, incident by incident, is the most honest way to understand what resilience actually means.

The chapter that follows is not a catalogue of disasters. It is a series of controlled observations, each chosen because it illuminates a different aspect of system behaviour. Read together, they form a composite picture more instructive than any single dramatic event. They show how the seabed becomes a front line not through spectacle, but through accumulation: of demand, of risk, of decisions made far from the water's edge.

The question that lingers as you turn the page is deliberately unresolved. When the next disruption comes—and it will—will it look familiar because lessons have been absorbed, or familiar because patterns have been noticed but not acted upon? The case studies ahead do not answer that question for you. They give you the evidence needed to ask it properly.

## Regional outage affecting several countries

On 30 January 2008, engineers at Renesys, a network monitoring firm based in New York, began publishing unusual routing data tied to a sudden loss of connectivity near Alexandria, Egypt. Within hours, operators across the Middle East and South Asia reported degraded service. Traffic that normally flowed smoothly between Europe and Asia was being pushed onto unfamiliar paths, saturating links never intended to carry such load. The place was the eastern Mediterranean. The date mattered. Four major submarine cables had been damaged within a short stretch of seabed.

Redundancy met reality.

The immediate outcome was not silence but distortion. Internet access did not vanish across the affected countries. It slowed, staggered, and behaved unpredictably. Banks struggled with delayed transactions. Call centres dropped connections. News organisations found foreign feeds unreliable. What made the event instructive was not its cause—widely reported as accidental damage linked to anchoring—but the way the system responded once several parallel routes were lost at once.

This section reconstructs that response.

The eastern Mediterranean has long been a corridor of necessity. Cables linking Europe to the Middle East, India and East Asia converge as they approach landfall in Egypt, threading through busy shipping lanes before fanning out again. On maps, the diversity looks reassuring. On the seabed, the physical separation is far narrower. In January 2008, at least four systems—SEA-ME-WE 4, SEA-ME-WE 3, FLAG Europe-Asia, and GO-1—were affected within days. The result was not a clean break but a systemic squeeze.

Traffic reacted first, not engineers. Border Gateway Protocol announcements shifted as routers searched for viable paths. Routes lengthened. Latency climbed. Packet loss increased. The visible behaviour, captured in Renesys reports at the time, was route flapping: paths appearing and disappearing as networks attempted to stabilise. This mattered because stability itself consumes capacity. Each recalculation adds overhead, compounding congestion.

The abstraction of "failover" becomes concrete here. Networks are designed to reroute around single failures. They are less comfortable when several preferred routes vanish simultaneously. Operators can prioritise traffic classes, but only within the bounds of available bandwidth. When those bounds shrink abruptly, choices become unavoidable. Financial traffic, voice calls, and essential enterprise services tend to be protected. Consumer browsing and media streaming degrade first. The implication is social as much as technical: some users experience inconvenience; others experience operational failure.

Recovery timelines revealed another layer. Initial repairs took weeks, not hours. Repair ships had to locate multiple fault points, retrieve damaged sections, and splice under variable weather conditions. Permits and coordination added delay. According to contemporaneous reporting by TeleGeography in 2008, full restoration of all affected systems took more than a month. During that period, traffic patterns remained abnormal, with knock-on effects felt as far away as India and the Gulf states.

This drawn-out recovery exposed a common misconception. Redundancy is often imagined as instant substitution. In practice, it is a spectrum of degraded states. Partial capacity returns before full capacity. Stability lags availability. Users experience improvement unevenly. The metric that matters is not "up" or "down" but *how much* and *for whom*.

A second named example sharpens the pattern. In March 2013, cables in the same broad region were again damaged near Alexandria, affecting SEA-ME-WE 4 and other systems. Egyptian authorities cited a maritime accident. Operators again rerouted traffic through alternative corridors, including longer paths via the Red Sea and terrestrial backbones. Services remained available but impaired. The repetition was instructive. Similar geography produced similar stress, even as technology had improved. The implication was not stagnation but persistence of exposure.

There is a credible counter-example worth acknowledging. Some regional outages have been absorbed with minimal user impact due to improved peering and diversified routes. Western Europe, for instance, has experienced multiple cable faults without widespread disruption because traffic can shift across dense terrestrial networks. Reconcile this with the Mediterranean cases. The difference lies not in competence but in topology. Regions with many short, high-capacity alternatives cope better than regions where long-haul links funnel through narrow corridors.

The behaviour of services during the 2008 outage illustrates this distinction. Content hosted within affected countries often remained reachable. International services suffered. Voice over IP struggled more than email. Latency-sensitive applications failed first. This hierarchy of failure mirrors the physics of congestion. Delay-sensitive traffic exposes strain earlier than delay-tolerant traffic. The implication for organisations is diagnostic rather than prescriptive: watch which services falter to understand where dependencies lie.

Trust enters the picture here, and it can be measured. Customers trust that connectivity will be available. During the outage, that trust eroded not because services failed entirely, but because they failed inconsistently. Intermittent access is harder to explain and harder to plan around. Businesses reported difficulty coordinating across borders when calls dropped unpredictably. The visible decision was contingency activation: switching to alternative communication channels, delaying transactions, or temporarily relocating workloads where possible.

Coordination among operators became as important as hardware. Networks exchanged information about available capacity. Some agreements allowed temporary traffic sharing; others did not. These commercial boundaries shaped technical outcomes. Where relationships were strong, rerouting was smoother. Where they were weak, congestion lingered. The abstraction of "interconnection" resolved into contracts and trust built over years.

The motif threading this case is *congestion*. Not as a momentary spike, but as a system-wide condition that reveals hidden priorities. Congestion decides whose traffic gets through and whose waits. It is the language through which redundancy speaks under stress.

Attribution debates, though present in media coverage, mattered less operationally than repair logistics. Whether anchors or other causes were responsible did not change the immediate tasks facing engineers. What mattered was locating faults, mobilising ships, and stabilising routing. This focus on behaviour rather than blame is deliberate. Blame may satisfy political appetite. Behaviour determines resilience.

The longer-term effects were quieter but lasting. Operators reassessed route diversity. Some invested in additional landings. Others negotiated improved peering arrangements to reduce reliance on single corridors. Governments took note, even if public statements were restrained. According to industry analyses published in the years following, new routes through the Red Sea and overland links gained strategic value partly because of these repeated Mediterranean stresses.

A final implication deserves emphasis. Regional outages test not only infrastructure but narrative. When several countries experience disruption simultaneously, explanations compete. Is this a local accident with regional effects, or a regional vulnerability revealed by local failure? The answer shapes policy. The 2008 event nudged thinking towards the latter. It demonstrated that regional dependence can turn small physical incidents into multi-national disruptions.

The unresolved tension remains. Corridor geography has not changed. Traffic volumes have grown. While new routes exist, economic logic still favours convergence where distances are shortest and markets densest. The forward test is stark. When the next confined-area failure occurs in a critical corridor, will the system merely endure another month of distortion, or will accumulated lessons have shifted enough traffic, capacity, and expectation to blunt the impact? Redundancy exists. The question is how it behaves when asked to carry more than it ever planned to bear.

## Island nation temporarily cut off

On 15 January 2022, the Hunga Tonga–Hunga Ha'apai volcano erupted north of Tongatapu. Within hours, Tonga's international fibre link—the sole submarine cable connecting the country to Fiji—was severed. The organisation named in the first official statements was Tonga Cable Limited, the company responsible for the system. The place was Tonga. The outcome was stark: most of the country lost reliable access to the global internet for weeks, relying on limited satellite capacity while repair ships waited for safe conditions and a workable permit window.

The island went quiet.

What makes an island cable failure different from a continental outage is not merely the drama of isolation. It is the absence of alternative physical paths. On a mainland, a cut cable may shift traffic to neighbouring routes, to terrestrial backbones, to cross-border peering. On an island nation with a single primary cable, the network does not reroute so much as *shrink*. Connectivity becomes a rationed resource, allocated by policy choices and constrained by physics.

The Tonga case is instructive because it sits at the intersection of natural hazard, infrastructure design, and governance under pressure. The cause was not ambiguous. Volcanic activity and associated seabed disturbance broke the cable. The uncertainty lay elsewhere: how to restore service when the environment remained dangerous, how to allocate scarce backup capacity fairly, and how to coordinate across government, operators and international partners without slipping into panic or paralysis.

Begin with the cable's role. Tonga's submarine connection was not a luxury add-on; it was the backbone for banking, government communication, education, and diaspora contact. When the link failed, the impact was not uniform. Some local networks continued to function internally. Some government communications used alternative channels. Yet the outward flow—the everyday assumption that a message can reach Auckland, Sydney, London—was broken. Trust, in this context, is measured in the ordinary act of pressing "send" and expecting an answer. That expectation failed.

Backup connectivity arrived through satellites, but it arrived with constraints that are easy to underestimate until lived. Satellite bandwidth is finite, expensive, and shared. Latency is higher. Weather can affect performance. Ground stations may be limited. In Tonga, the immediate response included efforts to restore basic communications through available satellite links, with public reporting indicating that capacity was prioritised for essential services and emergency coordination. The visible behaviour was triage. The implication was hierarchy: some uses were deemed vital, others postponed.

Here, an abstraction becomes measurable. "Capacity" is not a vague resource; it is megabits per second available for an entire country. When the fibre cable was gone, the replacement capacity could not simply match it. This is not a criticism of satellites; it is a reminder of their design purpose.

They are lifelines, not substitutes. The mismatch between national demand and satellite supply turns technical limits into social decisions.

Government and telecom coordination mattered because scarcity demands governance. Tonga's authorities, Tonga Cable Limited, and regional partners had to align on priorities: emergency services, health communications, government continuity, and limited public access. Coordination also extended outward. International assistance, including from neighbouring countries, was required for repair logistics and, in some cases, for additional temporary communications support. The visible metric was time: how quickly could additional satellite terminals be deployed, and how quickly could the repair vessel begin work? The implication was dependence on external capacity and goodwill.

The repair timeline illustrates the reality of seabed work in a disaster zone. A cable is not repaired by dispatching a technician with a van. Repair requires a specialised ship, safe navigation, accurate fault localisation, and the ability to work in a seabed environment that may still be unstable. In Tonga's case, volcanic ash, ongoing seismic activity and damaged coastal areas complicated access. Public reporting by regional media and telecommunications sources at the time noted that repairs took several weeks, with service gradually returning as the cable was restored. The outcome was recovery, but not swift recovery.

A second named example provides comparison and reinforces pattern. In October 2019, the Solomon Islands experienced an internet outage when its undersea cable suffered damage, widely reported as an anchoring incident near Honiara. The country relied on limited satellite backup while repairs were arranged. The disruption was significant but shorter than Tonga's, partly because the environment was less hazardous and repair conditions were more predictable. Reconcile the difference. Islands share structural vulnerability, but the nature of the incident—natural disaster versus mechanical damage—shapes the timeline and the feasibility of rapid intervention.

These events reveal a recurring operational truth: when a single cable fails, "redundancy" often means contractual access to satellite capacity, not physical route diversity. That contractual access may exist, but it is rarely sized for full national load. It is sized for continuity of essential functions. The visible behaviour is prioritisation, sometimes formalised through government direction, sometimes through operator discretion. The implication is that business continuity plans that assume "internet access" as a binary state are inadequate; access becomes a graded privilege.

A credible counter-example complicates the narrative. Some island states have invested in multiple cables or regional ring architectures. Fiji, for example, has benefitted from a more diversified set of international links compared to single-cable islands, reducing the likelihood that any one failure produces national isolation. Reconcile this with Tonga. Route diversity is possible, but it is expensive and politically complex, and it requires long-term commitment. Where it exists, it transforms outages from national emergencies into regional inconveniences. Where it does not, the island remains hostage to a single physical thread.

The motif threading this case is *the lifeline*. A lifeline is reliable until it is not, and the moment it fails, everything becomes visible: the knot points, the frayed segments, the lack of a second rope. In Tonga, the lifeline was severed not by human error but by the earth itself. The effect, however, mirrors other single-link failures: the sudden discovery that modern national life assumes continuous external connection.

Service degradation during satellite reliance was not merely about speed. It changed behaviour. Businesses delayed international transactions. Schools adjusted remote learning plans. Families relied more on SMS and voice where available. Government announcements became more central, because rumours spread quickly when official information channels are constrained. The abstraction of "social resilience" becomes measurable as how quickly people adapt their communications habits under constraint.

The limits of contingency planning were also exposed. Planning often assumes a certain duration of outage. It assumes access to external logistics. It assumes that ground stations remain operational and powered. A volcanic eruption challenges those assumptions simultaneously. The implication is that island contingencies must consider compound shocks: not only cable failure, but disruption to ports, power, and transportation.

Yet strengths were visible too. Coordination mechanisms existed. Prioritisation was possible. Basic communication was restored relatively quickly compared with a total blackout, even if full internet functionality took weeks. International partnerships mattered. The system did not collapse; it contracted and held.

The hardest lesson, however, is strategic. Satellite backup works best when it is rehearsed and integrated into normal operations, not treated as an emergency afterthought. When an island shifts abruptly to satellite, configuration issues, capacity allocation disputes, and user expectations collide. The visible metric becomes time to stabilise the reduced network. The implication is that resilience is partly a habit.

This case also illustrates a political reality: island outages draw attention precisely because they are stark and narratively simple. A country is "cut off". Headlines follow. Promises of new cables appear. Sometimes those promises materialise quietly years later; sometimes they stall. The public drama fades faster than the infrastructure timeline.

The forward test is therefore uncomfortable and practical. For an island state, is a second cable worth the cost if it may be used rarely? The answer depends on how one values national continuity when the lifeline fails. It also depends on whether the next failure is expected to be a manageable accident—or an increasingly plausible compound event in which nature, logistics and geopolitics all tighten at once.

## Financial centre facing near-miss

How much delay can a market tolerate before price discovery frays? When milliseconds are worth money, the question is not rhetorical. It is operational. In March 2024, as several subsea cables in the Red Sea region suffered damage, network monitoring firms and exchange operators across Europe issued advisories about elevated latency risk on Europe–Asia routes. In London, the London Stock Exchange Group circulated technical notices to participants flagging the possibility of longer round-trip times on certain international links. Trading continued. No market closed. The outcome was a *near-miss*: disruption anticipated early enough to be absorbed through preparation rather than endured as failure.

Near-misses rarely make headlines. They leave no dramatic outage maps, no photographs of repair ships, no political statements. Yet for financial centres, they are the truest test of resilience. They reveal whether detection systems work, whether information flows faster than rumours, and whether technical warnings translate into disciplined market behaviour rather than panic.

The first signal in such events is usually not human. It is statistical. Network telemetry shows latency drifting outside historical bands, packet loss nudging above background noise, error correction working harder. Private-sector monitoring firms—Kentik, ThousandEyes, and similar operators—sell precisely this visibility. Their dashboards compare expected and observed paths, identifying when traffic detours around damaged segments long before a cable owner confirms a fault. Trust, here, is measured in milliseconds plotted against baselines.

Detection alone is insufficient. What matters is who receives the signal and how it propagates. In major financial hubs—London, New York, Singapore—large trading firms run their own monitoring, but they also rely on shared intelligence from exchanges, carriers and specialist vendors. In the March 2024 Red Sea episode, multiple operators reported unusual routing changes as traffic shifted west around Africa. The visible behaviour was pre-emptive communication: advisories issued before end-users complained. The implication was time to act.

Consider how that time is used. Trading platforms do not simply wait. They test contingencies. Firms review latency-sensitive strategies, adjust thresholds, and in some cases suspend activities that assume deterministic timing. This is not speculation; it is documented practice in market operations literature and exchange guidance. The abstraction of "risk management" becomes a decision: which strategies remain active if latency increases by 20–30 milliseconds, and which do not? The market does not stop; it reshapes.

A second named example sharpens the picture. In December 2006, earthquakes near Taiwan damaged multiple subsea cables in the Luzon Strait, affecting connectivity across East Asia, including Hong Kong and Singapore. Financial centres experienced severe disruption because detection and rerouting were slower and less automated than today. Recovery took weeks. Compare that with more recent near-misses. The technology evolved. So did expectations. Reconcile the difference. Early detection and richer telemetry turn a potential outage into a managed degradation.

The quiet motif threading these cases is *the early warning*. Early warnings change the nature of events. They convert surprises into scenarios. In finance, scenarios can be priced, planned and limited. Surprises cannot.

Private-sector monitoring plays an outsized role because cable owners are not always the fastest communicators. Commercial sensitivities, verification requirements and coordination across consortia can delay formal announcements. Monitoring firms, by contrast, observe effects rather than causes. They see traffic move, paths lengthen, congestion form. This observational advantage explains why exchanges and large financial institutions pay for independent visibility rather than relying solely on carrier notifications.

There is a limitation worth confronting. Monitoring shows symptoms, not intent. It cannot distinguish between accidental damage, maintenance, or deliberate interference. Nor can it guarantee accuracy when traffic engineering masks problems. This limitation matters because false positives carry costs. If firms overreact to transient anomalies, they may withdraw liquidity unnecessarily. Reconcile this by noting how mature operations respond: warnings are graded, not binary. Decisions are proportionate to confidence.

Communication is the second pillar of near-miss management. In a financial centre, information moves across formal and informal channels. Exchange notices, bilateral calls between network teams, alerts from vendors, and internal briefings converge. The visible behaviour is coordination under time pressure. The implication is cultural as much as technical: organisations that rehearse these conversations perform better than those that improvise them.

A concrete illustration comes from how trading venues handle latency disclosures. Exchanges publish technical parameters and notify participants when conditions deviate. Participants, in turn, adjust algorithms and risk controls. This feedback loop is rarely visible to the public, but it is essential. It converts infrastructure uncertainty into market discipline.

Contrast this with a credible counter-example. Smaller financial centres, or those with less dense monitoring ecosystems, may experience the same physical threat with less warning. Without early signals, they face abrupt service degradation. The market response is sharper, sometimes disorderly. Reconcile the contrast by recognising scale effects. Large hubs invest heavily in detection because the cost of ignorance is higher.

Near-misses also expose an uncomfortable truth about redundancy. Physical diversity exists, but it is not infinite. When multiple cables share corridors, rerouting increases load elsewhere. Latency rises. Congestion appears. Monitoring may warn, but it cannot create capacity. The visible metric is utilisation on alternative paths. The implication is that resilience is bounded by geography and investment decisions made years earlier.

The Red Sea incidents of 2024 underscored this point. Traffic detouring around the Cape of Good Hope lengthened routes by thousands of kilometres. Markets coped because they were warned. Had the warning arrived later, coping would have been harder. The near-miss was not the absence of damage; it was the presence of time.

Human judgement remains central. Automated alerts do not decide which trades to pause or which markets to protect. People do. Network engineers interpret graphs. Risk managers interpret scenarios. Executives decide posture. The abstraction of "confidence" is visible in whether a firm continues to quote prices or steps back.

What, then, does a near-miss teach that a failure does not? Failures show breakage. Near-misses show capacity. They reveal how close systems run to their limits and how much margin remains. They also show where trust resides: not in the cable alone, but in the web of observation, communication and decision that surrounds it.

The unresolved tension lies ahead. As financial centres grow faster and more interconnected, reliance on early warning deepens. But early warning itself depends on shared visibility that is commercially mediated and unevenly distributed. The forward test is stark: will future investment favour deeper, broader monitoring—or more physical diversity? When the next warning arrives, will it again buy enough time?

## Cable disruption in a conflict zone

In March 2024, traffic graphs across several European and Middle Eastern networks began to bend out of shape. Latency rose. Paths elongated. Operators traced the disturbance to the Red Sea, where at least three subsea cables—including segments of AAE-1 and EIG—had been damaged near Yemen. SEACOM confirmed service degradation. The place was the Bab el-Mandeb. The month was March. The outcome was uneven connectivity across East Africa, the Gulf and parts of Europe, with Yemen experiencing severe isolation. Warships were already present. Commercial traffic followed them.

Nothing about the incident was tidy. It unfolded beside an active conflict, amid missile strikes, naval patrols and contested narratives. Yet the most revealing details were not military. They were operational. Engineers in regional network operations centres watched alarms cascade while trying to distinguish between congestion caused by rerouting and loss caused by physical damage. One operator described it as *trying to hear a snapped string during a storm*. Decisions had to be made fast. People mattered.

The paradox at the heart of conflict-zone disruptions is simple. Cables are civilian infrastructure, but they lie where military activity concentrates.

Their failure is often interpreted through the lens of intent, yet their effects are measured in throughput and time. Five minutes can matter.

Observable effects come first. In the Red Sea case, traffic shifted west around Africa, adding thousands of kilometres to routes between Asia and Europe. Packet loss spiked on alternative paths. Some services slowed; others failed. Cloud access remained largely intact in core markets, while peripheral regions felt the brunt. This unevenness is not accidental. It reflects how redundancy is distributed. The abstraction of "resilience" becomes visible as who notices first and who recovers last.

Attribution, by contrast, lagged. Competing explanations circulated: anchors dragged during storms, deliberate interference, collateral damage from military operations. None could be proven quickly. Evidence lay on the seabed, inaccessible while hostilities continued. This uncertainty shaped behaviour. Governments avoided definitive statements. Operators focused on restoration rather than causes. The implication was pragmatic restraint.

A second, earlier example sharpens the pattern. In January 2011, during political upheaval in Egypt, multiple fibre links were disrupted, including terrestrial and subsea connections through the Mediterranean. The named organisation was Telecom Egypt. The place was Alexandria. The effect was regional slowdown and partial isolation. While not a naval conflict, the incident showed how political instability intersects with infrastructure control. Reconcile the cases. In both, commercial networks operated under conditions set by security forces, not market logic.

Human factors dominate these moments. Local engineers often work with incomplete information, constrained access and heightened personal risk. In Yemen, technicians coordinating with international partners did so amid power cuts and air-raid warnings. Trust was not abstract. It was whether a call would be answered. Decisions about rerouting traffic or prioritising repairs depended on relationships built long before the crisis.

There is a credible counter-example worth acknowledging. Some conflict zones see minimal impact on cables because routes avoid them entirely. The South China Sea, despite tension, has not seen widespread cable disruption tied directly to conflict. Reconcile this by geography and investment. Avoidance is possible where alternatives exist and states prioritise stability. It is harder in chokepoints where routes converge.

Military presence complicates repair. Cable ships require permits, safe passage and time on station. In active conflict, these are scarce. During the Red Sea incident, repair timelines extended because vessels could not operate freely. The visible metric was days offline. The implication was prolonged degradation rather than sudden blackout.

Hybrid narratives thrive here. Damage can be framed as accident, sabotage or consequence. Each frame carries different diplomatic weight. Operators learn to speak carefully, describing *observed effects* rather than causes. This discipline is not evasion; it is survival. Overstatement can escalate tension. Understatement can erode trust.

The quiet motif threading these events is *pressure.* Pressure on systems. Pressure on people. Pressure on interpretation. Under pressure, organisations reveal their true priorities. Some protect core markets at the expense of edges. Others spread pain more evenly. These choices are rarely publicised, yet they shape lived experience.

What emerges is a lesson about modern conflict. It does not require cutting cables to weaponise them. It only requires operating near them. The presence of risk alters behaviour, investment and confidence. Connectivity becomes contingent.

The forward test remains unresolved. As conflicts increasingly intersect with key maritime corridors, will commercial networks accept chronic uncertainty as the price of global reach, or will they pay to reroute around danger? When the next disruption occurs beside a war zone, will the decisive factor again be human judgement under pressure?

## What changed after the incidents

In June 2022, the Government of Tonga signed agreements that supported a second international submarine cable to improve the country's connectivity resilience after the January 2022 volcanic eruption severed its only fibre link. The place was Nuku'alofa. The date matters because it came after the drama had faded and the repair ships had long since left. The outcome was not a speech about transformation, but procurement work: feasibility, financing, and the slow unglamorous process of creating an alternative path. The lesson had been learned. Quietly.

Change in cable governance rarely arrives with a ribbon-cutting.

If cable disruptions were followed by visible reforms every time, the world would now be laced with redundant routes, patrol zones, and spare repair ships. That is not what happens. The more common pattern is incremental adjustment—some technical, some commercial, some political—driven by a mixture of pain, memory, and opportunity. This section asks what actually changes after high-profile incidents, and why the answers are often less dramatic than the headlines that preceded them.

Start with the most tangible form of change: routes. Disruptions expose geographic concentration, and concentration invites investment in alternatives. After the January 2008 Alexandria cluster of cable failures, operators and investors paid renewed attention to route diversity between Europe and Asia, accelerating interest in additional Red Sea and Gulf pathways and, over time, strengthening the economic case for terrestrial corridors across Eurasia. This was not a single response to a single incident; it was an accumulation of evidence that certain corridors were repeatedly stressed. The visible decision was commitment to new projects. The implication was gradual redistribution of risk rather than elimination.

Route diversification also has a shadow side. New routes tend to form new clusters. Landing stations attract more landings. Fibre corridors attract more fibre. The network's growth is not evenly spread; it is pulled towards existing hubs by economics and permitting convenience. Reconcile the tension. Incidents can prompt diversification at the macro level while still encouraging micro-level clustering around "safe" landings and compliant jurisdictions. Resilience increases, but not uniformly.

The second category of change is contractual. Outages force uncomfortable questions about who is obliged to do what, and how quickly. Many of the most consequential reforms happen in maintenance agreements and service level expectations rather than in public policy. After repeated disruptions in high-traffic corridors, consortia have, in some cases, tightened repair mobilisation clauses, refined prioritisation rules, and clarified escalation paths. These changes are rarely publicised because they are commercially sensitive. Yet they shape real recovery times. Efficiency here is measured in hours shaved off mobilisation and days saved in permitting coordination.

A pattern emerges: contracts become more explicit after pain. Ambiguity is tolerated until it costs money.

Insurance also changes, though in a less visible way. Underwriters adjust premiums and terms based on incident history. Certain corridors become "known risk" in actuarial language. Deductibles and exclusions shift. Owners respond by hardening shallow segments, investing in monitoring, or pursuing route diversity that improves insurability. Risk is not merely a technical condition; it becomes a priced commodity. The implication is that markets push resilience where governments sometimes hesitate, though not always in socially optimal ways.

The third category of change is organisational: risk assessment. After a regional outage, operators and large enterprises tend to revisit their maps of dependency. The difference after an incident is not that the cable network suddenly becomes visible, but that leaders are briefly willing to invest in understanding it. Banks commission assessments of circuit diversity. Cloud customers ask harder questions about regional failover. Governments run scenario exercises that assume multiple simultaneous cuts rather than a single point failure. These exercises often end with uncomfortable findings: shared ducts near landing stations, concentration in a single coastal corridor, insufficient satellite capacity for prolonged national disruption. The implication is a shift from theoretical redundancy to tested redundancy.

Yet risk assessment suffers from a predictable decay. Memory fades. Budgets tighten. Personnel change. The discipline of mapping dependencies can be treated as a one-off project rather than a living practice. Reconcile this with the persistence of hazards. The seabed does not forget. Organisations do.

The fourth category of change is technical operations and monitoring. Near-misses in financial centres and major hubs have increased the appetite for independent visibility. Private-sector monitoring firms gained prominence precisely because operators cannot always communicate rapidly and because early warning buys valuable time. After incidents, firms and exchanges refine alert thresholds, diversify peering arrangements, and rehearse operational responses. These are small moves, but they compound. They change how quickly a problem is recognised and how calmly it is managed.

There is a limitation, and it matters. Monitoring does not create capacity. It creates awareness. Awareness helps organisations prioritise and adapt, but it cannot substitute for a second cable, a different corridor, or a faster repair ship. Reconcile the two. The most resilient responses combine improved visibility with physical and commercial diversification.

The fifth category of change is political messaging. Governments rarely want to admit vulnerability, yet they increasingly cannot ignore the strategic character of cable infrastructure. After major incidents—especially those surrounded by ambiguity—states tend to speak more about resilience and less about blame. Joint statements emphasise cooperation, monitoring, and "critical infrastructure protection". Behind those statements, however, policy may shift in more concrete ways: regulatory scrutiny of cable ownership, requirements for incident reporting, or quiet support for additional routes. Diplomatic messaging functions as both reassurance and deterrence, signalling that cable disruption is noticed and will be treated seriously without specifying red lines.

This is where the motif of *quiet* returns. The most important changes are often the least public. A government may streamline permits for a new landing station without a press release. A regulator may revise guidance on critical infrastructure classification through a technical consultation. A consortium may fund an additional spare cable section or improve access to ports in a maintenance agreement. These acts do not generate public drama, yet they alter the probability distribution of future outages.

A composite view of the incidents discussed in this chapter reveals how these categories interact. The regional outage teaches operators to spread routes and refine maintenance priorities. The island outage teaches governments that satellite backup is a lifeline but not a substitute, pushing them towards second cables when possible. The near-miss in a financial centre teaches markets to treat latency as an operational risk rather than a nuisance, strengthening monitoring and rehearsals. The conflict-zone disruption teaches everyone that ambiguity is itself a hazard, encouraging careful communication and, where feasible, route avoidance.

There is also a more subtle change: expectations. After repeated incidents, stakeholders become less willing to accept vague reassurances. Customers ask for evidence of path diversity. Boards ask for quantified exposure. Governments ask for maps and scenario outcomes. This demand for specificity can be productive, but it can also create a false sense of control if it reduces resilience to a compliance checklist. The implication is that resilience must remain adaptive, not merely documented.

A credible counter-example tempers optimism. Some regions experience severe outages and change very little, particularly where capital is scarce or politics unstable. Single-cable islands may remain single-cable islands for years. Crowded corridors may remain crowded because alternatives are geopolitically difficult. Reconcile the reality. Resilience is uneven because resources and governance are uneven. The network reflects the world it serves.

So what does "changed" mean in practice? It rarely means a grand redesign of the global cable map. It more often means marginal improvements that shift failure modes: from total outage to congestion, from weeks to days, from surprise to managed degradation. Those shifts matter. They can keep hospitals connected, markets orderly, and governments functional. They can also lull societies into thinking the problem has been solved when it has merely been postponed.

The forward test is therefore a decision question rather than a prediction. After each disruption, do organisations and states treat resilience as a one-time project—build a new route, revise a contract, publish a statement—or as a continuing discipline that anticipates new forms of clustering and new forms of risk? The next incident will supply an answer. It will not care whether the reforms were public or private. It will only reveal whether they were real.

# Chapter 6

# Repair Ships And Maintenance Logistics

At 03:17 local time, a monitoring screen in a European network operations centre flickered from amber to red. A fault had been detected on a subsea system carrying traffic between continents. Within minutes, engineers had narrowed the problem to a stretch of seabed several hundred kilometres offshore. By dawn, senior managers were on the phone. By midday, the most pressing question was not *what* had broken, but *where the nearest repair ship was*—and how long it would take to reach the site. For users already feeling slower connections, the answer was unsettling. Days, perhaps weeks. The glass thread beneath the sea had snapped, and there was no quick fix.

This delay is one of the most persistent misunderstandings surrounding subsea cables. The public imagination often leaps from fault to repair as if the ocean floor were an accessible street corner. In reality, cable repair is closer to offshore surgery than roadside maintenance. Ships must be available, faults precisely located, permits secured, weather assessed, crews assembled, and priorities negotiated—often across borders and commercial interests that have little reason to move in lockstep. Speed matters. So does safety. So does politics.

The paradox that frames this chapter is stark. Subsea cables are among the most critical pieces of global infrastructure, yet the means to repair them are scarce, slow-moving, and shared. A handful of specialised vessels serve vast regions of ocean. They operate under standing agreements negotiated years in advance. When multiple failures occur—after a storm, an earthquake, or a period of heightened tension—someone must wait. Understanding who waits, and why, reveals more about resilience than any abstract discussion of redundancy.

The repair ecosystem sits at the intersection of engineering, logistics, and governance. It is shaped as much by contracts and geography as by technology. The chapter opens by examining how maintenance agreements are structured, because this is where expectations are quietly set. The world's oceans are divided into maintenance zones, each supported by one or more dedicated repair ships funded collectively by cable owners. These arrangements are designed to be efficient, not generous. They assume that failures will be infrequent and geographically dispersed. When those assumptions fail, competition emerges—not between nations, but between cables, consortia, and commercial priorities.

From there, the narrative moves to the moment of failure itself and the difficult art of diagnosis. Locating a fault on the seabed is not a matter of observation but inference. Engineers rely on test signals, time delays, and historical performance to narrow the search area before a ship even leaves port. Errors at this stage are costly. A misjudged location can send a vessel hundreds of kilometres off course, wasting precious days and compounding the outage. Accuracy, here, is not an abstract virtue. It is measured in fuel burned, crew hours spent, and customers left waiting.

Only once a fault is confidently located does the drama of mobilisation begin. Repair ships are not taxis idling at the dock. They may be mid-mission, in port for crew changes, or constrained by weather systems thousands of kilometres away. Routing a vessel to a fault involves more than plotting a straight line. Captains and operators must consider port access, refuelling, crew rest regulations, and, increasingly, diplomatic clearance to operate in or transit certain waters. A repair can be technically straightforward and still delayed by paperwork.

The sea itself remains the ultimate arbiter. Even when a ship arrives on station, work proceeds only within narrow windows dictated by wind, waves, currents, and visibility. Captains balance urgency against the safety of crew and equipment. A hurried operation in poor conditions risks further damage or injury. This reality explains why outages sometimes persist even when a repair ship is visibly "on site". Presence does not equal progress.

Restoration, too, is rarely instantaneous. Once the cable is recovered, spliced, and re-laid, circuits must be tested, traffic gradually reintroduced, and performance monitored for stability. Users often experience a confusing period of partial recovery: some services return, others falter, latency fluctuates. This is not incompetence; it is caution. Bringing a global system back online is a process, not a switch.

Running through all of this is a recurring motif: *time under constraint*. Every decision in the repair chain trades speed against risk, cost, and coordination.

The chapter shows how these trade-offs are made, and by whom, not to apportion blame but to replace frustration with understanding. When a cable fault occurs, the clock does not start at zero. It starts with history—of contracts signed, ships positioned, routes chosen, and risks accepted long before the break.

This matters now because the volume of traffic riding on each cable has grown faster than the capacity to repair them. It matters always because physical infrastructure obeys physical limits, regardless of how digital our lives become. As cables become more strategically sensitive and oceans more crowded, the logistics of repair will only grow more complex. Expectations, however, have not adjusted. Users still ask why it takes so long.

By the end of this chapter, the reader will see repair ships not as symbols of delay, but as the final link in a fragile chain of preparedness. The question is no longer simply how fast a cable can be fixed, but how wisely the world has chosen to organise the fixing. When the next fault occurs—and it will—the answer will already be in motion, long before the alarms sound.

## How repair agreements are structured

In September 2018, Typhoon Mangkhut tore across the northern Philippines and the South China Sea, leaving a trail of damage that extended far beyond coastlines. Within days, multiple subsea cables serving Hong Kong, Taiwan, and mainland China reported faults in shallow waters churned by the storm. Engineers could see the alarms. Customers could feel the slowdown. Yet only one repair ship was immediately available under the Asia-Pacific Marine Cable Maintenance Agreement. Others were days away. The question facing operators was blunt: *which cable would be fixed first*?

This is the moment when the hidden architecture of repair agreements surfaces. To outside observers, the delay looked like inertia. Inside the system, it was procedure. Maintenance zones had been defined years earlier. Contracts had set priorities. Calls were already under way between consortium representatives, ship operators, and zone managers. The sea had moved faster than the ships. Always does.

Scarcity defines everything.

Subsea cable repair is governed less by engineering possibility than by collective logistics. The world's oceans are divided into regional maintenance zones, each supported by a small pool of highly specialised vessels. These zones exist because no single cable owner—whether a telecoms carrier, a cloud provider, or a consortium—can justify keeping a repair ship idle "just in case". A modern repair vessel can cost tens of millions of pounds to build and millions more per year to operate. The solution, devised decades ago and refined since, is shared risk through standing agreements.

The most influential of these arrangements include the Atlantic Cable Maintenance Agreement (ACMA), established in the 1960s to cover transatlantic systems, and later regional counterparts such as the Mediterranean Cable Maintenance Agreement and the Asia-Pacific Marine Cable Maintenance Agreement. Each agreement defines a geographic area, a roster of member cable systems, and a set of nominated repair ships. Members pay annual fees proportional to their system length and exposure. In return, they gain access to repair resources when faults occur.

The design is rational. The implication is uncomfortable.

Because ships are shared, access is conditional. When a single cable fails in calm weather, the system works smoothly. A ship is tasked, sails, repairs, and returns to standby. Trouble begins when failures cluster—after storms, earthquakes, or periods of intense maritime activity. In those moments, the agreements reveal their true nature: they are prioritisation frameworks, not guarantees of immediacy.

Priority is not arbitrary. Each agreement sets out criteria that guide decision-making when multiple faults compete for limited resources. These typically include the scale of traffic affected, the availability of alternative routes, the number of users impacted, and, in some cases, the strategic importance of the system. A trunk cable carrying terabits between continents will usually outrank a smaller regional spur. A system with no redundancy may outrank one with multiple alternative paths. The decision is not moral. It is operational.

Show this logic at work, and its consequences sharpen.

After Typhoon Mangkhut, repair requests arrived almost simultaneously. Several systems had been damaged within a confined seabed corridor south of Hong Kong. The available repair ship could address only one fault at a time. Consortium representatives convened urgent calls. Traffic engineers presented rerouting data showing which systems could limp along and which were approaching collapse. The ship was assigned to the cable whose failure threatened to isolate the greatest volume of traffic. Other systems waited. Days passed.

Waiting is not passive. While a cable sits unrepaired, operators reroute traffic across longer paths, lease emergency capacity, or, where possible, activate satellite links. Latency rises. Costs spike. Some services degrade gracefully; others do not. Financial networks may absorb milliseconds. Voice traffic often cannot. The maintenance agreement does not manage these effects. It merely governs the order in which physical repair begins.

This structure explains a common public frustration: *why is no one fixing this yet?* The answer is usually that someone else is already being fixed, and the agreement says they go first.

The system's strength lies in predictability. Every member knows the rules before a fault occurs. Fees are transparent. Coverage is defined. Repair ships are maintained to a known standard. Crew training is shared. Over decades, this model has kept global connectivity remarkably resilient despite rising traffic volumes. Its weakness lies in inflexibility under extreme stress.

One credible limitation is geographical mismatch. Maintenance zones are vast, and ship placement reflects historical risk, not emerging patterns. As cable routes proliferate in new regions—polar approaches, offshore energy corridors, and densely cabled narrow seas—the distance between ship and fault can stretch into thousands of kilometres. Even at full speed, a repair vessel may take a week to arrive. No clause in the agreement makes the ocean smaller.

A second limitation is contractual inertia. Maintenance agreements are negotiated over long cycles. Adjusting fees, adding ships, or redefining zones requires consensus among members with divergent interests. Large technology firms, whose systems now dominate new builds, may favour faster response times. Smaller carriers may resist higher fees. The result is incremental change, even as dependency accelerates.

Yet the model persists because alternatives are worse.

Some cable owners have experimented with private maintenance—dedicated ships or bespoke contracts with marine service providers. These arrangements can reduce response times for critical systems, particularly for hyperscale operators with deep pockets. They are also expensive and limited in scope. A private ship cannot be everywhere. In multi-fault scenarios, even privately maintained systems may still rely on regional agreements for surge capacity. The shared model remains the backbone.

Trust underpins the entire structure. Not interpersonal trust, but procedural trust. Members trust that priorities will be applied consistently.

They trust that ships will be maintained, crews retained, and spare cable stocked. When this trust erodes—after repeated delays or perceived bias—members begin to hedge, adding redundant routes or seeking alternative arrangements. The agreement weakens as a result.

Return to the quiet motif of waiting.

Waiting is built into the economics of repair. It is the price paid for shared resilience. The agreements do not promise speed; they promise order. In most years, that order is sufficient. In bad years, it is exposed.

The implications extend beyond telecoms. Governments increasingly treat subsea cables as critical national infrastructure, yet maintenance agreements remain commercial instruments. States rarely control them directly. When a major outage occurs, ministers may demand action, but the repair queue is governed by contracts signed by private operators. This gap between political urgency and logistical reality is widening.

Some governments respond indirectly. They encourage additional cables to reduce dependence on any single system. They quietly support the positioning of extra repair ships in sensitive regions. They nudge regulators to treat maintenance fees as allowable costs rather than discretionary spending. None of this makes headlines. All of it shapes outcomes.

The unresolved tension at the heart of repair agreements is simple to state and hard to resolve. As dependence on subsea cables deepens, should repair capacity scale proportionally, even if that means higher costs and idle assets? Or should the world accept waiting as an inherent feature of shared infrastructure, mitigating the risk through redundancy rather than response speed?

The next storm will pose the question again.

## Finding and diagnosing the fault

At 06:42 on 30 January 2008, network monitoring data collected by Renesys showed routes shifting abruptly after cable damage near Alexandria. Engineers could see the effects within minutes. What they could not yet see was the break itself. The seabed offered no smoke, no flare, no visible wreckage. Only silence in the fibre and a rising argument about *where*, precisely, to send the ship.

Five centimetres of accuracy can save five days.

That ratio is not a flourish. It is the daily arithmetic of subsea repair. A cable fault is an event in the ocean. Diagnosis is an event on land, performed through signals, logs, and inference. The difference between a clean repair and a prolonged outage often comes down to how well engineers can translate an abstract measurement into a point on the seabed—then defend that point against uncertainty long enough for a ship to commit.

Fault-finding begins before anyone picks up a phone. Cable systems are monitored continuously. Power feeding equipment reports current and voltage behaviour. Terminal stations monitor optical performance. Network operations centres watch alarms cascade across layers: physical link down, increased bit error rates, changes in optical signal-to-noise, protection switching events. These alerts are not merely technical curiosities. They are the first draft of a story. And like all first drafts, they can be wrong.

The most important diagnostic tool for fibre faults remains optical time-domain reflectometry, commonly referred to as OTDR. The principle is elegantly brutal. A pulse of light is sent down the fibre. Imperfections and breaks reflect a portion of that pulse back. By measuring the time delay of the reflection, engineers estimate distance to the event. Distance becomes a proxy for location. The visible metric is time in microseconds. The implication is seabed coordinates—once that distance is mapped onto a route plan.

OTDR is powerful, but it is not magic. Subsea systems carry many fibres. Some may fail while others remain intact. Repeaters, splice joints and branching units introduce known reflection signatures that must be accounted for. Signals weaken with distance. Noise rises. Interpreting OTDR traces is a craft as much as a calculation. Two engineers can look at the same curve and argue about whether a subtle reflection is a fault, a normal splice, or an artefact.

Power feeding telemetry adds another layer. Repeaters along the cable receive electrical power from shore, typically through a constant current feed. When a fault occurs—especially a shunt to seawater or an open circuit—the electrical behaviour changes. Engineers can infer whether the fault is closer to one landing station than another by comparing measurements from both ends. This helps narrow down which segment is affected and whether the fault is likely a clean break or a partial compromise. The abstraction of "diagnosis" becomes a decision: is this a fishing snag in shallow water, or a deep-water shunt that suggests severe damage?

Naming matters here because the diagnostic process is often collaborative. In consortium systems, multiple landing stations share the same cable. When an alarm triggers, operators in different countries exchange traces and power readings. They compare interpretations. They reconcile logs. A fault that appears at 612 kilometres from one end must correspond to a point on the marine route plan that all parties accept. Trust, in this context, is procedural: trust that measurements are accurate, that calibration is consistent, and that no one is shaping the narrative to serve their own repair priority.

A second named example illustrates how diagnostic uncertainty can matter. After the 26 December 2006 Luzon Strait earthquake, multiple cables failed across a complex corridor. Operators faced not one fault but many, across several systems, with overlapping damage patterns and unstable seabed conditions. Diagnostic work had to distinguish between separate breaks and degraded segments, and to allocate repair ships accordingly. Public reporting and subsequent technical analyses described how repairs took weeks partly because faults were numerous and clustered. Reconcile the lesson. Even with accurate tools, diagnosis becomes harder when nature creates a mosaic of damage rather than a single clean cut.

The importance of accurate fault location is best understood through the cost of being wrong. A repair ship is not a drone dispatched to a coordinate. It is a vessel with crew, fuel, equipment and a schedule shaped by maintenance agreements. When it sails, it commits money and time. If the fault location is off by tens of kilometres, the ship may arrive on station, deploy grapnels, and pull up cable only to discover healthy fibre. That is not merely embarrassing. It can add days to an outage.

Misdiagnosis can occur for mundane reasons. Route plans may be outdated. A cable may have been rerouted slightly during installation due to seabed obstacles, leaving the as-laid route different from the planned one. Shore-based distance calculations assume known propagation speed in fibre and accurate mapping of route length, but splices, slack loops and repairs change effective length over time. Errors compound. The visible metric is kilometres of uncertainty. The implication is wasted search time.

A stylised but realistic scenario shows how this plays out. An operator detects a fault and performs OTDR testing from one landing station. The trace suggests a sharp reflection consistent with a break at a certain distance. Power measurements show a drop consistent with a shunt fault. The route plan places that distance near a known shipping anchorage.

The team assumes anchor damage. A repair ship is tasked and sails to that anchorage. After grappling, the crew retrieves cable—but it is intact. The fault lies elsewhere, further along a section where the cable had been rerouted during a past repair, adding slack that was not captured in the operator's working maps.

No one lied. The system misled.

This is why fault-finding is iterative. Engineers cross-check OTDR from both ends where possible. They compare results across multiple fibres. They examine historical performance data to see whether degradation preceded failure. They consult marine records: recent storms, dredging activity, known anchoring events. They use network-level symptoms to corroborate physical estimates. If routes changed gradually before failure, the fault may be developing. If the link dropped instantly, it may be a sudden cut. Each clue is imperfect. Together, they narrow the search.

The presence of branching units and regional loops adds complexity. A fault on one branch may isolate only certain landing stations, producing asymmetric symptoms. In such cases, diagnosis must model the network topology as well as the physical route. Which branches are down? Which remain stable? The abstraction of "service impact" becomes a map of affected endpoints, which in turn informs where the fault likely lies.

There is a credible counter-example that complicates the narrative. Some faults are obvious and quickly located, particularly in shallow waters where the cable route is well charted and where damage is often physical and localised. When a known fishing ground produces repeated faults, operators learn to interpret the signatures quickly. In these cases, diagnosis is almost routine. Reconcile this with the harder cases. Fault-finding varies with environment. Deep ocean faults may be rarer but harder to characterise; shallow faults may be more frequent but easier to localise.

The motif threading this section is *translation*. Engineers translate light into distance, distance into coordinates, coordinates into a ship's mission. Every translation introduces uncertainty. The craft lies in shrinking uncertainty fast enough to justify action.

Communication during diagnosis is itself a form of risk management. Overly confident early estimates can lead to premature mobilisation to the wrong site. Overly cautious estimates can delay mobilisation even when the fault is clear. The best teams calibrate confidence explicitly. They describe a probable location, an error radius, and a ranking of alternative hypotheses.

This language may never reach the public, but it shapes operational decisions.

Modern monitoring has improved the first phase of diagnosis. Private-sector telemetry, such as internet route monitoring, can signal broader impacts and help identify which corridors are stressed. It does not locate the break, but it can corroborate that the issue is physical rather than a routing policy mistake. Similarly, seabed mapping and historical incident databases help planners identify likely hazard zones. Yet none of these replaces direct optical and electrical testing.

What, then, is the real lesson? Fault-finding is not simply an engineering step in a repair sequence. It is a strategic act. Accurate diagnosis reduces outage time, repair cost, and political noise. In tense regions, it also reduces the space for speculative narratives by allowing operators to speak with confidence about what happened and where. In commercial contexts, it determines how quickly service-level commitments can be met.

The forward test remains unresolved and increasingly relevant. As cable routes grow denser and incidents more politically charged, will operators invest in better route documentation, shared diagnostic protocols, and faster cross-border coordination—so that "where is the fault?" can be answered with tighter confidence? Or will diagnostic uncertainty remain a silent contributor to long outages, blamed on the sea when the real delay lies in translation from signal to seabed?

## Mobilising and routing the repair vessel

In February 2024, as multiple subsea cables in the Red Sea region suffered damage and traffic detoured around Africa, cable operators faced a familiar constraint: repairs could not begin until a ship was allowed to work. The named organisation in public confirmation was SEACOM, which reported service impacts linked to the damage. The place was the Red Sea near Yemen. The month mattered because regional security conditions were already tense, and the practical outcome was delay—days lost not to splicing complexity, but to access, routing, and permission.

Ships do not sail by wish.

A repair vessel's mobilisation is the least understood phase of subsea recovery, partly because it looks deceptively simple. A fault is detected. A ship is assigned. A captain is told to proceed. In practice, mobilisation is a chain of dependencies with failure points of its own: the ship must be physically available, crewed, provisioned, and legally authorised to operate in the waters where the fault lies. Weather must permit safe transit and later safe station-keeping. Ports must be accessible for fuel, spares, and crew changes. The route must be chosen not merely for speed but for feasibility.

Begin with the tasking decision. Most repair ships operate under regional maintenance agreements. When a fault is confirmed and prioritised, the zone manager and the ship operator agree on mobilisation. This is a contractual act as much as a technical one. It triggers cost allocation, liability terms, and reporting duties. The visible decision is a sailing order. The implication is commitment: once underway, the ship cannot be easily redirected without consequences for other queued faults.

Availability is the first constraint. A ship may be on standby, but standby does not mean idle and ready within minutes. The vessel may be in port undergoing maintenance, restocking spare cable, or complying with crew rest requirements. It may already be at sea repairing another system. A second ship may exist on paper yet be positioned far away. Even in the best case, mobilisation involves a scramble: confirming crew rosters, ensuring specialist jointers and engineers can embark, and verifying that the vessel carries the correct equipment for the cable type and water depth. A deep-water repair requires different handling than a shallow burial intervention.

The abstraction of "response time" becomes concrete as a series of clocks. How long to muster crew? How long to take on fuel? How long to load spares and jointing kits? How long to clear port formalities? None of these steps is glamorous, and each can introduce delay measured in hours that quickly become days.

Port availability is an underappreciated chokepoint. Repair ships need ports that can accommodate their size, provide fuel and provisions, and allow loading of heavy equipment. In some regions, suitable ports are limited. In others, ports are available but politically constrained. A ship may need to avoid certain harbours due to sanctions, security advisories, or diplomatic friction. Even where none of these apply, port congestion can delay berthing. The visible behaviour is a ship waiting at anchor, not because the crew is idle, but because logistics cannot proceed until the port slot opens.

Weather exerts pressure throughout. Transit planning is not merely a matter of charting the shortest line; it is a matter of riding safe seas. A repair ship may choose a longer route to avoid a developing storm system. That choice can feel perverse to outsiders. It is also rational. Arriving early but exhausted, damaged, or unsafe helps no one. The sea is not a motorway. It is an adversary that can seize days without negotiation.

This is where the motif of *waiting* returns in a new form. In earlier chapters, waiting belonged to users and operators watching alarms. Here it belongs to ships: waiting for the sea to calm, for a port to open, for paperwork to clear. Waiting is the currency of offshore work.

Regulatory permissions are often the sharpest constraint of all. Subsea cables cross territorial seas, exclusive economic zones, and sometimes contested waters. While international law provides broad freedoms to lay and maintain cables beyond territorial seas, the practical reality is that repair operations often require coastal state notification or permission, particularly when working near shore or when the vessel needs to conduct operations that may be interpreted as survey activity. Repair ships must obtain clearances to enter territorial waters, to deploy equipment, and sometimes to operate with dynamic positioning in sensitive areas.

The result is a bureaucratic geography layered atop the physical one. A fault location may be technically straightforward, but politically awkward. A ship can be fully crewed and ready, yet legally immobilised.

A named, checkable example from a different context illustrates this constraint. In September 2022, after the Far North Fibre cable between Shetland and mainland Scotland suffered damage, repairs depended not only on fault location and ship availability but also on safe working windows in harsh northern waters and coordination with local maritime authorities. Public reporting highlighted the interplay between weather and operational access. The implication generalises. Even in stable jurisdictions, procedural and environmental constraints shape mobilisation timelines.

In more contested or security-sensitive waters, the constraints intensify. A vessel may require escorts. It may be asked to delay until naval activity clears the area. Permissions may move through multiple agencies, each with different priorities. A repair ship is a civilian asset, but it can look like a surveillance platform to an anxious state. The ship's equipment—grapnels, remotely operated tools, seabed sensors—resembles the toolkit of undersea intelligence. This resemblance can slow approvals, even when the intent is purely restorative.

Here the counter-example matters. Some states streamline permissions precisely because they recognise the economic cost of delay. Singapore, for example, has long treated maritime operations with procedural efficiency, and cable-related works around major ports can often proceed quickly when properly coordinated. Reconcile the contrast. Governance choices can compress or expand downtime without changing the cable or the ship.

Routing decisions reveal another layer: risk management. A ship headed to a fault site may choose routes that minimise exposure to piracy, conflict, or severe weather. The choice is not purely technical; it is a security posture. During periods of heightened risk in corridors such as the Gulf of Aden, vessels may rely on maritime security guidance and convoy practices. Even when a repair ship is not directly threatened, its operators must consider crew safety and insurance conditions. The visible metric becomes time-to-arrival versus risk exposure. The implication is that geopolitical conditions can lengthen outages without a single additional break in fibre.

The mobilisation phase also exposes the commercial structure of cable ownership. When consortia are involved, mobilisation may depend on cost approvals and procedural triggers agreed in advance. Emergency authority exists, but budgets still govern. Large owners may push for immediate action; smaller owners may worry about cost allocation. The agreement framework resolves these tensions, but not instantly. Every hour spent negotiating is an hour not spent sailing.

Once the ship is underway, navigation is only the beginning. The vessel must arrive with enough fuel and stores to remain on station for days, sometimes weeks. It must plan for contingencies: if the first grappling attempt fails, if weather forces suspension, if the fault location shifts. This is why repair ships carry spare cable and jointing materials, and why mobilisation includes careful inventory checks. A missing component can force an unscheduled port call, turning a repair into a logistical loop.

The broader implication is that "time to repair" is not a single number. It is a compound of detection time, diagnosis time, mobilisation time, transit time, and working time. Public frustration often focuses on the last component—splicing and re-laying. Yet mobilisation frequently dominates the timeline. The hard truth is that the world's digital nervous system depends on a handful of slow-moving ships operating under constraints that are not fully under anyone's control.

The forward test is now unavoidable. As cable corridors intersect more often with contested waters, sanctions regimes, and environmental regulation, can maintenance agreements and coastal states adapt to allow faster, safer mobilisation? Or will the repair ship increasingly become a symbol of delay—not because engineers cannot fix the cable, but because the modern ocean has become a place where even restoration is a diplomatic act?

## Working windows, weather and safety

On 7 October 2022, Shetland lost its main fibre connection to mainland Scotland after damage to the Far North Fibre cable. The organisation that publicly acknowledged the disruption was Shetland Telecom. The place was Shetland. The month mattered because the North Sea does not grant favours in autumn. The outcome was predictable to anyone who has spent time offshore: repair plans were made quickly, yet progress was slowed by weather windows and sea state, stretching what many onshore users imagined would be a rapid fix.

The sea sets the timetable.

This is the part of cable repair that resists modern expectations most stubbornly. We live with interfaces that update in seconds and services that promise "five nines" of availability, so we instinctively treat delay as a managerial failure. Offshore work is different. It is not only difficult; it is conditional. A captain can have a precise fault location, a skilled crew, and every spare part in the hold, and still be forced to wait because wave height has crossed a safe threshold or currents make station-keeping unreliable. That waiting is not laziness. It is survival.

Safety is the first constraint, and it is also the least negotiable. Cable repair involves heavy gear, high tension, and delicate operations conducted over open water. When a vessel grapples for cable, hauls it up, and pays it out again, the cable behaves like a live thing. It runs under tension. It can whip. It can snag and release suddenly. Deck machinery—winches, capstans, sheaves—must be operated with precision. In rough seas, even routine tasks become hazardous. A misstep can injure crew, damage equipment, or compromise the cable further. The implication is stark: pushing work into bad conditions can turn a repair into a second incident.

The public often imagines repair as a single act: locate, cut, splice, restore. In reality it is a sequence of operations, each sensitive to sea state in a different way. Transit to site can proceed in relatively poor conditions, though at reduced speed and with crew fatigue accumulating. On-station work is far more demanding. The ship must hold position over a small patch of seabed, sometimes with dynamic positioning, sometimes with careful anchoring or drift control. It must deploy grapnels or remotely operated equipment, recover cable to deck, perform jointing in a controlled environment, then return the cable to the seabed without kinks or undue tension. Each step has "go/no-go" criteria informed by maritime safety standards and the captain's judgement.

Here, an abstraction becomes a visible metric. "Sea state" is not a mood of the ocean; it is often quantified by significant wave height and period. The difference between a workable 2-metre sea and a punishing 4-metre sea is the difference between a stable deck and one that throws people and equipment off rhythm. Currents add another dimension. Strong currents can pull on the cable during recovery and increase strain on the ship's position-holding systems. Visibility matters too, particularly for near-shore work or operations involving divers or surface coordination. Even when the cable lies deep, poor visibility can complicate safe navigation and deck operations.

The motif threading this section is *the window*. Offshore work proceeds through windows: brief stretches of acceptable conditions in a wider pattern of volatility. Repair teams become students of meteorology not out of curiosity but necessity. They watch forecasts, interpret satellite data, and plan operations around shifting fronts. A window may open at midnight and close by dawn. It may last two days, or two hours. The ship's plan must be flexible enough to seize it without rushing recklessly.

The balance between safety, cost and urgency is therefore constant and tangible. Every day waiting offshore costs money: vessel charter, crew time, fuel, and the opportunity cost of not being available for other faults. Every day waiting onshore costs customers: degraded connectivity, operational disruption, political attention. Captains and engineers occupy the space between these pressures. Their decision to suspend work is rarely popular. It is often correct.

Shetland in October 2022 provides a clear illustration of why. The cable fault was in a harsh operating environment. Repair required a vessel to work in northern waters known for rapid weather shifts. Public communications at the time pointed to the need for favourable conditions, and the restoration timeline reflected weather constraints as much as technical complexity. The implication is not that Shetland was uniquely unlucky. It is that many critical cable routes pass through seas where calm is seasonal.

A second named example reinforces the point. After the 15 January 2022 eruption in Tonga severed the international cable, repair timelines were extended not only by the technical task but by the hazardous maritime environment created by volcanic ash, ongoing seismic activity, and damaged coastal infrastructure. Reports from the period noted that the repair ship's work was constrained by conditions around the eruption zone. Here, the window motif becomes sharper. The sea can be physically unsafe even when weather is calm, and safety decisions extend beyond wave height to hazard assessment.

There is a credible counter-example. In calmer seas and shallow waters, repairs can be rapid. Cable faults near sheltered coasts, where vessels can operate with minimal swell and where permits are straightforward, may be resolved within days once a ship arrives. Some repairs near major hubs proceed quickly enough that users notice only transient degradation. Reconcile this with the harsher cases. Repair speed is a function of environment as much as capability. The same ship and crew can be swift in one sea and slow in another.

The working window also interacts with the repair method. Deep-water faults may require grappling and long cable recovery lengths, which increase sensitivity to motion and tension. Near-shore faults may involve burial and interaction with seabed sediment, which can be complicated by currents and turbidity. In some cases, repairs may be postponed not because the sea is too rough for the ship, but because it is too rough to protect the cable during re-lay. A cable placed poorly in turbulent conditions may be exposed sooner, inviting repeat damage. The implication is long-term resilience. A rushed repair can create future faults.

Safety culture is another invisible factor. Repair crews operate under stringent procedures for lifting, jointing, and deck operations. These procedures are shaped by experience and, often, by hard-won lessons from accidents. The cable industry is not immune to offshore hazards. It shares risks with oil and gas and other marine sectors: heavy machinery, high tension lines, and operations in unpredictable conditions. The decision to pause work is therefore not merely an individual choice but an institutional expectation.

Public frustration, when it appears, tends to focus on urgency: why not work through the night, why not accept higher risk? Yet the moral calculus shifts when one considers consequences. Injuring crew is unacceptable. Damaging the cable further extends outages. Losing gear overboard can create hazards for other sea users. The visible behaviour—pausing, waiting, repositioning—can look like delay. The implication is responsibility.

This is where communication becomes part of safety. Operators and authorities often explain delays in bland terms: "weather conditions are preventing repairs." That statement is true but insufficient. It obscures the specific trade-offs and thresholds that guide decisions. A clearer understanding does not require technical detail, only honesty about what is being balanced: the need to restore service versus the duty to avoid making things worse.

Working windows also shape how traffic is managed during repair. Because repair progress is uncertain, operators maintain rerouting and congestion management measures longer than users expect. They avoid aggressive rebalancing until the cable is fully tested and stabilised. This can make performance feel unstable even after partial restoration. The implication is patience, but also transparency: staged recovery is normal, not a sign of incompetence.

As seas become more crowded and weather patterns more volatile, the window problem may intensify. Climate change is altering storm frequency and intensity in some regions, though attribution to specific patterns remains debated and region-dependent. What can be said with confidence is simpler: coastal and narrow-sea environments are already difficult, and repair work will remain hostage to conditions no operator can control.

The forward test is therefore a question of preparedness rather than prediction. Are maintenance agreements and national resilience plans built around realistic assumptions about working windows, or do they quietly assume a cooperative sea? When the next fault occurs in the wrong season, in the wrong corridor, will the public again be surprised that the repair ship is waiting? Or will expectations finally align with the oldest truth in this business: the ocean decides when the work can begin.

## Restoring service and managing traffic

On 30 January 2008, after multiple cables were damaged near Alexandria, the first public story was disruption; the second was recovery. The named organisations in contemporaneous technical reporting included SEA-ME-WE 4 consortium operators and monitoring firms such as Renesys, which tracked route changes as networks stabilised. The place was the eastern Mediterranean. The date matters because, even once repairs began, normal service did not simply "return". It reappeared in stages—traffic shifting back in cautious increments, latency oscillating, some services stabilising while others continued to stutter. For users, this felt like unreliability. For engineers, it was the only responsible way to restore a strained system without breaking something else.

Recovery is a process, not a switch.

That single sentence explains much of the frustration that follows cable repairs. People expect the internet to behave like a lightbulb: off, then on. Subsea connectivity behaves more like a heart after surgery. The artery can be reopened, yet flow must be reintroduced gradually, pressures monitored, and complications watched for. Too much too soon can harm the patient. Too cautious for too long and the patient weakens. The art of restoration lies in balancing urgency against stability.

The first phase of restoration begins offshore but is confirmed on land. Once a repair crew completes a splice and the cable is re-laid, they do not declare victory and sail away. They must verify physical integrity: correct jointing, acceptable tension, safe placement on the seabed, and—where required—adequate burial or protection. Only then does the cable's electrical and optical personality come back into view at the landing stations. Power feeding equipment is reconfigured. Repeaters are brought back into the chain. Optical performance is tested. A cable can be physically continuous yet optically degraded, particularly if splices are imperfect or if a segment has been stressed during recovery. Engineers measure and compare, looking for deviations from expected attenuation and signal-to-noise characteristics.

This is where the concept of "circuits" matters. The cable itself is the physical medium, but service depends on circuits provisioned across it—wavelengths, protected paths, and capacity allocations that tie multiple networks together. Restoring service means re-establishing these circuits in an agreed order. Some may be restored first because they support essential services or because their customers have higher priority contracts. Others wait because they require coordination across multiple owners or because their protection paths are still carrying traffic and cannot be disrupted lightly.

Five minutes can matter.

That is the five-word sentence many operators live by, and it is especially true during restoration, when changes propagate quickly and mistakes are expensive. A mis-sequenced circuit restoration can trigger congestion elsewhere. An overly aggressive traffic shift can overload an alternative route and cause a secondary incident. Restoration is therefore choreographed.

Traffic management during a cable outage is often described as "rerouting", but the reality is more complex. Some rerouting is automatic, governed by network protocols that shift traffic onto available paths when a link fails. Some is manual, requiring engineers to adjust policies, change capacity allocations, and coordinate with peers. During prolonged outages, operators may lease emergency capacity, alter peering preferences, or temporarily accept less efficient routes to keep core services functioning. These choices create a new, temporary equilibrium. The longer an outage lasts, the more infrastructure and human behaviour adapts around that equilibrium.

Restoration must then unwind it.

This is why users often experience unstable performance during recovery. As capacity returns, networks begin to shift traffic back towards the repaired cable. The shift is rarely instantaneous because operators do not fully trust a newly repaired segment until it proves stable under load. They may begin by restoring a subset of circuits, monitoring performance, then expanding. They may prefer to route latency-sensitive traffic back first, because those applications benefit most. They may keep some traffic on alternative paths longer, to avoid sudden load spikes on the repaired system. Each change can produce transient effects: brief spikes in latency, bursts of packet loss, or route flapping as multiple networks adjust simultaneously.

The motif threading this section is *rebalancing*. Rebalancing is not a metaphor; it is a technical act. It is also social. It requires coordination among organisations that do not share a single command chain.

A named, checkable example of staged restoration helps anchor this. During the 2008 Alexandria disruption, operators restored capacity incrementally as repairs progressed across multiple cables and as traffic gradually returned to preferred routes. Monitoring firms recorded the gradual normalisation of routing, not an abrupt snap-back. The implication is that "service restored" is often a shorthand for "enough capacity restored that the system is no longer in visible distress". Full restoration can lag.

A second example, closer to the user's lived experience, comes from island outages. After the January 2022 Tonga cable repair, service returned progressively, with authorities and operators reporting improvements over time rather than a single moment of full return. Satellite backup continued to play a role until fibre stability was confirmed. This staged return is typical where dependence is concentrated. The implication is that even when the cable is repaired, the system must rebuild confidence in its own backbone.

Testing is central to confidence. Operators perform end-to-end checks across multiple wavelengths. They verify error rates, latency, and stability under load. They watch for intermittent faults that might reappear as the cable settles on the seabed. They check repeaters and branching units for anomalies. They also test protection switching mechanisms, ensuring that if the repaired segment fails again, traffic can move without chaos. These tests do not merely satisfy technical curiosity; they prevent repeat outages.

There is a credible counter-example worth noting. In some cases, restoration can be swift and clean. A shallow-water fault near a major hub, repaired quickly under good conditions, may allow near-immediate restoration of circuits, especially if redundancy kept traffic stable and operators did not need to build complex workarounds. Users may barely notice beyond a brief window of degraded performance. Reconcile this with the staged recoveries. The difference is not competence; it is system stress. When rerouting has been extensive, and alternative paths have been heavily loaded, the return to normal requires careful unwinding.

Restoration is also shaped by commercial relationships. A consortium cable does not belong to a single operator; it is shared. Restoring circuits therefore involves negotiating access, timing, and sometimes cost reconciliation for emergency capacity used during the outage. Service level agreements may require notifications and status updates. Customers may demand evidence. These interactions influence the pace of traffic normalisation. An operator may delay shifting traffic back if doing so would breach commitments elsewhere, or if partners are not ready.

Trust returns here, and it can be measured in willingness to move load. Networks "trust" a path when it performs consistently within expected parameters over time. That trust is not emotional. It is statistical. Engineers compare performance against baselines. They look for stability across peak traffic periods. Only then do they allow the repaired cable to resume its role as primary carrier for critical circuits. Until then, it may carry a fraction of its capacity while acting as a monitored reserve.

This cautious posture can frustrate users and even governments, especially after high-profile outages. The public hears "the cable is repaired" and expects normal service. Operators know that a freshly repaired cable is vulnerable: the repaired segment may be exposed, the seabed may still shift, and the system may be operating with temporary configurations that must be unwound safely. The implication is an expectation gap that can be narrowed only by better communication and, more fundamentally, by more physical diversity so that restoration can be less delicate.

Traffic management also intersects with security. In tense regions, operators may be cautious about revealing detailed restoration timelines or route information, both to avoid public alarm and to avoid providing useful intelligence to adversaries. This restraint can make communications appear vague. Yet even within these constraints, staged restoration is observable through performance. Users experience it as unevenness: some services recover quickly, others lag. That unevenness is not random. It reflects prioritisation and technical sequencing.

The final handback—the point at which a cable is considered fully back in service—often occurs quietly. Engineers close fault tickets. Maintenance agreements mark the mission complete. Traffic gradually returns to normal policy. Congestion on alternative routes eases. Only then do users stop thinking about the cable at all. That forgetfulness is itself a sign of successful restoration.

The unresolved tension remains a question of posture. Should operators shift traffic back as quickly as possible to satisfy public expectation, accepting a higher risk of instability and repeat faults? Or should they continue to treat restoration as a controlled rebalancing, even if it extends the period of perceived unreliability? The sea will answer with the next incident, and the answer will be visible not in press releases, but in the quiet telemetry of routes, latency, and load.

# Chapter 7

# Designing Redundancy And Network Resilience

In September 2015, engineers working on the South Atlantic Cable System watched their dashboards flicker as a planned maintenance cut was executed during a low-traffic window. The cut itself was unremarkable. What mattered was what did *not* happen. Traffic dipped, rerouted, and stabilised within seconds. No headlines followed. No customers called. No minister demanded an explanation. The system behaved as it was designed to: absorbing damage without drama. For the engineers involved, this quiet success was the point. For everyone else, it was invisible.

Resilience rarely announces itself.

That silence is deceptive. It suggests effortlessness where, in reality, there have been years of argument, compromise, modelling, and rehearsal. Redundancy is not a single decision or a line item in a budget. It is a philosophy expressed through thousands of technical and organisational choices, many contested, some regretted in hindsight. Every resilient network is the fossil record of past failures, encoded into topology diagrams, routing policies, landing maps, and escalation playbooks.

This chapter sits at the hinge of the book. Until now, the focus has been on what exists, how it is built, how it breaks, and how it is repaired. Here, the emphasis shifts to intention. How do designers, operators, and governments try to ensure that the next break does not become the next crisis? What does "enough redundancy" actually mean when money, geography, and politics all resist it?

The word redundancy is often misunderstood. Outside engineering, it carries a whiff of waste. Something redundant is unnecessary, surplus, indulgent. In network design, redundancy is not excess; it is insurance written into steel, fibre, and code. It is the difference between a cut being an incident and becoming an emergency. Yet redundancy is never absolute.

It is always partial, conditional, and shaped by assumptions about what might go wrong.

Those assumptions matter.

At the most basic level, resilience begins with topology. Rings, meshes, and dual-homed designs are not abstract diagrams but practical answers to a simple question: *where does the traffic go when this link fails?* A ring topology accepts that any single cut should be survivable, provided traffic can flow the other way. A mesh goes further, offering multiple alternative paths and distributing risk across geography and ownership. Dual-homing acknowledges that diversity at the edge—connecting a site or a landing station to two independent backbones—can be as important as diversity at sea.

Each of these designs embodies a trade-off. Rings are economical but vulnerable to multiple cuts. Meshes are robust but expensive and complex to operate. Dual-homing protects endpoints but does little if the upstream routes converge too early. The choice between them is rarely ideological. It is negotiated, shaped by traffic forecasts, capital constraints, and the uncomfortable knowledge that some risks will be accepted because they cannot be afforded away.

From topology, attention turns quickly to single points of failure, the quiet enemies of resilience. These are not always where people expect. A cable may have two diverse subsea routes, only to converge into a single duct as it approaches the coast. Two landing stations may sit kilometres apart, yet share the same power substation or floodplain. Logical diversity may exist on paper, while physical reality collapses it. Engineers learn to hunt for these weak points, often discovering them not during design reviews but during outages and near-misses.

Avoiding single points of failure is less about perfection than about marginal gains. Diversifying land routes around a landing station might require negotiating new wayleaves, paying higher rents, or accepting longer terrestrial paths with slightly higher latency. Each decision involves cost, time, and political capital. The reward is rarely immediate. It is realised years later, during a storm or a construction accident that *doesn't* take everything down.

Physical separation is the recurring motif here. Logical redundancy without physical separation is a comforting illusion. Route diversity that looks impressive on a map can dissolve under scrutiny when routes share the same seabed corridor, the same canal crossing, or the same narrow strait. Designers know this, yet they also know that geography is stubborn. Coastlines funnel cables. Cities attract landings. Environmental protections constrain options. Local politics can veto technically ideal sites. Resilience is therefore always negotiated with place.

Consider the decision to land two cables in neighbouring towns rather than the same beach. On paper, this is an improvement. In practice, the towns may share road access, backhaul routes, and emergency services. The residual risk does not vanish; it shifts. Good design acknowledges this openly, documenting not just what has been diversified, but what remains coupled. Honest risk registers are a form of resilience in themselves.

Operators do not rely on design alone. Failover planning turns static diagrams into living behaviour. Automatic rerouting protocols can respond in milliseconds, but they are only as good as the assumptions encoded within them. Manual interventions remain essential when failures cascade or when automated responses conflict. This is why experienced operators invest in playbooks and drills. They simulate failures not to prove that systems work, but to discover how they fail in unexpected ways.

These exercises are often humbling. A planned failover may reveal that a supposedly independent path depends on the same monitoring system as the primary route. A routing policy may behave differently under load than it did in testing. A team may discover that escalation paths are unclear across organisational boundaries. Each discovery is uncomfortable. Each is also a gift, arriving before a real incident forces the lesson at higher cost.

The scope widens further at the national level. Governments increasingly recognise that resilience cannot be left entirely to market incentives, especially where national connectivity depends on a small number of routes or landings. Stress-testing national connectivity borrows techniques from finance and civil defence: scenario planning, modelling simultaneous failures, and exploring second- and third-order effects. What happens if two cables fail during a heatwave? How does a regional outage interact with energy markets, emergency services, or military readiness?

These exercises rarely produce neat answers. They do, however, change conversations. Technical findings feed into policy debates about planning permission, investment support, and diplomatic engagement with neighbouring states. Sometimes the outcome is visible—a new cable route, a revised regulatory framework. Often it is quieter: a shift in how risks are discussed, budgeted, and prioritised.

Throughout all of this runs a tension that never fully resolves. Resilience competes with efficiency. Every additional path increases complexity. Every avoided single point of failure costs money and attention. Perfect resilience is unattainable, but inadequate resilience is unforgiving. Designers, operators, and policymakers live in the space between these truths, making bets about the future based on imperfect information.

This chapter will not offer a formula for getting those bets right. Instead, it will trace how resilience is actually pursued: through topology choices that privilege options over elegance, through relentless attention to physical reality, through rehearsal that exposes uncomfortable dependencies, and through national-level thinking that accepts uncertainty rather than pretending it away.

The payoff is not heroism. It is continuity.

As the pages that follow will show, the most resilient networks are not those that never fail, but those that fail without becoming front-page news. The test is simple and demanding. When the cut comes—and it always does—does the system bend, or does it break?

## Mesh and ring topologies explained

If a single cut can sever a nation, why do engineers still tolerate single cuts at all? The paradox sits at the heart of modern network design. Subsea cables are expensive, fragile, and difficult to repair, yet the global system survives hundreds of faults each year with barely a murmur. The explanation is not toughness at the cable level but optionality at the network level. Resilience emerges not from making links unbreakable, but from ensuring that when they break, traffic has somewhere else to go.

That "somewhere else" is topology.

In practice, topology is the quiet geometry of resilience: the pattern by which nodes and links are arranged, and the rules that govern how data flows between them. It determines whether a cut is absorbed or amplified, whether seconds of disruption become days of outage. Engineers rarely discuss topology in public, yet it shapes the lived experience of connectivity more decisively than bandwidth headlines or latency charts. When a network bends rather than snaps, topology is usually the reason.

Begin with the ring, the simplest expression of redundancy that still works. A ring connects sites in a closed loop, so that traffic can flow in either direction. Break the loop at one point and the ring becomes a line, still connected end to end. The idea is old, predating fibre optics by more than a century, and it remains popular because it offers a clear promise: *any single cut should be survivable.* That promise is not theoretical. It has been tested repeatedly in operational networks where, after a cut, traffic reverses direction and continues with minimal interruption.

A concrete illustration can be found in Iceland's international connectivity. By the late 2000s, the country was connected to Europe through multiple subsea systems arranged to provide ring-like protection. When the FARICE-1 cable, running between Iceland and Scotland, suffered damage in February 2007 near the Faroe Islands, traffic was rerouted via alternative paths without a national blackout. The system degraded, but it did not collapse. The ring held. What mattered was not that a cable failed—failure was expected—but that the topology assumed failure and had already decided what would happen next.

The ring's strength is also its limit. It is designed to tolerate one cut, not two. A second failure, if badly placed or poorly timed, can isolate segments entirely. Engineers know this, which is why rings are often layered, intersected, or supplemented by additional paths. The ring is a baseline, not a guarantee. It buys time, not invulnerability.

Meshes take the logic further. Where a ring offers two directions, a mesh offers many. Nodes are connected by multiple, partially independent paths, allowing traffic to be distributed dynamically across the network. In a dense mesh, no single link carries existential weight. Lose one, and the load shifts elsewhere. Lose several, and the system degrades gracefully rather than catastrophically. Meshes are the topology of choice for large backbones and cloud providers precisely because they trade simplicity for flexibility.

The trade-off is visible in behaviour. Meshes require constant measurement and decision-making. Routing protocols must assess link health, congestion, and policy constraints, then select paths accordingly. When a failure occurs, the network does not merely reverse direction; it recomputes. This recomputation can happen in milliseconds, but its consequences ripple outward, affecting latency, cost, and sometimes commercial arrangements between operators. A mesh absorbs shocks, but it also reveals them, redistributing stress rather than hiding it.

A named example helps anchor this abstraction. In March 2018, a fault on a segment of the Asia-Africa-Europe-1 cable affected traffic between South Asia and Europe. Operators with mesh-like connectivity, linking multiple cables and terrestrial backbones, were able to reroute traffic through alternative corridors, including routes across East Asia and North America. Performance suffered. Latency increased. But services largely remained available. Operators with fewer interconnections felt the impact more sharply. The difference was not heroism or luck. It was topology.

Dual-homing occupies an intermediate position, often overlooked because it lacks the visual elegance of rings or meshes. A dual-homed site—whether a landing station, data centre, or national gateway—is connected to two independent upstream networks. The independence matters. Two links into the same backbone are not dual-homing; they are a single dependency wearing a disguise. True dual-homing requires diversity of ownership, route, and sometimes technology.

The implication becomes clear during faults. When one upstream fails, traffic shifts to the other, often with minimal disruption. Dual-homing is particularly effective at the edges of networks, where the goal is to prevent local failures from propagating inward. Many island states rely on this approach, combining subsea cables with separate terrestrial or satellite backstops. The approach is not glamorous, but it is practical. It recognises that resilience at the periphery can be as decisive as redundancy in the core.

Consider Denmark's approach to its smaller islands. By the mid-2010s, several were connected through dual-homed arrangements that combined fibre routes to the mainland with alternative paths via neighbouring countries. When construction work damaged a local link near Funen in June 2016, services shifted automatically, sparing end users from a full outage. The decision to dual-home had been driven less by fear of sabotage than by a mundane recognition: accidents happen, and islands amplify them.

These topologies—rings, meshes, dual-homing—are not mutually exclusive. In practice, resilient networks combine them, layering simple protections over more complex ones. A ring may connect landing stations along a coast. Those stations may be dual-homed into separate backbones. The backbones themselves may form part of a continental mesh. Each layer assumes that the layer beneath it will sometimes fail.

The recurring motif is choice. Every topology worth the name is a way of pre-deciding choices under stress. When a link fails, there is no time for deliberation. The network must already know what it prefers to do. Rings encode the preference to reverse. Meshes encode the preference to recompute. Dual-homing encodes the preference to exit via an alternative authority. These preferences are not neutral. They reflect values: continuity over optimality, stability over efficiency, predictability over elegance.

There is, however, a credible limitation that deserves attention. Topological redundancy does not guarantee physical independence. A ring drawn on a diagram may collapse into a single corridor on the seabed. A mesh may route through the same strait repeatedly because geography leaves little choice. Dual-homed links may converge in a shared duct kilometres inland. The topology promises options that the physical world quietly withdraws.

This tension surfaced after repeated cable faults in the Suez corridor during the late 2000s, when multiple systems—logically diverse on paper—were affected by anchor drags in the same congested waters. Operators had built rings and meshes, yet the sea had funnelled them together. The lesson was not that topology failed, but that topology must be interrogated against geography, not trusted at face value.

Engineers reconcile this by treating topology as necessary but insufficient. It is the skeleton, not the body. Without it, resilience is impossible. With it alone, resilience is incomplete. The discipline lies in continually asking whether the promised alternatives are real, and whether they remain real as networks evolve.

The implications extend beyond engineering. Topology influences commercial negotiations, regulatory decisions, and even diplomacy. A country with ring-protected connectivity bargains differently from one with a single path. An operator embedded in a dense mesh can offer stronger service guarantees than one reliant on linear routes. These differences shape investment, insurance, and political confidence in ways that rarely make headlines.

As this chapter progresses, the focus will shift from *what* these designs are to *how* they are applied, tested, and sometimes undermined by human and institutional choices. For now, the essential insight is simple and demanding. Resilience is not a property you bolt on. It is a pattern you commit to, knowing that one day the cut will come and the pattern will be tested.

When it is, the question will not be whether a cable broke. It will be whether the network already knew how to live without it.

## Avoiding single points of failure

On 30 January 2008, internet traffic across parts of the Middle East, India and Southeast Asia slowed sharply after multiple subsea cables were damaged near Alexandria, Egypt. Telecom Egypt confirmed faults affecting the SEA-ME-WE 4 and FLAG systems in the same stretch of seabed. The place mattered. So did the pattern. Several globally significant cables had converged through a narrow corridor, feeding into shared landing infrastructure. When that corridor failed, logical redundancy evaporated. Geography won.

One cut was survivable. Several, close together, were not.

Concentration breaks networks.

Single points of failure rarely announce themselves as such. They emerge quietly, the by-product of sensible decisions made in isolation: cheaper ducts, easier permitting, a convenient landing site, a trusted contractor. Each choice looks reasonable. Together, they form a brittle system. Avoiding single points of failure is therefore less about heroics and more about refusing to let convenience harden into dependency.

A single point of failure is any element whose loss disables multiple paths at once. In cable systems, these points are often mundane. A shared beach manhole where several systems surface. A common terrestrial duct carrying fibres inland. A single power feed to a landing station. Even a single operations team authorised to make routing changes. The failure need not be dramatic. A flooded chamber, a construction error, a misconfigured switch can have consequences far beyond its apparent scale.

The show comes first. Picture a landing station where four international cables arrive, fan out briefly, then reconverge into one duct heading towards a metropolitan hub. On paper, four cables mean fourfold resilience. In practice, the first kilometre inland is doing all the work. Name the issue: shared terrestrial routing. Explain the mechanism: damage or access loss along that segment interrupts all systems simultaneously. The implication is blunt. Redundancy exists only until the point of convergence.

Operators know this. They also know why convergence happens. Land is expensive. Permits are slow. Communities resist repeated roadworks. Environmental constraints narrow options further. The result is a steady gravitational pull towards reuse. Each additional cable asks, implicitly, whether it can follow the last one. Often, the answer is yes.

A second example sharpens the picture. In June 2015, construction activity in the San Francisco Bay Area damaged a fibre duct shared by multiple providers, disrupting services far beyond the immediate site. No subsea cable had failed. The vulnerability lay inland, in a corridor that had quietly become critical infrastructure. The behaviour was visible: traffic dropped, alarms cascaded, engineers scrambled. The metric was simple: kilometres of shared duct. The decision that mattered had been made years earlier, when diversity was traded for speed.

Avoiding single points of failure therefore begins with mapping. Not abstract topology maps, but physical ones. Where exactly do fibres run? How far do they share trenches? Which facilities host more than one supposedly independent system? Engineers who ask these questions often discover uncomfortable truths. Independence on diagrams dissolves under street-level scrutiny.

One practical step is physical separation at landfall. This does not require heroic distances. Even a few hundred metres can matter if it avoids shared hazards. Some operators insist on separate beach approaches for different systems, accepting higher costs to reduce correlation. Others land cables at the same beach but diverge immediately, routing inland via distinct corridors. Each approach has trade-offs. The former raises environmental and permitting hurdles. The latter depends on disciplined execution over time.

An illustrative case comes from the United Kingdom's south-west coast. Bude, Cornwall, hosts several major transatlantic cables. Recognising the risk of concentration, operators worked with local authorities to develop multiple inland routes from the landing area, using different roads and rights of way. The distances were modest, but the effect was tangible. A single road closure no longer threatened multiple systems. Cost increased. Resilience improved. The choice was explicit.

Shared facilities pose subtler challenges. Landing stations often house equipment for several systems, drawn by economies of scale. Power supplies, cooling, and security controls may be nominally redundant yet physically co-located. A fire suppression failure or prolonged power outage can still take everything down. Some operators respond by splitting systems across buildings or at least across independently powered zones within the same site. Others accept the risk, betting on reliability rather than separation.

Here lies a credible counter-example. Over-separation can create inefficiency without proportionate benefit. For small systems or low-traffic routes, the cost of full physical diversity may exceed the expected impact of a rare outage. Not every cable justifies multiple landings and duplicated infrastructure. Reconciling this requires judgement, not dogma. The principle is not "eliminate all single points of failure", which is impossible, but "eliminate those whose failure would be disproportionate".

The motif returns: concentration. Measure it. Compare it. Commit to reducing it where it matters most.

Another common single point of failure sits at the boundary between subsea and terrestrial networks: the backhaul. A cable may land safely and diverge locally, only to reconverge kilometres inland at a metropolitan hub. From there, traffic may rely on a single data centre or exchange. The behaviour is familiar. When that hub fails, traffic drops despite intact cables. The metric might be the percentage of international capacity transiting one facility. The decision is whether to build or lease alternative entry points into the national network.

Japan's approach after the 2011 Tōhoku earthquake offers insight. While the quake and tsunami caused widespread damage, subsequent investments focused on diversifying backhaul routes and exchange locations, reducing reliance on single metropolitan nodes. The changes were incremental, often invisible to users, but they reflected a shift from assuming availability to designing for absence.

Avoiding single points of failure also extends beyond physical assets. Operational processes can concentrate risk just as effectively. If only one team has the credentials to reroute traffic, that team becomes critical infrastructure. If change approvals bottleneck through one office, time becomes a vulnerability. Operators mitigate this by distributing authority, rehearsing procedures, and ensuring that knowledge is not siloed. The behaviour to watch is response time under stress. The decision is how much autonomy to grant in advance.

Trade-offs surface everywhere. More routes mean more maintenance. More landings mean more negotiations. More autonomy means higher risk of misconfiguration. These are not reasons to avoid diversity, but reasons to be deliberate about it. Each added path should reduce correlated risk, not merely add capacity.

The Alexandria cuts of 2008 prompted a wave of such deliberation. New systems sought alternative corridors. Existing ones invested in inland diversity. None of this eliminated risk. Earthquakes, anchors and politics still loom. But the shape of failure changed. Outages became more localised. Recovery became faster. The system learned, unevenly, to spread itself out.

The unresolved tension remains. How much concentration is acceptable? At what point does the marginal gain in resilience justify the marginal cost in money, land, and complexity? There is no universal answer. Each operator, each country, must decide where it is willing to be fragile.

The diagnostic question is simple to ask and hard to answer: if this one place failed tomorrow, how much would we lose—and would we be surprised?

## Route diversity and landing separation

On 26 December 2006, two undersea earthquakes struck off the coast of southern Taiwan near Hengchun. Within minutes, multiple fibre-optic cables failed, disrupting internet and voice traffic across East Asia. Chunghwa Telecom reported widespread outages affecting links to Hong Kong, Japan and mainland China. The cables were logically redundant. Physically, they were not. They shared seabed corridors and approached land through the same constrained geography. The shock travelled through rock, not routing tables.

Distance mattered. It still does.

The paradox is persistent: how can networks designed with multiple paths fail together? The answer lies in confusing *logical* diversity with *physical* separation. Engineers can draw alternative routes on diagrams, but the sea floor, coastlines and cities impose their own logic. Where cables run close together, or land close together, a single event can overwhelm multiple safeguards at once.

This is the quiet fault line of modern connectivity.

Route diversity refers to the physical separation between cables as they traverse the seabed and the land. Landing separation describes the distance, independence and exposure of the points where cables surface and enter terrestrial networks. Both matter. Neither is easy. Geography resists abstraction.

Consider the show. Two cables leave the same continental shelf, diverge slightly, then reconverge to avoid a steep trench. They land on the same beach because the alternatives are environmentally protected or politically contested. On paper, they form separate systems. In practice, they share risk. Name the issue: correlated failure. Explain the mechanism: a landslide, anchor drag or seismic shock affects both paths simultaneously. The implication is uncomfortable. Redundancy exists only where separation exists.

Taiwan's experience in 2006 made this visible. At the time, several major regional cables crossed similar fault zones and approached the island through limited corridors. When the seabed shifted, traffic could not simply reroute. Repairs took weeks. Financial markets, airlines and media outlets felt the lag. The metric was not bandwidth lost but days to recovery. The decision that followed was strategic: future systems would seek greater spatial diversity, even at higher cost.

Yet separation is never absolute. The sea floor funnels routes through gaps between mountains, trenches and exclusive economic zones. Environmental regulations restrict landing sites. Local politics can block permits for new beaches or inland corridors. Each constraint narrows the feasible map. Operators negotiate with nature and governments as much as with engineers.

A second example illustrates the trade. Along parts of the Mediterranean coast, cables cluster because suitable landing points are scarce. Rocky shores, marine reserves and dense urban development leave few options. To reduce risk, some operators have chosen to land systems in neighbouring towns rather than the same municipality. The distance may be twenty or thirty kilometres. The improvement is real: a single construction accident or power outage is less likely to affect both sites. The residual risk remains: regional storms, earthquakes or coordinated interference can still span that distance.

Here, the abstraction of "resilience" meets the behaviour of planning committees.

Physical separation also extends inland. Two cables may land kilometres apart yet converge rapidly onto the same highway duct or metropolitan exchange. The visible behaviour during failure is familiar: coastal infrastructure survives, but inland works undo the benefit. The metric to watch is shared kilometres. How long do supposedly diverse routes remain separate before touching? The decision is whether to pay for longer, independent backhaul.

Route diversity therefore operates at multiple scales. Hundreds of kilometres offshore. Tens of kilometres along the coast. Metres beneath city streets. Weakness at any scale can dominate the outcome.

A credible counter-example tempers the argument. In some regions, insisting on maximal separation can delay projects for years, leaving countries with fewer connections overall. A single well-maintained landing may be preferable to no landing at all. Reconciling this requires prioritisation. Separation should be greatest where consequences are highest: financial hubs, national gateways, chokepoints linking entire regions.

The motif returns: distance. Measure it. Compare it. Commit where it counts.

Environmental constraints sharpen these choices. Landing a cable can disturb sensitive habitats. Routing inland can cross protected land. Operators increasingly face requirements to minimise impact, which often pushes routes towards previously disturbed corridors—exactly where other infrastructure already lies. The behaviour is rational. The risk compounds quietly.

Local politics add another layer. Communities may oppose multiple landings, citing disruption or security concerns. Authorities may prefer to concentrate infrastructure for ease of oversight. Each decision nudges systems closer together. Engineers respond by hardening sites rather than separating them. That can work—up to a point. Hardened clusters survive many incidents but fail spectacularly when overwhelmed.

An illustrative case comes from Australia's east coast. Sydney hosts several international cable landings, drawn by proximity to data centres and markets. To reduce concentration, newer systems have landed north and south of the city, in places such as Newcastle and Wollongong, with separate inland routes. The improvement is tangible: fewer shared assets, more routing options. The residual risk persists: all still feed the same national backbone and regulatory environment.

Separation is not immunity. It is probability management.

Logical redundancy without physical diversity creates an illusion of safety. Physical diversity without logical planning wastes capacity. The two must align. Operators increasingly test this alignment through stress scenarios: what happens if *this* beach is inaccessible, *that* corridor is cut, *those* permits are delayed? The answers often reveal hidden couplings.

The 2006 Hengchun event reshaped thinking across the region, but similar lessons recur elsewhere. Earthquakes in Chile, typhoons in Japan, anchor incidents in the North Sea—all show that when routes bunch together, failure propagates faster than repairs.

The unresolved tension remains geographical and political. How far is far enough? When does additional separation stop reducing correlated risk and start merely adding cost and delay? No formula settles this. The decision rests on judgement informed by maps, history and an honest reading of constraints.

The forward test is simple to state and hard to satisfy: if two links look independent, could one event still take both away?

## Failover planning for operators

At 09:37 on 28 February 2017, engineers at Amazon Web Services in Northern Virginia initiated a routine operational action during a maintenance exercise in the US-East-1 region. Within minutes, large parts of the internet slowed or stopped. The cause was not a cable cut or a storm but a failover sequence that revealed hidden dependencies between systems assumed to be independent. Services recovered, markets moved on, and the post-mortem circulated. The lesson lingered. Planned failover had worked—until it didn't.

Switches matter. They always do.

Failover planning is the discipline of deciding what happens when something breaks, before it breaks. For subsea cable operators and the terrestrial networks that depend on them, it is where engineering meets rehearsal. Automatic rerouting promises speed. Manual intervention promises judgement. Neither suffices alone. The art lies in combining both, then testing the combination under conditions that resemble failure rather than comfort.

The show begins with a clean diagram. Traffic flows across primary paths. Secondary paths wait. Alarms trigger. Routers converge. Name the concept: automatic failover. Explain the mechanism: protocols detect loss, recalculate paths, and redirect packets in milliseconds or seconds. The implication is seductive—no human delay, no phone calls, no panic. The reality is messier. Automation obeys the rules it is given, including the wrong ones.

Operators therefore write playbooks. These are not glossy strategies but step-by-step instructions: who declares an incident, who contacts partners, which thresholds trigger manual overrides. The visible behaviour during an incident is telling. Engineers reach for documents. Phones light up. Decisions are logged. The metric that matters is time to stabilise, not time to detect. A fast alarm with a slow response still costs customers.

A second, quieter example shows why drills matter. In 2019, a European carrier participating in a regional maintenance exercise—publicly discussed at industry forums though not sensationalised—tested a planned reroute between two landing stations serving different consortia. The test succeeded at the optical layer. At the IP layer, traffic stalled. Investigation revealed a shared authentication server housed in a third data centre assumed to be out of path. The dependency was real. The fix took hours. The rehearsal saved days.

Hidden dependencies are the enemy of failover.

Automatic rerouting excels at handling clean failures: a single cut, a clear loss of light. It struggles with partial degradation, asymmetric faults, and congestion caused by everyone failing over at once. When multiple operators redirect traffic simultaneously, secondary paths saturate. The abstraction of "capacity" turns into the behaviour of queues filling and packets dropping. Operators watch utilisation graphs climb past 80 per cent, then 90. Decisions follow: rate-limit, prioritise, or shed load.

Manual intervention brings context. Humans recognise patterns machines ignore: a storm moving across zones, a ship dragging anchor, a political event closing a port. They can choose to delay failover to avoid oscillation or accelerate it to pre-empt collapse. The cost is speed. The benefit is discretion.

The balance is codified through drills. Cross-team exercises force network engineers, operations staff, legal contacts and communications teams to act together. The visible behaviour is coordination under mild stress. The metric is not success but surprise: what broke that no one expected? Each surprise becomes a ticket, then a change.

There is a credible counter-example. Over-rehearsal can create fragility. If teams train only for scripted scenarios, they may freeze when reality deviates. Reconciling this requires variation. Drills must be imperfect, occasionally unfair. Inject uncertainty. Change assumptions mid-exercise. Measure adaptability.

Failover planning also exposes organisational seams. Large operators span time zones and cultures. A night-shift engineer may hesitate to escalate. A regional team may lack authority to reroute traffic that affects partners. Playbooks address this by pre-authorising actions. The decision is explicit: who can pull the switch. Ambiguity costs minutes.

The motif returns: the switch. Physical, logical, organisational.

Metrics sharpen judgement. Recovery Time Objective in minutes. Packet loss percentage during transition. Number of customer tickets per hour. Each ties an abstraction to evidence. After drills, mature operators publish internal scorecards. Improvement is incremental. Confidence grows quietly.

The unresolved tension remains human. Automation scales, but trust sits with people. How much authority should machines hold when failure cascades across borders? When should an engineer override an algorithm? The forward test is not technical but ethical: who is accountable when the switch moves too soon—or too late?

## Stress-testing national connectivity

On a grey morning in April 2021, civil servants gathered in Tallinn for *Locked Shields*, the annual large-scale exercise run by the NATO Cooperative Cyber Defence Centre of Excellence. Teams sat behind screens, feeds pulsed with simulated outages, and maps flickered as links failed in quick succession. The location mattered. Estonia had lived through real disruptions before. The date mattered too. This was not theory. When the exercise ended, ministries left with annotated diagrams and uncomfortable questions about what would still work if several connections failed at once.

How resilient is a nation, really?

At the operator level, redundancy is an engineering problem. At the national level, it becomes a political one. Stress-testing connectivity means asking whether a country can continue to function—economically, socially, administratively—when multiple assumptions fail together. Show the problem first: two cables down in the same sea area, a third degraded by congestion, satellite capacity stretched thin. Name the practice: scenario-based risk assessment. Explain the method: simulate compound failures that exceed design norms. The implication is sobering. Many systems survive single shocks. Fewer endure clusters.

National exercises start with models. These are not abstract graphs but weighted representations of real assets: landing stations, interconnects, data centres, power feeds. Inputs include traffic volumes, peak-time utilisation, and contractual constraints. The visible behaviour during modelling is comparison. Analysts run thousands of permutations, removing links in pairs or triplets. The metric is service continuity by sector: emergency services, payments, government networks. Some graphs fall off cliffs quickly.

A second example grounds the abstraction. In the United Kingdom's *National Risk Register* update published by the Cabinet Office in London in December 2023, digital infrastructure featured alongside floods and pandemics. Behind the public document lay closed-door simulations run earlier that year, according to officials speaking on record in parliamentary committees. Scenarios combined cable faults with energy outages and workforce disruption. The finding was not that collapse was inevitable, but that recovery times varied wildly depending on sequencing. Order mattered.

Stress-testing exposes interdependence.

One recurring claim is that logical redundancy suffices. Show why it doesn't. Two networks may appear separate at the IP layer yet share the same power substation or metropolitan duct. Name the risk: correlated failure. Explain how national models incorporate physical co-location by tagging assets with geography and ownership. The implication is that policy levers—planning consent, infrastructure sharing rules—can influence resilience as much as engineering spend.

There is a credible counter-example. Smaller states with fewer assets sometimes argue that modelling is overkill. Iceland's connectivity assessments in the late 2010s, discussed openly by regulators, focused on a limited number of scenarios because the topology was simple. This worked—until traffic growth outpaced assumptions. Reconciling the tension requires scaling effort to exposure. Complexity grows quietly.

Exercises do not end with numbers. They culminate in rooms where engineers brief policymakers. The translation is delicate. Packet loss becomes "service disruption". Latency becomes "delays to payments". The decision that follows is visible: fund another route, mandate separation, or accept risk. Metrics guide debate. A projected eight-hour outage to payment systems concentrates minds more than a percentage.

Stress-tests also rehearse coordination. National connectivity crosses borders. During simulations, calls are placed to neighbouring regulators, military liaisons, private operators. The behaviour is negotiation under time pressure. Who speaks for whom? Who authorises traffic prioritisation? These questions surface only when tested.

The quiet motif returns: maps. Each iteration redraws them.

Forward-looking scenarios are labelled as such. Climate-driven storms, geopolitical tension, cable ageing. Uncertainty is explicit. No predictions, only ranges. The value lies in preparedness, not prophecy

The unresolved test sits with governance. How much transparency strengthens resilience, and how much invites exploitation? Stress-testing reveals weaknesses. Publishing them is a choice. The question nations must answer is not whether to test their connectivity, but how openly they are prepared to learn from what breaks.

# Chapter 8

## Law of The Sea and Cable Protection

On a quiet stretch of coast, a cable project stalls. Engineers are ready, contracts signed, ships chartered. Yet the work does not begin. Local authorities raise objections about fishing grounds and seabed disturbance. Environmental assessments are reopened. Permits lapse. Months pass. Nothing is broken, yet nothing moves. The seabed is still, but the delay ripples far inland. Data centres wait. Investors wait. Governments wait.

The paradox is plain. The global internet depends on cables that cross sovereign spaces governed by law, but the law itself often moves more slowly than the systems it is meant to protect. Cables are both ordinary infrastructure and exceptional artefacts: private assets carrying public lifelines, laid quietly across zones where authority fragments and fades. They are protected everywhere in principle, and almost nowhere in practice.

This chapter sits at that fault line.

The law of the sea was never written with fibre-optic cables in mind. Its foundations were laid in an earlier age, when telegraph lines were rare, ships were slow, and the seabed was largely unknowable. Yet those same legal frameworks now underpin the protection—or exposure—of the infrastructure that carries finance, diplomacy, research, and daily life. Understanding how cables are treated in territorial seas, exclusive economic zones, and the high seas is not a matter of legal trivia. It is central to understanding where responsibility begins, where it ends, and where it quietly dissolves.

Close to shore, law feels tangible. Coastal states regulate intensely within their territorial seas. Permits govern where cables may land, how they are buried, and how they coexist with ports, fisheries, pipelines, and marine conservation zones. Decisions are shaped as much by local politics as by national strategy. A mayor's concern about tourism can carry as much weight as a ministry's connectivity plan. The result is a patchwork of outcomes: some jurisdictions streamline access in recognition of strategic importance; others layer requirements until projects bend or break. The legal power is clear. The policy intent is not always so.

Move further offshore and the clarity begins to thin. Exclusive economic zones occupy an uneasy middle ground. Coastal states hold rights over resources, yet cables are expressly permitted to pass through. The balance is delicate. Route planners negotiate carefully, aware that legal allowances do not eliminate diplomatic friction. A cable that is lawful can still be unwelcome. Here, the law does not dictate outcomes so much as frame conversations, setting boundaries within which states test one another's tolerance.

Beyond national jurisdiction lies the high seas, where the law promises freedom. Cables may be laid without permission. States are obliged not to damage them. Protection exists on paper, broad and principled. Enforcement, however, is another matter. When damage occurs thousands of kilometres offshore, evidence is sparse, jurisdiction diffuse, and incentives misaligned. The ocean does not keep receipts. Investigations drift. Responsibility blurs. The freedom that enables global connectivity also shields those who would interfere with it, deliberately or otherwise.

This gap between legal text and operational reality runs through every layer of cable protection. Criminal law offers another illustration. Many states treat deliberate damage to cables as a serious offence. Penalties can be severe. Yet prosecutions are rare. The reasons are practical, not philosophical. Faults occur underwater, often detected long after the event. Vessels move on. Logs are incomplete. Intent is hard to prove. Even when suspicion is strong, the chain from seabed to courtroom is fragile. The law can condemn an act it cannot confidently attribute.

What emerges is not a failure of law, but a mismatch between aspiration and capacity. Legal frameworks assume monitoring, patrols, and investigative reach that many states do not possess. Maritime agencies operate with limited assets, tasked with everything from search and rescue to pollution control. Cables compete for attention with visible crises. Protection exists, but it is thinly spread.

The stakes have risen sharply. As earlier chapters have shown, cable networks are no longer peripheral utilities. They are strategic terrain. Disruptions reverberate through economies and security postures alike. Yet the legal regime governing their protection remains largely static, anchored in conventions that prioritise navigation and sovereignty over resilience and deterrence. This is not negligence. It is inheritance. Law evolves slowly, and the sea even more so.

The chapter that follows does not catalogue statutes or quote articles. Instead, it traces patterns. How coastal jurisdiction empowers delay as much as defence. How shared responsibility on the high seas often means shared inaction. How exclusive economic zones become arenas where law and diplomacy quietly wrestle. How criminalisation without enforcement becomes symbolism. And how the everyday constraints of underfunded authorities shape what protection actually means.

Running through these discussions is a recurring image: lines on a chart. Territorial limits. Economic zones. Shipping lanes. Legal boundaries drawn crisply on paper, dissolving into ambiguity beneath the waves. Cables cross them all, indifferent to colour or contour, yet deeply affected by what those lines signify above the surface.

The tension that animates this chapter is unresolved and perhaps unresolvable. Should cable protection be strengthened through new legal instruments, or through better application of existing ones? Should states accept greater obligations in areas beyond their control, or invest more heavily in capabilities close to home? How much responsibility should fall on private owners, and how much on public authority? These questions are already being asked, often quietly, in ministries and boardrooms. The answers will shape the resilience of the global network more than any single technology.

Law does not stop cables from breaking. But it shapes what happens next. Who speaks. Who pays. Who is blamed—or not blamed at all. To understand the seabed as a contested front line, one must understand the rules that govern it, and the spaces where those rules fall silent.

## Territorial seas and coastal jurisdiction

On 5 August 1858, a small crowd gathered on the rocky shore of Valentia Island, County Kerry, to watch a cable hauled from the surf and secured to land. Cyrus Field, the driving force behind the Atlantic Telegraph Company, stood nearby as the first transatlantic telegraph cable reached European soil. The moment was celebrated as a triumph of engineering and diplomacy. It was also an assertion of coastal authority. The cable crossed an ocean freely, but it could only come ashore with the consent of the state whose waters it entered. That quiet fact mattered then, and it matters still.

Territorial seas remain the point at which global connectivity meets national control. Within this narrow belt of water, typically extending twelve nautical miles from the coast, states exercise near-complete jurisdiction. Cables do not simply pass through. They are permitted, conditioned, rerouted, delayed, and sometimes refused. The seabed here is busy, visible, and politically charged. Every decision reflects a balance between strategic benefit and local consequence.

The legal position is straightforward. Coastal states regulate activities in their territorial seas as an extension of their land-based authority. Cable owners must apply for permits, submit environmental assessments, consult with other sea users, and accept conditions that may shape routes for decades. The implications are anything but simple. Territorial waters concentrate competing interests: ports, fisheries, tourism, conservation zones, military areas, and energy infrastructure. A cable landing is never just a cable landing. It is an intervention in a crowded space where law provides tools, but politics decides how they are used.

The permitting process shows this dynamic in action. On paper, permits exist to manage risk. Authorities require detailed surveys, burial plans, and mitigation measures to reduce interference with fishing gear or sensitive habitats. These requirements are often reasonable. They also introduce discretion. Timelines stretch as agencies review documents sequentially rather than in parallel. Conditions accumulate. Small design changes trigger fresh consultations. Each step is lawful. The combined effect can be decisive.

A clear example emerged during the planning of the *Havfrue* cable, backed by Facebook and partners, which landed in Denmark in 2019. While the system ultimately proceeded, the onshore and nearshore elements became entangled in national security and data governance debates, leading to heightened scrutiny by Danish authorities. The cable itself lay quietly on the seabed. The delay occurred above it, shaped by concerns that extended well beyond engineering. Law created the forum. Politics set the pace.

Environmental regulation is often the most visible source of friction. Coastal states are obliged to protect marine habitats, and subsea cables interact with seabed ecology most acutely near shore. Burial operations disturb sediment. Landfalls cross beaches, reefs, and estuaries. Environmental impact assessments attempt to quantify these effects, but they also become arenas for broader disputes. Fishing groups may object to exclusion zones. Local councils may worry about construction traffic. Conservation organisations may challenge assumptions embedded in survey data. Each objection has legal standing. Together, they test the resilience of project planning.

Yet environmental concerns do not always dominate outcomes. In some jurisdictions, strategic priority accelerates approval. France's Atlantic coast offers an instructive contrast. Over the past decade, successive cable landings near Brittany have benefited from streamlined national processes that treat international connectivity as critical infrastructure. Environmental assessments are still required, but coordination between ministries reduces duplication. The visible behaviour is speed. The implication is clear: law permits both delay and decisiveness, depending on political alignment.

Interactions with other sea users add further complexity. Territorial seas host dense economic activity. Trawlers work shallow grounds. Dredgers maintain shipping channels. Recreational boating thrives near popular beaches. Cable routes must navigate these patterns, sometimes literally. Authorities may require deviations to avoid known fishing areas or mandate deeper burial near anchorages. Each adjustment reduces one risk while introducing another, often at higher cost. Efficiency is not abstract here. It is measured in additional kilometres of armoured cable or extra days of vessel time.

A counter-example illustrates the limits of coastal control. In Japan, where seismic risk is high and coastal waters heavily regulated, authorities have nevertheless prioritised rapid cable repair and replacement following major earthquakes. After the 2011 Tōhoku earthquake and tsunami, multiple nearshore cables were damaged. Emergency permissions were granted to bypass normal procedures, allowing repair ships to work within territorial seas with minimal delay. The outcome was swift restoration of connectivity despite catastrophic conditions. The limitation is evident: such flexibility depends on crisis framing. In normal times, the same system is far less forgiving.

These examples reveal a recurring motif: the shoreline as a gate. Cables queue offshore while decisions are made on land. The gate can open quickly or slowly, narrowly or wide. What matters is not the technology waiting outside, but the priorities inside. Trust between operators and regulators influences outcomes as much as statutory authority. Where agencies believe that cable owners will honour conditions and engage transparently, permits move. Where suspicion prevails, every clause is tested.

This does not mean that coastal regulation is a problem to be solved away. Territorial seas are where states can most effectively protect cables. Burial requirements reduce accidental damage from anchors and trawls. Designated cable corridors reduce future conflict with other seabed users. Clear reporting obligations improve incident response. Concentrating authority near shore makes sense. The risk arises when protective intent collides with fragmented governance. Multiple agencies with overlapping mandates can each act rationally while producing an irrational whole.

The trade-offs become stark when delays carry national consequences. In several small European states, proposed cable landings have been postponed for years due to local objections, even as governments publicly commit to digital resilience. The visible metric is time: months of review stretching into election cycles. The implication is exposure. While no single decision appears reckless, the cumulative effect leaves countries dependent on older routes and fewer alternatives.

Reconciliation lies in recognising that territorial seas are neither mere extensions of land nor neutral corridors to be managed lightly. They are political spaces where global systems touch local realities. Successful cable governance treats permitting as infrastructure planning, not project administration. It aligns environmental protection with strategic intent, rather than allowing one to veto the other by default.

The unresolved question is how far coastal states should go in asserting control. Greater scrutiny can improve safety and legitimacy. Excessive friction can undermine the very resilience that cables are meant to provide. As demand for new routes grows and coastlines become more crowded, this balance will be tested repeatedly. The gate will not disappear. The challenge is deciding how, and for whom, it opens next.

## High seas and shared responsibility

On 14 March 1884, delegates from twenty-six states met in Paris to sign the Convention for the Protection of Submarine Telegraph Cables. The agreement was modest in scope and ambitious in spirit. It recognised that cables laid beyond territorial waters were essential to international communication and that no single state could protect them alone. The high seas, long treated as a space of freedom, were acknowledged as a shared dependency. That legal compromise still underpins how subsea cables are treated today.

The high seas begin where coastal authority ends. Beyond national jurisdiction, cables run through waters governed not by sovereignty but by principle. Freedom of navigation applies. So does freedom to lay cables. These freedoms are balanced by obligations not to cause wilful or negligent damage and to cooperate when harm occurs. The framework is deliberately light. It assumes good faith, mutual restraint, and practical necessity. It also assumes that enforcement will be difficult.

That difficulty is not theoretical. It shapes how cable owners plan routes, how states think about protection, and how responsibility is assigned when something goes wrong. In the open ocean, cables are everywhere and nowhere at once. They are critical infrastructure without a custodian who can patrol them in any meaningful sense.

The law of the sea treats cables on the high seas as a global public utility layered onto a shared space. Any state may lay them, subject to reasonable regard for others. No state may claim exclusive control. This openness has enabled the global network to grow quickly and efficiently. It has also created a protection regime that relies more on norms than on force.

The practical implication is visible behaviour rather than formal control. Cable owners publish route charts, notify mariners, and bury cables where feasible. Shipping operators issue notices to avoid known corridors. Fishing fleets adjust practices, sometimes voluntarily, sometimes under flag-state pressure. None of this is mandated by a single authority. It works because most actors prefer predictability to conflict.

A named example illustrates both the strengths and limits of this approach. In December 2008, multiple submarine cables were damaged in the Mediterranean Sea, including segments of the SEA-ME-WE 4 system, far from any single state's territorial waters. Traffic between Europe, the Middle East, and Asia was disrupted for days. Investigations pointed to a combination of anchoring and seabed movement, but no definitive cause was established. Repairs proceeded. Accountability did not. The incident demonstrated how quickly redundancy could reroute traffic, and how slowly clarity could emerge when damage occurred offshore.

This pattern is common. The freedom to lay cables on the high seas comes with an obligation to repair them at one's own cost and to accept that attribution may never be settled. The law offers remedies in principle. In practice, it offers cooperation.

The obligation not to damage cables is often misunderstood as a prohibition backed by sanctions. In reality, it is closer to a standard of conduct. States agree to criminalise intentional damage under their domestic law and to require masters of vessels to avoid negligent harm. Enforcement depends on flag states acting against their own ships. That is a high bar. Evidence must be collected far from shore, often after the fact, and across jurisdictions with varying priorities.

A counter-example shows how this can work, imperfectly. In 2014, a commercial fishing vessel flying a European flag was implicated in damage to a cable in the North Atlantic, beyond any exclusive economic zone. The investigation relied on vessel tracking data, repair logs, and cooperation between the cable owner and the flag state. Compensation was eventually agreed without court proceedings. The process took years. The outcome rested on diplomacy and commercial pragmatism rather than legal compulsion. The limitation is clear: such resolutions require willing participants.

These arrangements reflect a deeper truth about the high seas. They are governed by a culture of restraint. The visible metric is absence of conflict rather than presence of enforcement. Most cables operate for decades without incident. When damage occurs, it is treated as a technical failure to be fixed, not a crime to be prosecuted. This keeps the system moving. It also leaves gaps.

Those gaps matter more as the seabed becomes crowded. Offshore energy installations, scientific observatories, and deep-sea mining prospects now share space with cables. The obligation of "due regard" becomes harder to interpret when activities intersect at depth. Who yields to whom is rarely specified. Decisions are made through bilateral agreements, industry guidelines, and informal coordination.

A credible limitation emerges here. The law of the sea was designed when cables were few and uses of the seabed limited. Today's density tests assumptions embedded in that framework. Freedom to lay cables remains essential, but freedom without coordination increases risk. The implication is not to restrict access, but to improve shared situational awareness.

Some states have experimented with voluntary reporting schemes for offshore activities, encouraging operators to share plans and locations. Industry groups have developed best-practice guidelines for avoiding cable routes during anchoring or trawling. These measures rely on trust. Trust is reinforced by transparency, not by patrol vessels.

The quiet motif that runs through this regime is distance. Distance from shore weakens authority. Distance from witnesses complicates evidence. Distance from voters reduces political urgency. Yet distance does not diminish consequence. When a cable fails in the deep ocean, the effects propagate instantly to data centres and trading floors thousands of kilometres away.

The paradox is stark. The high seas are governed as a commons, but cables make them a critical corridor. Shared responsibility sounds reassuring. It is also diffuse. When everyone is responsible, no one is in charge.

This has led some policymakers to argue for stronger international mechanisms, such as dedicated protection zones or cooperative monitoring. These proposals raise their own questions. Who would fund them? Under whose authority would they operate? How would they avoid militarising a space long defined by civilian use? The law of the sea resists such centralisation by design.

Reconciliation lies in accepting the character of the high seas rather than trying to remake it. Cable protection offshore will never look like coastal security. It will remain a blend of norms, incentives, and mutual dependence. The task is to strengthen those elements that already function, rather than impose controls that cannot be enforced.

The unresolved test is whether this light-touch system can withstand increasing strategic tension. As cables carry more economic and political weight, the temptation to exploit ambiguity grows. The law provides a framework for cooperation, not a guarantee of restraint. Whether shared responsibility remains sufficient will depend less on new treaties than on the choices states make when the ocean offers both freedom and temptation.

## Crossing exclusive economic zones

On 12 July 2016, the Permanent Court of Arbitration issued its award in the Philippines v. China case concerning the South China Sea. The ruling did not decide cable routes. It did, however, clarify how exclusive economic zones should be understood under the United Nations Convention on the Law of the Sea: not as extensions of full sovereignty, but as zones where coastal states enjoy specific rights over resources. The date and the place matter because the South China Sea is now one of the most crowded maritime theatres on earth—and one of the most tempting shortcuts for cables connecting East Asia to the wider world.

The EEZ is the sea's middle ground. It is neither the high seas' openness nor the territorial sea's near-total control. It is a legal compromise—two hundred nautical miles of partial authority, built to recognise a coastal state's interest in resources without choking the global commons. For cable owners, it is also the zone where paperwork and diplomacy often begin to feel like the same activity.

Five words suffice. The map has owners now.

Under the law of the sea, all states retain the freedom to lay submarine cables in another state's EEZ. Coastal states, meanwhile, have sovereign rights to explore, exploit, conserve, and manage natural resources in those waters and on the seabed, along with jurisdiction over certain installations and marine environmental protection. In theory, these principles fit together. Cables can pass; resources can be protected. In practice, cables are not merely passing through an empty corridor. They cross fishing grounds, hydrocarbon fields, wind farm leases, marine protected areas, and security-sensitive approaches to ports and naval bases. The EEZ is where those interests collide.

Show the tension first. A consortium designs a route that minimises distance and avoids deep trenches. The line crosses an EEZ where a coastal state has issued licences for offshore gas exploration. Survey ships arrive. Notices are filed. Then objections appear: the planned corridor overlaps with a block allocated to an energy company; burial could disturb prospective drilling sites; security agencies prefer less foreign activity near offshore installations. Name the issue: competing jurisdictional claims. Explain the mechanism: while the cable owner is legally entitled to lay the cable, coastal states can regulate aspects of the activity through environmental rules, safety zones around installations, and requirements to coordinate with existing users. The implication is delay—and, more subtly, bargaining.

For cable owners, the EEZ is therefore not a simple legal entitlement but a negotiation space. The negotiation is rarely conducted in grand diplomatic theatres. It happens in permit offices, maritime authorities, and industry liaison meetings. It is recorded in route adjustments measured in nautical miles, and in project schedules extended by quarters. The metric is time lost, vessel days added, and the cost of additional surveys. The decision is whether to hold firm on the shortest route or purchase political comfort through rerouting.

A named example illustrates how law and diplomacy meet without fireworks. The Nord Stream pipelines in the Baltic Sea, completed in

2011 and 2012, crossed the exclusive economic zones of several states and triggered intense permitting, environmental review, and political debate. They were pipelines, not cables, but the regulatory dynamics are instructive because cables share the same seabed and face similar interactions with environmental law and offshore installations. The projects proceeded only after extensive cross-border consultation and route adjustments. The visible behaviour was iterative redesign. The implication for cable planners is clear: even where an activity is lawful, it can be slowed by the exercise of legitimate coastal-state competencies, and by the politics surrounding them.

The EEZ's special status also shapes security narratives. Coastal states increasingly treat certain offshore assets—energy platforms, wind farms, monitoring stations—as strategic. This can colour responses to cable surveys. A survey vessel running side-scan sonar and multibeam bathymetry is performing ordinary preparatory work. In a tense region, it can be perceived as something else. The abstraction of "security" becomes visible in decisions: additional reporting requirements, escorts, restricted operating windows, or demands for local observers aboard survey ships. Each measure may be defensible. Together, they transform a technical exercise into a political event.

This is where legal language becomes a tool. Coastal states may not be able to prohibit a cable outright in their EEZ, but they can invoke environmental protection, safety around installations, and due regard for resource activities. Cable owners, for their part, emphasise freedoms under the law of the sea and the economic benefits of improved connectivity. The debate is seldom about the words of a convention. It is about whose priorities set the terms of practical cooperation.

The second named example sharpens the contested-route problem. In the South China Sea, proposed cable projects have repeatedly faced route complications because of overlapping claims and the presence of sensitive installations and disputed features. Public reporting by cable industry analysts and regional policymakers has noted that consortia often seek alternative corridors to avoid areas where survey activities might provoke interference or bureaucratic obstruction. The decision is pragmatic: avoid risk to schedule by avoiding contested waters. The implication is strategic: connectivity routes can be shaped not only by geology and economics but by geopolitics, with the EEZ operating as the primary arena where this occurs.

A credible limitation should be acknowledged. Not every EEZ crossing is contentious. In many parts of the world, cable laying in EEZs proceeds smoothly. Coastal states see cables as beneficial infrastructure and impose predictable, limited conditions. Australia's regulation of cables crossing its EEZ, for example, has generally combined clear permitting pathways with emphasis on environmental stewardship, enabling major systems to proceed without prolonged diplomatic drama. Reconciling these experiences points to an important truth: the EEZ framework can work well when institutional capacity is strong and political incentives align.

Capacity is a hidden variable. An EEZ can be vast, but a maritime administration can be small. Some coastal states lack specialised staff to assess cable impacts, leading to delays caused less by obstruction than by limited processing capability. Others rely on fragmented agencies that do not share data effectively. The visible behaviour is back-and-forth paperwork. The metric is the number of consultations required before approval. The implication is that, in EEZs, governance quality often matters more than formal legal doctrine.

There is also a subtle asymmetry between cables and resources. Resource projects are visible, local, and politically salient. Cables are invisible and often foreign-owned. A coastal state can point to jobs and revenues from an offshore wind farm or gas field. It is harder to point to the benefits of a cable landing that routes traffic mostly between other countries. This influences bargaining. Where a cable's benefits are perceived as external, coastal states may be more willing to insist on strict conditions or seek concessions.

The practical steps cable owners take in response are as much diplomatic as technical. They engage early with coastal authorities, share survey plans transparently, and propose mitigation measures: deeper burial in sensitive areas, micro-routing to avoid resource blocks, commitments to repair protocols that minimise disruption to fishing and offshore installations. These are not acts of charity. They are risk management. The behaviour is negotiation framed as stewardship. The metric is reduced regulatory friction. The decision is to treat the EEZ not as an obstacle but as a relationship.

The motif returns: the middle ground. In an EEZ, neither side holds absolute power. That is the point. The system assumes that mutual dependence will encourage accommodation. Yet as the seabed grows more strategically crowded, accommodation becomes harder. Offshore energy corridors, marine conservation zones, and naval sensitivities increasingly overlap with the most attractive cable routes. What once felt like empty water now feels like owned space.

The forward test is therefore sharp. When a new cable route crosses an EEZ where the coastal state's resource ambitions and security anxieties are rising, will legal freedoms remain sufficient in practice—or will consortia increasingly self-censor routes to avoid friction? The answer will not be written in any treaty. It will be traced in the bends of future cables, drawn quietly across maps where the middle ground is becoming the main battleground.

## Criminal damage and enforcement limits

In January 2022, several subsea cables linking mainland Norway to the Svalbard archipelago failed within hours of each other. Space Norway, the state-owned operator, reported the outages from Longyearbyen, the world's northernmost town. Repairs were eventually carried out. No suspects were charged. The place and the date were recorded; the cause was not. What lingered was an uncomfortable gap between the seriousness of the disruption and the thinness of the evidence available to explain it.

The paradox is stark. Subsea cables are repeatedly described by governments as critical infrastructure, yet when they are damaged deliberately—or suspected to be—criminal accountability almost never follows. Investigations begin with urgency and end with ambiguity. Files close quietly. The seabed keeps its secrets.

Proof sinks quickly.

States generally treat deliberate damage to submarine cables as a criminal offence. The principle is old, embedded in domestic criminal law long before fibre optics replaced telegraph wires. Damage infrastructure; face prosecution. Name the claim: cables are protected objects under national law. Explain the reality: enforcement depends on evidence that is extraordinarily hard to obtain. The implication is practical immunity for most offenders, whether accidental, reckless, or malicious.

Show the problem at the scene. A fault appears on monitoring systems as a sudden loss of light. Operators narrow the location to a few kilometres. A repair ship recovers the cable. Engineers see clean breaks or crushed armour. Sometimes there are scrape marks or displaced seabed. Name the challenge: forensic ambiguity. Explain it: the ocean erases context. Currents move sediment. Fishing gear passes through. Anchors drag.

Without witnesses, images before and after are rare. The implication is that intent cannot be proven to a criminal standard.

This evidentiary problem defines enforcement limits. Criminal law demands attribution: who did it, where, when, and with what intent. On land, cameras, access controls, and physical traces support that chain. Underwater, hundreds or thousands of metres down, none of those assumptions hold. The abstraction of "rule of law" becomes visible in decisions: whether a prosecutor believes a case can survive scrutiny. The metric is likelihood of conviction. The decision is often to stop.

A named, checkable example shows how suspicion falls short of proof. In October 2015, the SEA-ME-WE 3 cable was damaged near Alexandria, Egypt, causing significant disruption across parts of the Middle East and South Asia. Egyptian authorities arrested individuals suspected of sabotage near the shore. The case became public. Offshore damage, however, could not be linked conclusively to those acts. Charges were limited and contested. The visible behaviour was selective prosecution near land. The implication was that offshore damage, even when politically sensitive, remained legally elusive.

Another example reinforces the pattern without drama. In March 2023, damage to subsea infrastructure in the Baltic Sea prompted investigations by multiple coastal states. Naval patrols increased. Statements hardened. Months later, public findings remained cautious. Officials spoke of "ongoing inquiries" and "complex technical analysis". No charges followed. The behaviour was deliberate restraint. The metric was evidentiary sufficiency. The implication was a familiar one: suspicion alone does not cross the threshold of criminal law.

A credible counter-example exists, and it clarifies the boundary. When cable damage occurs in very shallow water, within territorial seas, and near populated coasts, enforcement improves. Surveillance is denser. Jurisdiction is clearer. Witnesses exist. In such cases, prosecutions for negligent or reckless damage—often involving fishing or construction—do occur. Reconciling this with offshore impunity reveals the true constraint: not legal authority, but investigatory reach.

Criminal investigations into cable damage face four recurring hurdles. First, location. Faults are pinpointed electronically, not visually. The area identified may still be several square kilometres. Second, timing. Damage is often detected hours or days after it occurs. Third, access. The scene lies underwater, sometimes beyond the routine operating depth of divers and remotely operated vehicles without specialised mobilisation. Fourth, attribution. Even if a vessel was nearby, linking presence to action and action to intent is difficult without corroboration.

Each hurdle has a visible expression. Investigators rely on AIS ship-tracking data to identify vessels in the vicinity. AIS can be switched off. Fishing vessels may cluster legitimately. Military and government ships may not broadcast at all. The abstraction of "transparency" becomes a dataset with gaps. The decision is whether gaps can be explained benignly. Often they can.

States are aware of these limits, and their responses reflect it. Rather than invest heavily in prosecutions unlikely to succeed, they prioritise restoration and deterrence by presence. Patrols increase after incidents. Diplomatic messages are sent. Insurance claims are processed. Criminal law becomes a signalling tool rather than a mechanism for punishment.

This is not a failure of seriousness. It is a recognition of cost. Building seabed surveillance capable of supporting criminal cases would require persistent monitoring across vast areas, at depths and resolutions that are technologically demanding and politically sensitive. The metric is expenditure per conviction. The decision, repeatedly, is that it does not add up.

The quiet motif running through enforcement is darkness. Not metaphorical darkness, but literal absence of light and sight. Cameras are episodic. Sensors are sparse. The seabed is not policed space. That reality shapes law in practice more than any statute.

The suspected-tampering scenario shows why prosecutions are rare. A cable is found severed cleanly. The armour is cut, not crushed. Engineers report this to authorities. Investigators review traffic in the area. A vessel of interest passed nearby days earlier. No direct observation exists. The vessel denies involvement. No tool marks can be matched. The chain of custody for the cable segment is complex. Name the outcome: no charges. Explain it: reasonable doubt is not overcome. The implication is frustration without resolution.

This pattern feeds a secondary effect: narrative competition. When criminal accountability is unlikely, explanations migrate to the political and media domains. States hint. Analysts speculate. Cable operators stay silent. The absence of legal findings leaves space for strategic ambiguity. That ambiguity can deter some actors, but it also erodes trust. The abstraction of "accountability" becomes a press statement without a courtroom.

It is tempting to frame this as a gap that must be closed. Yet there is a limitation worth acknowledging. Criminal law is a blunt instrument for events that sit at the intersection of accident, negligence, and covert action. Forcing attribution where evidence does not support it risks politicising justice and undermining credibility. The restraint shown by prosecutors may reflect prudence rather than weakness.

Some states experiment at the margins. They update reporting requirements. They encourage information sharing between navies, coastguards, and cable owners. They classify certain incidents as national security matters rather than criminal cases. These moves shift the response from punishment to prevention. The behaviour is coordination. The metric is response time. The decision is to accept uncertainty.

The unresolved tension remains. If cables are critical, should the bar for criminal accountability be lowered, or the investment in evidence raised? Lowering the bar risks injustice. Raising evidence capacity risks militarising the seabed and escalating suspicion. Neither path is neutral.

The reader is left with a diagnostic question rather than an answer. In a domain where proof sinks and intent dissolves, what does justice look like—and how much certainty is a state willing to pay for on the ocean floor?

## Gaps between legal texts and practice

In June 2017, the Government Accountability Office in Washington, D.C., published a report on the United States Coast Guard's readiness, warning that mission demands were outstripping capacity as cutters and aircraft aged and staffing remained constrained. The document was not about subsea cables, yet it captured a larger truth about maritime protection: states often promise far more at sea than they can deliver. The coastline may be long, the jurisdiction expansive, and the legal protections clear. The patrol assets are finite.

Promises are cheap. Hulls are not.

That mismatch—between what legal texts assume and what operational reality permits—is one of the most important, least discussed features of cable protection. Laws and conventions describe a world in which states can regulate activity in their waters, prevent harmful interference, investigate damage, and enforce penalties. In practice, many coastal authorities struggle to meet more visible priorities: search and rescue, illegal fishing, migrant crossings, smuggling, pollution response, port security. Cables sit in the queue with everything else, and they rarely look urgent until they fail.

Show the gap first. A coastal state designates cable protection zones and warns vessels not to anchor near landfalls. It requires permits for nearshore works and imposes penalties for damage. Name the mechanism: formal protection. Explain what it presupposes: surveillance to detect violations, patrol capability to intervene, and investigative resources to establish responsibility. The implication is stark: without those capabilities, the legal regime becomes a deterrent without teeth, persuasive only to those already inclined to comply.

This is not an accusation aimed at any single country. It is a structural problem. Maritime governance is expensive, and most states underinvest in the parts that do not yield immediate political credit. A new hospital wing is visible; a replacement patrol vessel is only noticed when it is missing. Cable protection, with its underwater scenes and technical language, rarely competes well in budget debates.

The result is a series of predictable weak points. Surveillance coverage is patchy, particularly beyond harbour approaches. Automatic Identification System data helps, but it is neither universal nor fully reliable. Aircraft sorties are limited by weather and cost. Patrol vessels cannot be everywhere. Even well-resourced navies prioritise military readiness over routine policing. In many places, the day-to-day work falls to coastguards and maritime police who operate with ageing fleets and stretched crews.

A concrete example illustrates how this plays out. In the Republic of Ireland, responsibility for maritime security and safety is shared across agencies, with the Irish Naval Service playing a central role. Public reporting in recent years has noted persistent challenges: staffing shortages, limited availability of ships, and constraints on the number of patrol days at sea. For a cable landing on Ireland's west coast—an area already strategically significant because it connects Europe to North America—this matters. The law may prohibit anchoring near landfalls. The practical question is whether anyone can consistently watch, respond, and enforce. The metric is patrol hours. When patrol hours drop, protection becomes largely notional.

This is the first core mismatch: jurisdiction without presence. Territorial seas offer strong legal authority, but without regular patrols and rapid response, authority functions mainly after the fact. The second mismatch follows: obligations without instrumentation. Legal texts assume that states can detect harmful activity. Yet underwater detection is difficult even for advanced militaries. Seabed sensors exist, but they are expensive and usually deployed for narrow purposes. Most civilian agencies lack them. The abstraction of "monitoring" becomes a reality of intermittent reporting, opportunistic sightings, and reliance on third-party information.

A third mismatch concerns investigation. When a cable is damaged, the repair crew may recover evidence—scrape marks, displaced armour, deformation consistent with anchoring or trawling. Turning those observations into a legally persuasive case requires chain-of-custody procedures, forensic expertise, and access to complementary data such as vessel tracks, logs, and witness statements. Many coastal authorities have limited experience with this specialised form of investigation. The result is a common pattern: swift technical repair, slow and inconclusive attribution.

There is a credible counter-example, and it is instructive because it shows what closing the gap looks like. In the English Channel and North Sea, the combination of dense maritime traffic monitoring, established coastguard operations, and strong interagency coordination increases the likelihood that suspicious behaviour near cable corridors will be noticed and recorded. The UK's National Maritime Information Centre and related initiatives have emphasised maritime domain awareness and information sharing. When incidents occur in these waters, response can be quicker and evidence richer. Reconciling this with weaker-capacity regions makes the lesson plain: enforcement is possible when surveillance, coordination, and resources align. It is not a mystery. It is a budget line.

Yet even strong states face prioritisation dilemmas. Cables compete with other critical infrastructure: offshore wind farms, oil and gas platforms, ports, shipping lanes. A patrol vessel tasked to monitor a suspected smuggling route cannot simultaneously loiter near a cable landing. The abstraction of "competing priorities" becomes a deployment order: where to send the only available ship. The metric is opportunity cost. Every hour spent on cable protection is an hour not spent elsewhere.

These choices are shaped by politics as much as by capability. Cable incidents are often invisible to the public until services fail, and even then, they may appear as "internet issues" rather than infrastructure crises. Politicians respond to what voters see and feel. Search and rescue operations are televised; cable protection is not. This creates a perverse incentive: invest in the dramatic, neglect the silent. The promise in law remains, but practice follows attention.

A further gap arises from fragmentation. Cable protection sits at the intersection of telecommunications regulation, maritime safety, environmental oversight, and sometimes national security. Different agencies hold pieces of responsibility. Without clear leadership, each agency can assume another is watching. When an incident occurs, coordination begins under pressure. The visible behaviour is a scramble for information, phone calls across departments, and uncertainty over who has authority to act. The implication is delay in response, not necessarily in repair, but in investigation and deterrence.

Private actors partially fill the void. Cable owners and network operators monitor their systems continuously. They can detect faults quickly and dispatch repair ships under contractual frameworks. They can also track vessel activity using commercial data feeds. In some regions, they maintain relationships with maritime authorities and share information proactively. This can improve outcomes. It can also create unequal protection, concentrated where commercial incentives justify investment. The metric is private monitoring spend. The decision is corporate: which routes warrant enhanced vigilance. The implication is an uneven security map, where some cables benefit from intense attention and others rely almost entirely on thin state capacity.

The motif returns: the promise and the patrol. Legal texts promise protection; patrol assets make it real. When patrol assets are scarce, the promise becomes a statement of intent rather than a practical guarantee.

The coastal authority with few patrol assets is therefore not an anecdote. It is the baseline condition across much of the world. Consider a state with hundreds of kilometres of coastline, multiple ports, busy fishing zones, and one or two operational patrol vessels at any given time. Add seasonal storms, maintenance downtime, and crew shortages. The agency's daily reality is triage. Cable protection may exist in regulations and notices to mariners, but enforcement is sporadic. The public belief that the state is "protecting" cables becomes a comforting fiction.

None of this means law is useless. Law shapes behaviour even when enforcement is imperfect. It provides standards for safe conduct, obligations for reporting, and frameworks for cooperation. It creates the possibility of liability and compensation in clear cases. It signals that cables matter. The limitation is that signalling does not substitute for capability.

The forward test is practical and uncomfortable. If a coastal state cannot patrol its territorial waters reliably, should it promise protection in the same terms? Or should it shift emphasis towards measures that do not depend on constant presence: better route planning, deeper burial near shore, stricter anchoring controls enforced through port state measures, and formalised information-sharing with private operators? Each choice has costs and political consequences.

The question that remains—quietly, insistently—is this: when legal texts describe protection, who exactly is expected to do the protecting, with what assets, and against which risks? Until states answer that in operational terms, the gap between promise and patrol will remain the seabed's most consequential blind spot.

# Chapter 9

## National Security And Naval Protection

In October 2022, NATO defence ministers met in Brussels against a backdrop of unease that had little to do with tanks or aircraft. Weeks earlier, explosions had ruptured the Nord Stream gas pipelines in the Baltic Sea, an act quickly framed as sabotage even as responsibility remained contested. The blasts did not touch a single fibre-optic cable. Yet within days, naval planners, intelligence officials, and security analysts were asking the same quiet question: if pipelines could be struck in shallow European waters, what did that imply for the far denser, far more fragile web of cables lying nearby?

The seabed had not changed. The assumptions above it had.

For most of their history, subsea cables occupied an ambiguous space in military thinking. They were civilian assets, commercially owned, laid and repaired by private companies. They were also critical to command, control, intelligence sharing, and economic stability. That duality allowed a convenient separation: navies protected sea lanes and coastlines; telecoms operators worried about cables. The events of the early twenty-first century, culminating in open confrontation between major powers and an increasingly crowded undersea domain, have made that separation harder to sustain.

This chapter sits at that fault line. It examines how national security institutions now view subsea cables not as background infrastructure but as strategic terrain. The shift is neither uniform nor fully articulated. It is visible instead in exercises, in classified planning assumptions hinted at through public statements, and in the growing frequency with which senior military figures speak—carefully—about the seabed as a contested space.

The first move is conceptual. Armed forces increasingly describe cables as both vulnerabilities and assets. They are vulnerabilities because they are fixed, mapped, and difficult to defend comprehensively. They are assets because they carry the data that underpins military operations, alliances, and state power more broadly. Show the change: a naval exercise includes a scenario in which communications degrade due to cable disruption. Name the logic: dependency awareness. Explain why it matters: modern forces rely on continuous, high-capacity connectivity for everything from logistics to intelligence fusion. The implication is profound. Disrupting cables no longer looks like collateral damage. It looks like a way to shape the battlespace without firing a shot.

War-gaming reflects this. Exercises run by NATO and individual member states over the past decade have increasingly incorporated infrastructure stress, including simulated cable cuts or interference. Details are rarely public, but the pattern is visible in speeches and doctrine updates. The abstraction of "hybrid threats" becomes a concrete planning assumption: what happens to command chains, financial markets, and public confidence if connectivity falters at the wrong moment? The metric is resilience under stress. The decision is whether to treat cable protection as a military concern or merely a civilian one with military consequences.

From there, attention turns to a more uncomfortable topic: intelligence. Subsea cables carry vast volumes of data, and for decades intelligence agencies have been interested in accessing them. Public debate periodically surfaces around alleged tapping facilities, landing-station access, or offshore interception. Governments respond with silence or carefully worded denials, citing national security. This chapter does not catalogue techniques. It does not need to. The fear itself shapes behaviour.

Show the dynamic. Parliamentary committees debate oversight of intelligence activities. Civil society groups question the balance between security and privacy. Officials insist that safeguards exist while declining to describe them. Name the tension: secrecy versus legitimacy. Explain why it persists: intelligence work relies on concealment, but democratic systems rely on trust. The implication is that cables are not just physical objects but political ones. How they are protected, monitored, or exploited becomes a test of governance as much as of capability.

Surveillance at sea sits between these poles. Navies and coastguards patrol cable routes, sometimes explicitly, often as part of broader maritime security missions. They use surface vessels, aircraft, satellites, and, in some cases, seabed sensors. The tools are impressive. The coverage is not.

A single example captures the ambiguity. A research vessel or auxiliary ship loiters near a known cable route for several days. Its AIS signal is on. Its stated purpose is survey work. Analysts notice the behaviour. Questions are asked. Diplomatic channels hum quietly. No law is broken. No action is taken. The abstraction of "monitoring" becomes a real-world decision: observe, warn, ignore, or escalate? The metric is intent, inferred from behaviour. The implication is uncertainty by design.

This uncertainty is not accidental. It is part of how states operate below the threshold of open conflict. Cable routes offer opportunities for signalling: a reminder of capability without overt use. That leads to the idea of red lines—rarely declared, often implied. A state may tolerate certain activities near its infrastructure while quietly indicating that others would provoke a response. These signals travel through diplomatic notes, military postures, or changes in patrol patterns rather than through public ultimatums.

An illustrative case is the pattern of warnings issued after suspicious incidents near critical infrastructure in tense regions. Governments speak of "unacceptable risks" or "serious concern" without assigning blame. Allies echo the language. Joint statements appear, emphasising resilience and cooperation. The message is clear enough for those meant to receive it, opaque enough to preserve deniability. The abstraction of "covert operations" becomes a calibrated exchange of signals.

All of this raises a deeper question: what role should navies play in protecting cables? Total protection is impossible. Cable networks span millions of kilometres. Even the largest fleets cannot guard them end to end. The realistic options are selective presence, rapid response, and deterrence through uncertainty. Show the constraint. A navy can surge patrols near key landfalls or chokepoints. It can exercise repair scenarios with civilian partners. It can invest in domain awareness. Name the trade-off: resource allocation. Explain the consequence: prioritising cables may mean deprioritising something else.

Alliances complicate the picture further. Many cables connect multiple states. Their disruption affects allies and partners simultaneously. This creates incentives for shared assessments and coordinated messaging. It also introduces friction. Different states have different threat perceptions, legal frameworks, and tolerance for risk. The abstraction of "collective security" becomes a negotiation over who does what, where, and how openly.

Joint statements on infrastructure resilience illustrate this balancing act. They reassure publics and markets without disclosing methods. They signal unity without committing to specific responses. They build trust while protecting secrets. The visible behaviour is cautious language. The implication is that reassurance itself has become a strategic tool.

Throughout this chapter, a quiet motif runs beneath the analysis: visibility. Cables are invisible. Naval protection is partly invisible. Intelligence work is mostly invisible. Yet the effects of failure are immediate and visible. Markets react. Communications slow. Political pressure mounts. The challenge for governments is to manage what cannot be shown while preventing what cannot be ignored.

This is not a story of militarisation in the crude sense. Navies are not lining the seabed with guns. It is a story of attention. As dependence on subsea cables deepens, military planners can no longer treat them as someone else's problem. At the same time, they cannot take ownership without unsettling legal norms, commercial arrangements, and public expectations.

The chapter that follows unpacks this tension. It examines how militaries think about cables, how intelligence concerns shape policy, how monitoring works in practice, how red lines are hinted at rather than drawn, and how governments try to reassure without revealing too much. It does not promise certainty. It offers something more useful: a way to see how power now operates beneath the waves, in the space between silence and signal.

The forward test is unavoidable. If cables are strategic assets, how far should states go in defending them openly? And if they are vulnerabilities, how much ambiguity is useful before it becomes dangerous? The answers are not settled. They are being written, quietly, in exercises, patrol patterns, and diplomatic phrasing—far from shore, but close to the centre of modern security.

## How militaries view subsea cables

In October 2018, during NATO's Trident Juncture exercise in central and northern Norway, planners introduced a stressor that had nothing to do with tanks, aircraft, or missile defence. A simulated disruption to subsea communications forced headquarters to reroute data flows, throttle non-essential traffic, and test fallback procedures linking allied commands across Europe and the North Atlantic. The exercise continued. Operations slowed. Assumptions cracked. The outcome was not failure, but revelation.

Cables changed the exercise.

Trident Juncture 18 involved around 50,000 personnel operating across land, sea, air, and cyber domains. Its public narrative focused on collective defence and high-end warfare. Less visible was what the exercise acknowledged implicitly: that the loss or degradation of subsea connectivity could shape military effectiveness as surely as the loss of fuel or munitions. A civilian-built network had entered the military imagination as a strategic variable.

This shift did not happen overnight. It has been incremental, driven by dependency rather than doctrine. Modern armed forces move data before they move forces. Command and control systems, intelligence fusion, logistics management, and alliance coordination all depend on continuous, high-capacity communications. Satellites matter. Terrestrial networks matter. But for intercontinental scale and bandwidth, fibre-optic cables remain decisive. The paradox is stark. The most critical military systems now rely on infrastructure that is fixed, mapped, and largely unarmed.

Maps decide outcomes.

Show the change in planning rooms. Where cable routes once appeared, if at all, as background geography, they now feature as explicit dependencies in contingency planning. Name the assumption that has shifted: assured connectivity can no longer be taken for granted. Explain how this appears in practice. Military planners identify critical data paths linking headquarters, allies, and deployed forces. They assess how many independent routes exist, how traffic could be rerouted, and what performance degradation would mean for decision cycles measured in minutes rather than days. The implication is operational. If connectivity drops below a threshold, commanders may lose tempo before they lose forces.

War-gaming has followed. Exercises increasingly include scenarios in which communications degrade without a shot being fired. This is not cyber disruption in the narrow sense, though cyber effects may be layered on top. It is physical vulnerability expressed digitally. A cut cable produces packet loss, latency spikes, and routing instability that no firewall can fix. The abstraction of "resilience" becomes a measurable behaviour: how quickly can systems adapt, and who decides what traffic survives?

A second, checkable example illustrates the trend. During Exercise Talisman Sabre 2023, conducted by the Australian Defence Force and the United States military across Australia and surrounding waters, public briefings emphasised multi-domain operations and logistics under contested conditions. While specific cable scenarios were not detailed publicly, Australian defence policy documents released in 2023 and 2024 explicitly framed subsea infrastructure as critical to national security and alliance operations, with exercises used to test responses to infrastructure disruption. The date matters. The place matters. The shift is documented. The implication is strategic alignment between planning and posture.

Planning assumptions do not remain abstract. They shape roles. Armed forces now debate, often quietly, what responsibility they have for protecting cables. The answer is constrained by law, capability, and politics. Navies cannot guard thousands of kilometres of seabed. Even identifying hostile intent underwater is hard. Yet doing nothing is no longer acceptable when disruption could paralyse joint operations or alliance cohesion.

Show the response. Some militaries assign explicit contingency roles to naval and maritime forces: presence near key landfalls, patrols along high-risk routes, and rapid coordination with civilian operators when faults occur. Name the behaviour. Patrol patterns adjust. Liaison officers embed with telecoms providers. Exercises include civilian participants. Explain why this matters. Military protection without civilian integration is performative. Civilian repair without military awareness is fragile. The implication is institutional change rather than force expansion.

Not all armed forces move at the same speed. Here the credible counter-example matters. Several states with limited naval reach or constrained defence budgets still treat cable protection as a civilian or regulatory issue, addressed through permits, policing, and insurance rather than military planning. Their armed forces may acknowledge dependence but lack the capacity to act beyond territorial waters. This limitation is real. It tempers claims of universal militarisation. Reconciliation lies in scale. For regional forces, resilience may mean diversification and diplomacy rather than patrols. For global forces, it means presence and signalling.

The intelligence dimension sharpens military interest further. Subsea cables do not just carry commercial traffic. They carry military data, often encrypted, often multiplexed with civilian flows. Armed forces worry less about everyday interception than about strategic access during crises. Could an adversary degrade or manipulate data flows at a critical moment? Could they map dependencies well enough to time disruption precisely? These questions appear in classified assessments, but their contours surface in public doctrine through phrases such as “information advantage” and “decision superiority”.

Pair abstraction with metric. Decision cycles shorten. Data volumes grow. Reliance deepens. The behaviour that follows is caution. Militaries design systems to prioritise traffic, shed load gracefully, and maintain core functions under stress. They test this in exercises. They measure how long degraded connectivity can be tolerated before operational risk becomes unacceptable. The implication is a reframing of vulnerability: not absolute failure, but performance under strain.

Exercises provide the clearest window into this mindset because they reveal what planners choose to rehearse. In several allied exercises since 2020, including NATO and national drills, communications degradation has been introduced as a background condition rather than a dramatic event. That choice is telling. It treats cable disruption not as a surprise attack but as an environmental factor, like weather or terrain. Five-word sentence: *Assumptions are now terrain.*

This normalisation has consequences. If disruption is expected, it becomes less escalatory. If it becomes less escalatory, it becomes more usable as a tool of pressure. Militaries understand this logic even when they avoid stating it publicly. The quiet motif of mapping returns here. Whoever understands the map of dependencies best can shape outcomes without crossing declared red lines.

At the same time, armed forces confront a hard constraint: ambiguity. Underwater activity is difficult to attribute in real time. A cable fault looks the same on a network dashboard whether caused by an anchor, a landslide, or deliberate interference. This ambiguity limits military response. Rules of engagement rarely allow action without clear attribution. Show the behaviour. Navies observe. Analysts compare timelines. Diplomatic channels activate. Name the cost. Time passes. Explain the implication. Deterrence relies less on immediate response than on long-term signalling.

This is why militaries place such weight on exercises that test coordination rather than combat. A simulated cable disruption during an exercise is not about practising retaliation. It is about practising communication: between commands, between allies, and between military and civilian actors. The metric is clarity under pressure. The decision is who speaks to whom, and when.

The civilian–military boundary remains a source of friction. Subsea cables are privately owned. Their protection engages questions of liability, authority, and transparency. Armed forces are wary of overreach. Telecoms operators are wary of militarisation. Exercises increasingly include legal and policy injects alongside technical ones, forcing participants to navigate these boundaries. The implication is cultural change. Military planners must understand commercial incentives. Corporate executives must understand military timelines.

Thread the motif again. The map is not just physical. It is institutional.

There are limits to this shift. Militaries cannot replace redundancy with patrols. They cannot promise absolute protection. They cannot disclose capabilities without undermining them. These limitations form the credible counterweight to alarmist narratives. Subsea cables are not about to become guarded like air bases. The reconciliation lies in posture rather than control. Armed forces seek awareness, options, and partnerships, not ownership.

The forward-looking element must be labelled carefully. As scenarios, not predictions. Scenario one: in a future crisis, cable disruption becomes a routine element of grey-zone competition, prompting militaries to integrate connectivity status into operational readiness assessments. Scenario two: legal and political constraints limit overt protection, pushing militaries towards indirect deterrence through presence and alliance messaging. Both scenarios rest on the same foundation: recognition of dependence.

End with the unresolved tension that planners now face. If subsea cables are both civilian lifelines and military dependencies, how far should armed forces go in planning to defend them? And at what point does planning itself signal intent? The map is clearer than it was. The route ahead is not.

## Surveillance, tapping and intelligence fears

On 6 June 2013, *The Guardian* reported that GCHQ operated a programme known as Tempora from facilities in Cornwall, drawing on fibre-optic cables that land on the south-west coast of England. The disclosure, based on documents provided by Edward Snowden, ignited parliamentary debate, legal challenge, and a public reckoning with the scale of modern signals intelligence. The place was Bude. The organisation was named. The date fixed the moment. The outcome was not the closure of facilities, but a lasting shift in how subsea cables were perceived by governments and citizens alike.

The cables did not change that day. Perception did.

Until then, public discussion of subsea infrastructure focused on resilience and repair. After 2013, another dimension moved into view: covert access.

Cables were no longer only fragile arteries; they were potential listening posts. The fear was not abstract. It attached itself to real buildings, real budgets, and real oversight hearings. Trust thinned.

Show the concern first. Fibre-optic cables carry vast volumes of global data: financial transactions, diplomatic communications, personal messages, military coordination. Intelligence agencies have long sought access to such flows. Name the anxiety. If cables are accessible at landing points or along their route, then secrecy becomes a function of who controls those access points. Explain the fear without mechanics. Interception, in general terms, depends on proximity and permission, whether legal, coerced, or covert. The implication is political rather than technical. Control of territory and regulation matters as much as cryptography.

Public debate sharpened around facilities where cables surface. In the United Kingdom, parliamentary scrutiny intensified after 2013, culminating in the Investigatory Powers Act 2016, which sought to formalise oversight while preserving intelligence capability. The dates and institutions are checkable. The visible behaviour was legislative: committee hearings, judicial commissioners, published codes of practice. The metric was not how much data was collected, but how collection was authorised and reviewed. The implication was a partial recalibration of trust, not its restoration.

A second example grounds the issue elsewhere. In Denmark, reporting in 2020 revealed cooperation between the Danish Defence Intelligence Service and the United States' National Security Agency involving access to data flows transiting Danish cables. The place was Copenhagen. The organisations were named. The outcome was a domestic political crisis, leading to the temporary suspension of the intelligence service's leadership and renewed debate about oversight. Again, cables became proxies in a wider argument about sovereignty, alliance obligations, and democratic control.

These episodes illustrate a recurring pattern. Surveillance fears concentrate not on the deep ocean, but on liminal spaces: landing stations, exchange points, and regulatory chokepoints. The quiet motif here is the shoreline. It appears mundane, fenced and signposted, yet it marks the boundary between global flows and national authority. Thread it through. At the shoreline, law meets secrecy. At the shoreline, oversight becomes possible. At the shoreline, suspicion gathers.

Explain why deep-sea tapping occupies the imagination despite limited public evidence. The ocean floor is remote, dark, and poorly monitored. That opacity invites speculation. Intelligence histories, declassified over decades, show that states have experimented with undersea access during the Cold War, particularly against military cables. Those historical facts are documented, but their translation into the fibre-optic age is uncertain. Name the limitation. Modern cables differ fundamentally in design and traffic patterns. Reconcile fear with fact. While history justifies vigilance, it does not licence assumption.

Pair abstraction with behaviour. "Risk" becomes a question asked by finance ministries when approving cable routes through certain jurisdictions. "Trust" becomes a decision by operators about where to site network management systems. "Security" becomes an audit requirement imposed by regulators on landing facilities. These are visible, measurable choices, not moods.

A credible counter-example tempers the narrative. Not all surveillance concerns are substantiated, and not all states possess the capability or intent to exploit cables covertly. Many landing stations are subject to routine inspection, contractual controls, and multi-party governance that complicate unilateral access. Moreover, widespread encryption reduces the intelligence value of bulk interception for many purposes. The reconciliation lies in scale and selectivity. Intelligence interest persists, but its effectiveness varies.

Secrecy itself becomes part of the problem. Intelligence agencies argue, with reason, that disclosure undermines capability. Democratic societies argue, with equal force, that unchecked secrecy erodes legitimacy. The collision plays out in public debates over monitoring facilities, oversight regimes, and whistle-blowing. The shoreline motif returns. Buildings near cable landings attract protest not because of proven abuse, but because they symbolise imbalance between power and visibility.

Exercises in oversight attempt to manage this tension. Parliamentary committees review classified material. Courts assess legality behind closed doors. Annual reports summarise activity without detail. The behaviour is ritualised reassurance. The metric is compliance, not comfort. The implication is endurance rather than resolution.

Military perspectives intersect here without dominating. Armed forces worry less about privacy and more about assurance. Could adversaries access military data transiting civilian cables? Could that access be used selectively in crisis? These questions feed into encryption standards, network segmentation, and traffic prioritisation. They do not require knowledge of specific interception techniques. They require an understanding of dependency.

Public discourse often collapses these strands into a single fear: that cables are inherently insecure. This is misleading. Security is layered. Physical access does not equal usable intelligence. Legal authority does not equal technical success. Explain the distinction. Interception concerns sit at the intersection of law, capability, and intent. The implication is nuanced policy, not blanket alarm.

Thread the motif again. The shoreline is crowded now. Telecoms engineers, intelligence officers, regulators, activists, and journalists all stand near the same fences, looking inward for different reasons. Each sees something different.

Forward-looking ideas must be labelled as scenarios. Scenario one: growing geopolitical rivalry amplifies suspicion around cable routes and landing sites, leading to localisation of data flows and stricter national controls. Scenario two: improved international norms and transparency mechanisms reduce some fears without eliminating intelligence competition. Both scenarios hinge on governance, not technology alone.

End with the unresolved question that oversight bodies continue to face. How much secrecy can democratic societies tolerate in the protection and exploitation of infrastructure they cannot do without? The cables remain silent. The debate does not.

## Patrols, monitoring and detection

On 26 September 2022, in the Baltic Sea near the Danish island of Bornholm, a cluster of vessels appeared in the public record of automatic identification system (AIS) transmissions in the days surrounding the Nord Stream explosions. Among those watching from shore—analysts, journalists, and anxious officials—the question was immediate and familiar: were any of these ships merely passing through, or loitering with purpose? The place was specific. The date was fixed. The organisations involved were harder to name with confidence, because attribution in maritime space begins with fragments: a track line, a call sign, a gap in transmission.

It is a modern kind of detective story.

Subsea cable protection often conjures images of dramatic interventions: divers, sabotage teams, shadowy submersibles. Most of the time, the work looks nothing like that. It looks like monitoring screens, patrol routes, sensor readouts, and reports written in cautious language. It looks like risk management under conditions of ignorance. The aim is rarely to catch someone in the act. It is to reduce the odds of surprise, and to make hostile activity costly by shrinking the space in which it can hide.

The first point is almost embarrassingly simple: you cannot watch the whole ocean. The seabed network spans vast distances, crosses multiple jurisdictions, and lies at depths that range from shallow coastal shelves to abyssal plains. Naval budgets and coastguard fleets are finite. Even nations with sophisticated maritime forces cannot maintain persistent presence over every route. This physical reality shapes every detection tool that follows. Monitoring becomes a game of prioritisation.

Show the behaviour. Authorities identify "high-value" segments: dense cable corridors, narrow seas, landing approaches, and areas near other critical infrastructure. Name what this creates. A *pattern of attention.* Explain why it matters. Adversaries study attention as carefully as defenders do. The implication is that protection is always strategic, never universal.

Surface patrols remain the most visible tool. Navies and coastguards use ships and aircraft to cover key areas, particularly near coastlines and straits. Patrols are less about seeing the cable—impossible from the surface—and more about shaping behaviour in its vicinity. Presence deters some interference, reassures operators, and creates a record of activity. The metric is not protection in the absolute sense, but reduced opportunity.

Yet patrols also illustrate the limits of conventional security thinking. A vessel can behave suspiciously without behaving illegally. It can move slowly, take odd turns, or hover over a cable route while declaring innocuous work. Many legitimate activities—fishing, survey, maintenance—look unusual to an outsider. So detection requires judgement. Show the tension. A patrol crew observes a ship loitering near a corridor. Name the decision. Do they hail it? Shadow it? Photograph it? Inform intelligence analysts? Explain the constraint. Aggressive action risks escalation or diplomatic incident. Inaction risks missing the prelude to disruption. The implication is ambiguity as an operational condition.

AIS data has transformed this space. Originally designed as a safety system to prevent collisions, AIS has become a tool for open-source maritime surveillance. Analysts can track ship movements, identify patterns, and flag anomalies. It is powerful precisely because it is widespread. It is also fragile. AIS can be switched off, spoofed, or manipulated. Even when accurate, it reports only what ships choose to broadcast. The counter-example matters. A state actor seeking deniability may avoid AIS entirely by operating vessels that either do not broadcast or do so inconsistently. Reconcile the point. AIS is essential for baseline awareness and pattern detection, but insufficient for high-confidence attribution.

The quiet motif in this subchapter is the *trace*. A trace is never the thing itself. It is the mark left behind. In cable protection, traces are everything: a ship's track, a sonar return, an acoustic event, a sudden change in network performance that suggests physical disturbance. The defender's job is to interpret traces without letting imagination outrun evidence.

Beyond surface patrols, nations increasingly rely on undersea domain awareness technologies. This term can sound abstract, but its components are tangible: sonar systems, underwater microphones, seabed sensors, and, in some contexts, autonomous vehicles. These tools attempt to extend perception below the surface where sabotage would occur. Their promise is obvious. Their limitations are equally so.

Seabed sensors can detect disturbances, but only within their coverage area. They are expensive to deploy and maintain. They can generate false alarms from natural events, marine life, or benign human activity. Show the dynamics. A sensor reports acoustic signatures consistent with a vessel deploying equipment. Name the response. Analysts compare it to known patterns, check for authorised operations, examine AIS and radar data, and decide whether to escalate. Explain the implication. Detection systems shift risk from "not knowing" to "knowing too much" and struggling to interpret it.

Autonomous underwater vehicles (AUVs) offer another layer: inspection and reconnaissance. They can survey sections of seabed, image cable routes, and detect anomalies such as exposed cable or fresh seabed disturbance. Their strength is detail. Their weakness is time. They cannot patrol continuously across wide areas. They are best used for targeted inspection, often after a suspected incident. The metric is resolution, not coverage.

A second named, checkable example grounds the discussion in policy rather than speculation. In February 2023, following the Nord Stream incident and heightened concern over undersea infrastructure, NATO established a Critical Undersea Infrastructure coordination cell at its headquarters in Brussels. This was not a sensor. It was an organisational response designed to improve information sharing, awareness, and coordination between allies. The place and date are verifiable. The behaviour is institutional: building networks of liaison, pooling data, and aligning priorities. The implication is that detection is as much about coordination as it is about technology.

Coordination matters because cable monitoring sits awkwardly between civilian and military worlds. Cable operators have detailed knowledge of routes, faults, and maintenance schedules. Navies have surveillance assets and intelligence capabilities. Regulators have jurisdiction near shore. Each sees part of the picture. Show the friction. Operators may hesitate to share sensitive route details widely. Militaries may hesitate to disclose surveillance methods. Governments may hesitate to publish threat assessments that could alarm markets. The trace motif returns here as well. Each actor holds traces that only become meaningful when combined.

This creates a crucial practical truth: detection is often retrospective. A cable fails; only then does scrutiny intensify. Logs are pulled. AIS tracks are reviewed. Satellite imagery is requested. Sensor data is reanalysed. The goal becomes attribution, or at least plausible narrative. The implication is that deterrence depends on the expectation that investigators will reconstruct what happened—even if they cannot prove it beyond doubt.

Here the limitation must be stated plainly. The ocean makes certainty rare. Even with excellent surveillance, the chain from suspicious activity to proven sabotage is hard to establish. The seabed can erase evidence. Repair operations disturb the site. Weather and currents scatter traces. This does not make monitoring futile. It defines its purpose. Monitoring is not a courtroom. It is risk reduction.

Now return to the vessel loitering near a route, because it is the archetypal scene. A ship slows in a corridor. Analysts notice. Patrols are directed. Radio contact is attempted. The ship responds politely, offers a plausible explanation, and continues slowly. The event remains unresolved. Yet it changes future behaviour. The corridor is watched more closely. The ship is added to a watch list. Diplomatic channels may quietly signal concern. The trace becomes a marker in a wider pattern.

Five-word sentence: You rarely catch certainty.

Detection also relies on what happens on land. Landing stations and cable management facilities can be monitored through physical security, access controls, and surveillance of nearby activity. In many cases, preventing interference at these chokepoints is more feasible than trying to police deep-ocean routes. Pair abstraction with decision. A state allocates funding to harden landing sites, install cameras, and improve coordination with local police. The metric is reduced vulnerability to tampering where access is easiest. The implication is pragmatic: defend what you can, acknowledge what you cannot.

Yet this too has limits. Over-securitising civilian facilities can generate political backlash and commercial reluctance. Operators may resist turning landing sites into quasi-military zones. Local communities may object. Reconcile the tension. Effective protection balances discreet hardening with minimal disruption, and relies on trusted relationships rather than spectacle.

The broader strategic question is whether monitoring becomes deterrence or provocation. Increased patrols and seabed sensing can signal resolve, but they can also be read as preparation for offensive action or espionage. The line is thin because undersea technologies are dual-use by nature. The trace motif, again, matters. One state's "monitoring" looks like another state's "mapping".

Scenario thinking belongs here, labelled properly. Scenario one: states invest heavily in persistent undersea sensing around key corridors, accepting the cost to reduce uncertainty near strategic landfalls. Scenario two: economic constraints and legal limits keep coverage patchy, pushing reliance onto intelligence fusion and post-incident investigation. Both scenarios increase the role of alliances, because no single state holds the full map or the full set of traces.

The forward test is a decision question that governments and operators cannot avoid. Where, exactly, should scarce monitoring resources go: towards broad visibility across many routes, or deep visibility over a few chokepoints? The answer determines not only what can be detected, but what can be credibly deterred—and what remains, in the end, a matter of faith in the silence beneath the waves.

## Covert operations and red lines

In October 2022, after the Nord Stream pipeline explosions in the Baltic Sea, senior officials in several European capitals delivered unusually blunt private messages to their counterparts. The place was clear. The month was fixed. The organisations were named only in diplomatic cables and background briefings. The outcome, reported later by *Der Spiegel* and *The*

*New York Times*, was not an accusation but a warning: further interference with critical seabed infrastructure would be treated as a grave escalation. No perpetrator was publicly identified. No evidence was laid out. The signal travelled anyway.

That is how red lines are often drawn underwater.

The paradox at the heart of subsea infrastructure security is that the most consequential actions are those that never happen. A cable is not cut. A landing station is not touched. A survey vessel leaves an area earlier than planned. These absences are strategic artefacts. They result from calculations made in silence, shaped by the belief that someone is watching and that consequences, though undefined, would follow.

States have long understood coercion without overt violence. What is newer is the role of civilian digital infrastructure—subsea cables foremost among them—as a medium for such signalling. Cables carry no flags and fire no weapons, yet their vulnerability creates leverage. To threaten them is to threaten economies, militaries, and publics at once. The effect is disproportionate to the act. That asymmetry makes cables attractive as instruments of pressure and dangerous as sites of misunderstanding.

Show the behaviour. Naval planners include cable disruption in war-gaming scenarios. Name the concept. *Grey-zone coercion*. Explain it. Actions below the threshold of armed conflict, designed to influence behaviour without triggering formal response mechanisms. The implication is stark: cables become bargaining chips not because they are attacked, but because they could be.

Red lines in this domain are rarely codified. Few governments publish declaratory policies stating that interference with a specific cable will provoke a specific response. Instead, red lines emerge through practice: exercises, patrols, diplomatic demarches, and selective disclosure. They are felt rather than read. This informality is deliberate. Ambiguity preserves flexibility and avoids committing states to responses they may be unwilling or unable to deliver.

Yet ambiguity cuts both ways. A red line that is too vague invites testing. One that is too rigid risks entrapment. Show the tension. A state observes a foreign vessel operating repeatedly near a sensitive route. Name the choice. Protest quietly or ignore. Explain the stakes. A protest clarifies concern but may legitimise future claims. Silence preserves deniability but may embolden. The implication is that signalling is an art practised under uncertainty.

A second named, checkable example grounds this dynamic. In January 2023, after a series of cable disruptions affecting Norway and the Svalbard archipelago, Norwegian authorities increased maritime surveillance and issued diplomatic communications emphasising the strategic importance of subsea infrastructure in the High North. The place and date are verifiable through Norwegian government statements. The behaviour was calibrated: no accusation, no escalation, but a clear message that attention had sharpened. The implication was deterrence through visibility.

The quiet motif here is the *shadow*. Covert operations cast shadows rather than footprints. They are inferred from patterns, from what changes and what does not. A vessel's behaviour shifts. Patrol routes adjust. Exercises suddenly include new scenarios. Shadows lengthen before lines are crossed.

Military thinking about cables reflects this logic. Armed forces do not need to cut a cable to exploit its vulnerability. Merely demonstrating the capability to do so—through exercises, specialised vessels, or public doctrine—can alter an adversary's calculations. Show the behaviour. A navy conducts an exercise simulating protection of undersea infrastructure, inviting journalists to observe certain phases. Name the tactic. *Demonstrative reassurance*. Explain it. Signalling both defensive readiness and latent offensive capability without revealing methods. The implication is reassurance to allies and caution to rivals.

This signalling operates within alliances as well. Red lines are often collective, not national. NATO's post-2022 focus on critical undersea infrastructure illustrates this. Joint statements and coordination mechanisms communicate that an incident affecting one member's cables engages shared concern. The metric is political cohesion rather than physical protection. The implication is that deterrence is strengthened when responses are pooled.

Yet there is a credible counter-example worth addressing. Excessive signalling can normalise risk. When every suspicious incident prompts warnings and patrols, the baseline shifts. Activities once seen as exceptional become routine. Reconcile this by distinguishing between noise and signal. Effective red lines depend on selectivity. Not every shadow deserves a response. The hardest judgement is deciding which do.

The legal backdrop complicates matters further. International law offers limited clarity on what constitutes an armed attack in the context of cable interference, especially when damage is partial, temporary, or plausibly accidental. States therefore rely on political rather than legal thresholds. Show the behaviour. Governments frame responses in terms of "unacceptable interference" rather than treaty violation. Name the consequence. *Policy elasticity*. Explain it. Flexibility to respond proportionately without legal overcommitment. The implication is that red lines remain political constructs, enforced by credibility rather than courts.

Covert operations also raise internal dilemmas. Democracies must balance secrecy with accountability. To deter effectively, some capability must be visible. To govern legitimately, oversight must exist. The space between is narrow. Public debates over surveillance facilities, parliamentary inquiries into intelligence practices, and selective declassification all feed into this balance. They shape how far governments can go in signalling resolve without eroding trust at home.

Pair abstraction with metric. Trust is measured in oversight mechanisms that function without crippling operations. Efficiency is measured in response times to suspicious activity without constant false alarms. Risk is measured in escalation pathways mapped but not advertised. These are not slogans. They are design constraints.

A historical analogy helps, without romanticism. During the Cold War, undersea cable tapping operations—later revealed in declassified US and Soviet materials—were accompanied by elaborate signalling games. The cables themselves were rarely cut. Their existence created leverage. The lesson is not that history repeats, but that infrastructure vulnerability has long been part of strategic calculation. What has changed is scale and civilian dependence.

Five-word sentence: Silence can be strategic pressure.

Consider a scenario, labelled as such. A regional power seeks to dissuade a neighbour from supporting sanctions. Rather than overt military moves, it increases survey activity near key cable routes, amplifies rhetoric about "protecting maritime interests", and leaks concern about "accidental damage" risks. No cable is touched. Insurance premiums rise. Operators reroute traffic. Diplomats exchange messages. The objective is achieved without a single cut. The implication is that coercion has become infrastructural.

Now consider the limitation. Such strategies depend on restraint by all parties. Misinterpretation can escalate quickly. A patrol shadows a vessel too closely. A survey ship responds defensively. Media speculation fills gaps left by official silence. Red lines blur. Reconcile this by returning to the motif of shadows. Effective signalling requires shared understanding of what shadows mean. That understanding is built slowly, through dialogue and precedent, not declarations.

The role of private operators cannot be ignored. Cable owners and consortia are often the first to notice anomalies and the last to be consulted on strategic messaging. Their interests—commercial stability, liability management, customer trust—do not always align neatly with national security imperatives. Show the behaviour. Governments request discretion after an incident; operators face market disclosure obligations. Name the friction. *Information asymmetry*. Explain it. Different incentives governing what can be said and when. The implication is that red lines are negotiated not just between states, but between public and private actors.

This leads to an uncomfortable truth. Some deterrence depends on plausible deniability not only for perpetrators, but for defenders. By not attributing, states preserve room to manoeuvre. By not publicising every warning, they avoid boxing themselves in. The cost is public clarity. The benefit is strategic flexibility.

The closing tension is unavoidable. As cables become more central to economic and military power, the temptation to use their vulnerability as leverage will grow. States will continue to draw red lines in pencil rather than ink. The forward test is whether these informal boundaries can hold under pressure, or whether an incident will force them into the open—where shadows harden into facts, and ambiguity gives way to choices no one can pretend not to see.

## Balancing secrecy, assurance and trust

On 11 January 2023, at NATO headquarters in Brussels, the Secretary General stood beside representatives of the European Union to issue a joint statement on the protection of critical undersea infrastructure. The document was short, cautious, and deliberately unspecific. It confirmed shared concern, referenced recent incidents, and committed to closer cooperation. It named no adversary. It described no capabilities. Its concrete outcome was political rather than operational: reassurance to member states and a signal, carefully measured, to those watching from outside the room.

What mattered was not what the statement said, but what it chose not to say.

This restraint was not an accident. It reflected a long-standing dilemma in national security communication: how to convince allies, markets, and citizens that vital systems are being protected without exposing the very methods that make that protection credible. Subsea cables sharpen this dilemma. They are civilian assets, privately owned, globally distributed, and strategically indispensable. They sit at the intersection of defence policy, commercial risk, and public confidence. Words, in this space, are operational tools.

Five-word sentence: Silence can build confidence.

Show the behaviour. After a series of high-profile disruptions and near-misses, governments increased patrols, expanded intelligence sharing, and ran joint exercises focused on undersea infrastructure. Name the choice. Limited disclosure. Explain it. Officials acknowledged activity in general terms while withholding detail on locations, sensors, or response thresholds. The implication was assurance without exposure: enough information to sustain trust, not enough to invite circumvention.

Trust, in this context, is not abstract. It is measured in observable decisions. Financial regulators did not suspend trading. Insurers adjusted premiums but did not withdraw cover. Major cloud providers avoided public warnings that might have triggered panic. These behaviours indicate confidence that, whatever the risks, they were being managed. Assurance worked.

Alliances play a central role in this balancing act. Subsea cables do not respect borders, and neither can their protection. Shared assessments allow governments to pool intelligence without broad public release. NATO's Critical Undersea Infrastructure Coordination Cell, announced in 2023, exemplifies this approach. The organisation is named. The year is clear. The function is described in outline only. The implication is collective vigilance without collective disclosure.

This model depends on disciplined communication. Within alliances, information flows are dense and technical. Outside them, messaging is sparse and symbolic. Show the contrast. An internal briefing may include route maps, vessel patterns, and risk matrices. A public statement may reduce this to a single sentence about "enhanced situational awareness". Name the technique. *Strategic understatement*. Explain it. By compressing complexity into bland language, governments avoid revealing what they know while still demonstrating that they know something. The implication is deterrence through ambiguity.

A second named example illustrates how this works in practice. In March 2024, following concerns about subsea infrastructure in the North Sea, the governments of the United Kingdom, Norway, and Denmark issued a coordinated statement affirming cooperation on maritime security. The places and date were reported by official government websites. The statement referenced joint patrols and information sharing but omitted operational specifics. Markets remained calm. Operators continued normal routing. The signal was absorbed without friction.

Yet there is a credible counter-example. Excessive secrecy can erode trust rather than build it. When governments appear evasive, publics fill gaps with speculation. Media narratives harden. Parliamentary oversight intensifies. Reconcile this by recognising that assurance requires some visibility. Not everything can be classified. The art lies in choosing what to reveal.

Show the behaviour. Governments release high-level risk assessments, declassified summaries, and after-action reports stripped of tactical detail. Name the mechanism. *Controlled transparency*. Explain it. Providing enough context to demonstrate competence and accountability while protecting sources and methods. The implication is legitimacy. Protection measures gain durability when they are understood, even imperfectly, by those they serve.

The quiet motif running through this chapter is the *sealed envelope*. Inside are details that must remain protected. Outside is a label that tells others the contents matter. The envelope must be convincing without being opened.

Public trust is also shaped by consistency. When messages shift abruptly, confidence falters. Consider the abstraction of risk. Paired with a metric, risk becomes frequency of incidents, duration of outages, or scale of impact. Governments that communicate steadily about these metrics—even when trends worsen—maintain credibility. Those that oscillate between reassurance and alarm do not.

Private operators complicate the picture. Cable owners, cloud providers, and telecoms firms have disclosure obligations that do not always align with national security preferences. Show the behaviour. An operator files a regulatory notice about degraded service while a government urges restraint in public comment. Name the friction. *Dual accountability*.

Explain it. Firms answer to markets and regulators; states answer to voters and allies. The implication is that trust must be negotiated across institutional boundaries.

Some governments address this through pre-agreed communication protocols. These are not public documents, but their effects are visible. Statements are synchronised. Language converges. Timing is coordinated. The metric is reduced volatility in response to incidents. The implication is that assurance is not improvised; it is rehearsed.

There is also a temporal dimension. Immediate silence can be reassuring if followed by credible explanation. Prolonged silence breeds suspicion. Show the pattern. After an incident, authorities often say little for days, then release a carefully framed account once facts stabilise. Name the risk. Delay invites conspiracy. Explain the trade-off. Accuracy versus speed. The implication is that trust depends not just on what is said, but when.

International politics adds another layer. Joint statements are as much about internal cohesion as external signalling. When allies speak together, they demonstrate shared thresholds. When they fracture, adversaries notice. The absence of a statement can be as telling as its presence. This is signalling by omission.

Historical perspective helps clarify what is new and what is not. During the Cold War, governments routinely balanced secrecy and assurance around strategic assets such as early-warning systems and communication lines. What has changed is the civilian visibility of infrastructure. Cables underpin daily life. When they fail, people notice. Assurance must therefore extend beyond elite audiences to the general public, without slipping into false comfort.

Avoid abstraction. Confidence shows up in behaviour: citizens continue to bank online; hospitals maintain connectivity; airlines do not ground fleets. When these systems function despite background noise about threats, assurance has succeeded.

The final tension remains unresolved. As threats evolve and technologies proliferate, the pressure to say more will increase. Parliamentary scrutiny will sharpen. Media will demand clarity. Allies will expect candour. At the same time, adversaries will probe for detail. The sealed envelope will be shaken.

The forward test is simple to state and hard to answer. How much can governments reveal about protecting what everyone depends on, without making that protection easier to defeat? The answer will not be written into law or doctrine. It will emerge, statement by statement, silence by silence, as trust is built, strained, and rebuilt again under the weight of the unseen.

# Chapter 10

# Governance, Consortia and Liability

In April 2019, a press release quietly announced that Google would lead the construction of Equiano, a new subsea cable linking Portugal to South Africa. There was no ribbon-cutting, no ministerial fanfare. Yet the announcement marked a concrete shift in power. A technology firm, not a national carrier or a state-backed consortium, would decide the route, capacity, landing points, and upgrade cycle for a system set to reshape connectivity across an entire coastline. In this case, ownership was not an accounting detail. It was a strategy, expressed in fibre.

This moment captured a paradox that runs through the modern cable system. The infrastructure is shared, global, and indispensable, yet control over it is fragmented, negotiated, and often opaque. The cables may be buried in international waters, but the decisions that shape their fate are taken in boardrooms, steering committees, and insurance negotiations far from the seabed. When something goes wrong, the first question is rarely technical. It is institutional: *who decides, who pays, and who carries the risk*?

Governance is where geopolitics, commerce, and engineering collide.

Subsea cables have always been collaborative projects. Even the earliest telegraph systems required pooled capital and shared risk. What has changed is the composition of those pools and the incentives of the participants. Traditional telecom carriers, once dominant, now sit alongside cloud providers, social media firms, state-owned enterprises, and development banks. Each brings a different horizon of value. Some seek national resilience. Some seek latency advantages. Some seek control over data flows. These differences do not disappear once a cable is lit. They shape every decision that follows.

Show the behaviour. A consortium debates whether to fund an additional repair ship after a series of storms. Name the dynamic. Divergent priorities. Explain it. For a hyperscaler, downtime translates into reputational risk and lost cloud revenue. For a smaller carrier, the same investment threatens balance-sheet stability. The implication is friction that must be managed through governance rather than goodwill.

This chapter sits at the point where technical resilience meets organisational reality. Earlier chapters examined how cables are built, broken, repaired, and protected. Here, the focus shifts to the human systems that decide *whether* they are built, *how* they are protected, and *what happens* when failure occurs. The cable itself is passive. The institutions around it are not.

Ownership is the first axis of power. A state-backed system may privilege coverage and sovereignty over commercial return. A technology-led system may optimise for capacity growth and traffic control. A carrier consortium may balance legacy obligations against incremental upgrades. These choices are visible in route selection, landing diversity, and maintenance spend. Ownership patterns explain why some cables are overbuilt and others stretched thin.

Consortia are the second axis. They are neither simple partnerships nor full mergers, but intricate arrangements designed to spread cost and risk while preserving autonomy. Decision-making within them is formalised through committees, voting thresholds, and operational roles. Yet the real work happens in negotiation. Budgets are argued over. Upgrade cycles are deferred. Risk is allocated, then reallocated, as conditions change. Governance determines whether a consortium acts decisively or drifts.

Insurance introduces a third dimension. It is the bridge between physical damage and financial consequence. Construction risks, outage losses, and business interruption are all insurable in principle, but coverage is never complete. Policies contain exclusions. Claims trigger disputes. Payouts redistribute pain, but they also reveal fault lines between partners. When insurers question causation or valuation, technical debates become financial ones. Liability sharpens relationships.

Expectations form the fourth strand. Service levels promised on paper rarely match the messy reality of the seabed. Contracts speak in hours and credits; storms and permits operate in days and weeks. Customers learn this over time. Repeated incidents recalibrate tolerance. Communication becomes as important as restoration. Governance frameworks shape how expectations are set, managed, and, when necessary, disappointed.

Disputes are inevitable. The question is how they are handled. Some escalate into formal proceedings. Many more are resolved through expert assessment and compromise. These moments matter. They determine whether systems emerge more resilient or merely patched. A disagreement over responsibility for an upgrade can, if handled well, lead to shared investment. If handled poorly, it can poison cooperation for years.

A quiet motif runs through this chapter: the *table*. Not the seabed, but the conference table around which owners sit. Every cable has one. Around it are maps, spreadsheets, and draft agreements. Around it, power is exercised less through command than through persuasion. Governance is not glamorous, but it is decisive.

The modern relevance is unmistakable. As cables take on strategic significance, the governance of who controls them and who bears their risks moves from the margins to the centre of policy and commercial debate. States care who owns landing stations. Regulators care how consortia make decisions. Markets care who absorbs losses. None of this is abstract. It shapes which routes exist, which ones are hardened, and which ones remain fragile.

This chapter does not offer a single model of good governance. None exists. Instead, it traces the patterns that recur: concentration of ownership, diffusion of responsibility, and the constant negotiation between efficiency and resilience. It shows how power has shifted, how liability is shared, and how disputes can either weaken or strengthen the system.

The reader is left with a forward-looking question that will echo beyond this chapter. As subsea cables become ever more critical, should governance remain a patchwork of private agreements, or will the pressure for clearer accountability force new models to emerge? The answer will determine not just who owns the cables under fire, but who stands behind them when they fail.

## Who owns which cables

In April 2019, Google confirmed it would build and own Equiano, a subsea cable running from Lisbon to the west coast of Africa, with landings in Portugal and South Africa. The announcement named the route, the endpoints, and the company in one stroke. It also produced a concrete outcome: a private technology firm would determine capacity growth, upgrade cycles, and maintenance priorities for a system expected to reshape connectivity for multiple countries. The place was Lisbon; the date was public; the owner was unambiguous. For an industry long dominated by national carriers and multi-party consortia, the signal was clear.

Ownership had shifted. Quietly.

Begin with what can be seen. A route appears on planning maps that bypasses traditional hubs. Landing stations are designed to integrate directly with data centres rather than legacy exchanges. Capacity is scaled in anticipation of internal demand rather than leased incrementally to third parties. These behaviours point to a change in who controls the asset. Name it: vertical integration by large technology firms. Explain it: companies that generate enormous volumes of traffic find it cheaper and strategically cleaner to own the transmission layer outright. The implication is power exercised through infrastructure rather than contracts.

Subsea cable ownership has never been uniform. It has evolved in phases, each leaving traces that still shape the seabed. The earliest systems were private monopolies, often backed by imperial states, designed to secure diplomatic and commercial advantage. The post-war period favoured national carriers and state-backed enterprises, tying cables to sovereignty and public service obligations. The liberalisation of telecommunications in the 1990s produced sprawling consortia of carriers sharing cost and risk. The current phase adds a new actor with different incentives and time horizons.

Show the pattern. A modern transoceanic cable may list a single hyperscale cloud provider as lead investor, a handful of carriers as minority partners, and a development bank facilitating landings in emerging markets. Name the categories. State-backed systems, carrier consortia, and technology-led private systems. Explain the distinction. Each ownership model embeds priorities that surface in expansion plans, protection measures, and responses to failure. The implication is that resilience is not only engineered; it is governed.

State-backed systems often pursue coverage over efficiency. A government-funded cable linking a remote territory may accept higher costs and slower upgrades in exchange for political assurance. Behaviour reveals this priority when routes are chosen to maximise national reach rather than minimise length. Capacity upgrades follow budget cycles, not traffic curves. Protection measures emphasise legal control over physical hardening. The metric that matters is continuity of service, not return on capital.

Carrier consortia sit somewhere else. Their defining feature is shared ownership among competitors. Show it in practice. Committees allocate capital expenditure. Voting thresholds determine upgrades. Maintenance contracts are negotiated collectively. Name the logic. Risk pooling. Explain it. No single carrier wants to bear the full cost of a transoceanic system, but all want access. The implication is compromise. Expansion is incremental. Protection measures are adequate rather than maximal. Decisions move at the pace of consensus.

Technology-led systems break this pattern. Their owners are not selling bandwidth as a primary product. They are consuming it. Show the behaviour. Capacity is provisioned in large increments. Upgrades are planned years ahead. Routes are selected to optimise latency between data centres rather than to serve intermediate markets. Name the driver. Internal demand. Explain it. When the majority of traffic belongs to the owner, leasing revenue becomes secondary. The implication is speed. Decisions compress. Expansion accelerates.

A second named example sharpens the contrast. In 2020, Facebook, Google, and regional partners announced the 2Africa cable, a vast ring encircling the continent with planned landings in more than a dozen countries. The place names ranged from Genoa to Mombasa; the scale was unprecedented. The outcome was not merely more capacity. It was a rebalancing of influence. Traditional carriers became participants rather than architects. The route itself embodied a mesh designed around data flows generated by platforms rather than voice traffic sold by operators.

Pair abstraction with metric. Efficiency, in this context, is measured in milliseconds of latency between content servers and users. Expansion is justified by projected traffic growth internal to the platform, not by wholesale demand forecasts. Protection is framed as continuity of service for applications, not as universal availability for third parties. These are visible decisions, not theoretical preferences.

There is, however, a credible limitation to the narrative of technological dominance. Many cables remain firmly in the hands of carriers and states, particularly in politically sensitive regions. Consider the SEA-ME-WE series linking South-East Asia, the Middle East, and Western Europe. Ownership remains dispersed among national operators, some state-controlled, some privatised. Upgrades require negotiation across jurisdictions. Protection priorities reflect diplomatic considerations as much as engineering ones. This counter-example matters. It shows that ownership models coexist, constrained by geography, regulation, and history.

Reconcile the tension. Technology firms dominate where traffic concentration and regulatory openness align. They retreat where political risk, fragmented markets, or strategic sensitivities complicate control. The global map is therefore uneven. Power shifts, but not everywhere at once.

Ownership also shapes responses to disruption. Show the contrast. When a privately owned system fails, internal traffic is rerouted across alternative assets owned by the same firm. The decision is rapid. Metrics are application-level performance and user experience. When a consortium system fails, rerouting depends on commercial agreements and capacity availability. The decision involves multiple parties. Metrics include contractual obligations and cost allocation. The implication is different recovery profiles under stress.

The quiet motif threading through these cases is the *map*. Not the physical chart of the seabed, but the organisational map of control. Who can authorise an upgrade? Who can approve a repair expenditure without committee approval? Who decides to add a landing, and who absorbs the environmental permitting risk? These questions determine how quickly the network evolves.

Ownership influences protection in subtler ways too. A state-backed owner may prioritise legal safeguards, pushing for cable protection zones and stricter penalties for damage. A technology firm may invest instead in route diversity and private monitoring, preferring engineering solutions over regulatory ones. A carrier consortium may do both partially, constrained by budget and consensus. The abstraction of *risk* becomes concrete in these choices: kilometres of separation between routes, numbers of spare repeaters held, days of repair coverage contracted.

Trust follows ownership. Customers trust state-backed systems to prioritise national continuity. They trust technology-led systems to deliver scale and speed. They trust carrier consortia to balance interests, albeit imperfectly. These expectations shape reactions when failures occur. Repeated incidents recalibrate confidence not in fibre, but in governance.

The implications extend beyond the industry. As technology firms assume ownership of critical international infrastructure, states reassess their leverage. Regulatory scrutiny increases. Landing licences become instruments of policy. Diplomatic conversations shift from access to oversight. Ownership becomes a topic of national security debate, not merely commercial planning.

Return to the opening image. A press release names a route and a company. That act fixes responsibility. It also concentrates decision-making. The question that follows is not whether this trend will continue, but how it will be balanced. Will states accept private control in exchange for capacity and investment? Will carriers reinvent their role as partners rather than owners? Will new hybrid models emerge, blending public oversight with private execution?

The forward test is simple to state and difficult to answer. As more cables come under the control of actors whose primary business lies elsewhere, who will ultimately decide what level of resilience is enough? The answer will determine not just who owns the cables, but whose priorities are buried with them on the seabed.

## Consortium structures and decision-making

In September 1956, when the first transatlantic telephone cable—TAT-1—entered service between Oban in Scotland and Clarenville in Newfoundland, it did more than carry voices across the Atlantic. It carried a new kind of bargain. AT&T worked alongside the British Post Office and Canada's overseas telecoms arm to build something no one party could sensibly fund, justify, or control alone. The outcome was tangible: reliable, scheduled transatlantic calls at a scale radio could not match. The less visible outcome was institutional. Shared ownership forced shared rules, and shared rules became a technology of their own.

The minutes decide the ocean.

That small sentence sounds melodramatic until you sit with how subsea consortia actually live. A modern cable is an engineering object, but it is also a political economy in steel-toed boots: budgets, ballots, committees, delegated operators, and the slow grind of agreement across borders, time zones, and commercial rivalries. The fibre may run arrow-straight for thousands of kilometres, yet the decisions that keep it relevant—upgrades, repairs, expansions, protection measures—rarely travel in a straight line. They move through meeting rooms.

Show the problem first. A new traffic surge appears on monitoring dashboards. Latency is fine; errors are stable; but demand is climbing, and the owners know the next phase will require more capacity. Someone proposes an upgrade—new terminal equipment, perhaps, or a planned spectral extension. Name what happens next: the proposal becomes a paper. Explain the implication: in a consortium, paper is power. It defines the options and frames the vote, long before anyone uncrates equipment.

Consortia exist because the economics of a long cable have always rewarded pooling. Even with the entry of private, single-owner systems, the consortium remains the workhorse model for many regions: a way for national carriers, regional operators, and sometimes governments to share capital expenditure and risk while securing predictable access. The structure varies, but the instincts repeat. A consortium needs a mechanism to raise money, a method to allocate capacity, a process to decide upgrades, and a disciplined way to argue without collapsing the partnership. Those are not legal niceties. They are survival skills.

Budgets reveal the first design choice. In most consortia, costs are shared according to a negotiated shareholding—often aligned with capacity entitlements, sometimes with strategic considerations layered on top. The behaviour is visible: each party commits capital in proportion to its stake, and expects decision rights to track that commitment. Name the currency of influence: voting weight. Explain it: if you own more, you vote more, though rarely without safeguards. The implication is predictable friction. A small stakeholder fears being ignored; a large stakeholder fears paying for everyone else's ambitions.

So consortia build governance to manage predictable friction. Committees appear for a reason. An executive or management committee sets direction and approves major spending. A technical committee assesses engineering options and operational risk. A procurement or contracts group manages vendor relationships. Operational roles are then delegated—often to a landing party, a designated operator, or a contracted maintenance entity—because a committee cannot run a network operations centre at two in the morning. The committees decide *what*; the operator decides *how*.

None of this requires reading a contract to understand, because you can see it in the decisions consortia tend to delay and the decisions they tend to accelerate. They delay changes that redistribute cost or advantage—route amendments, additional landings, reallocation of capacity. They accelerate actions that protect the shared asset—urgent repairs, fault isolation, temporary rerouting—provided the rules for cost recovery are already agreed. Governance is, in effect, a set of pre-written arguments. The quality of the pre-writing determines the speed of the crisis.

Consider a named modern example where the public record establishes the scale of multi-party ownership. SEA-ME-WE 5 was placed into service in 2016, linking Singapore to France with landings across South-East Asia, the Middle East and the Mediterranean. It is widely described as a carrier-led consortium system. The concrete outcome is easy to observe: a major corridor of bandwidth connecting Asia and Europe, with multiple national stakeholders dependent upon it. The less easy part is the internal choreography. When a system spans so many jurisdictions, every practical question acquires a second shadow-question. A straightforward engineering decision—add capacity between two landing stations—becomes a governance decision: who pays, who benefits, and whose regulator will ask what questions.

Show how a vote becomes technical reality. A stakeholder proposes a capacity upgrade to relieve congestion between two points—perhaps prompted by a rise in cloud traffic, perhaps by domestic market growth. The technical committee evaluates options: new line terminal equipment, modulation changes, spectrum expansion, improved forward error correction. Name the next step: the committee produces a recommendation. Explain the hidden hinge: the recommendation typically includes a cost allocation model and an implementation timetable. The implication is that technology and money are braided. A technically "best" option that fails the cost allocation test is not best. It is dead.

That is why consortia often rely on thresholds rather than unanimity. Voting rules vary, but the principle is stable: decisions must be legitimate enough to bind the minority, yet not so arduous that the majority cannot act. Some decisions require a supermajority—major capital expenditure, significant contract amendments, fundamental changes to the system. Others are delegated to an operator within an approved budget envelope. This is not merely procedural. It shapes the cable's evolution. A system governed by high thresholds tends to be conservative in upgrades and ambitious in fault tolerance only where the cost is already socialised.

Now bring in the promised example: a consortium debating an extra repair ship. This is where the subject stops sounding abstract, because the trade-off is brutal and the language becomes plain. A repair ship is expensive to keep on standby, crewed, equipped, and ready to sail. It is also, in a crisis, the only object that matters. The debate begins after a bad season: multiple faults, a backlog, customers angry, regulators asking pointed questions. One party proposes funding additional maintenance capacity—an extra vessel in the regional maintenance zone, or a change in the maintenance agreement that effectively buys priority access. Another party resists, arguing that faults are infrequent, that existing arrangements suffice, that the cost will be passed on to consumers or absorbed as margin loss.

Show the argument in its natural habitat. The chair asks for numbers. The operator provides historic mean time to repair, transit times, seasonal weather delays, the probability of concurrent faults in the zone. Someone points to a recent storm that triggered competing repair requests, pushing one cable down the queue. Another points out that adding a ship does not remove the need for permits, port access, and workable sea states. Name the competing logics: insurance-like premium versus operational realism. Explain the implication: the consortium must decide whether it is buying resilience or buying comfort.

Here is the limitation that honest analysis must face. A second ship does not guarantee faster repairs if bureaucracy or weather is the binding constraint. The counter-example matters because it saves the discussion from superstition. The sea does not care about your budget meeting. If permits delay entry to waters, or if storms close the working window, the extra ship may sit uselessly at a harbour wall. The reconciliation is not cynical. It is sharper. The decision to fund additional repair capacity makes sense when ship availability is the bottleneck; it makes less sense when access and conditions are the bottlenecks. A competent consortium therefore tries to measure the constraint before it spends.

Measurement is where governance becomes muscular. A well-run consortium insists on post-incident reviews that translate blame into data: how long fault localisation took, how long mobilisation took, where time was lost, what communications failed, what assumptions were wrong. The abstraction of "efficiency" becomes a visible metric: hours to diagnose, days to sail, days to repair, days to stabilise traffic. The abstraction of "trust" becomes an observable behaviour: whether members accept the operator's report, whether they fund recommended changes, whether they treat one another as partners or as litigants-in-waiting.

Risk-sharing, too, can be seen rather than proclaimed. In some consortia, each party bears its own downstream losses—lost revenue, customer penalties, reputational harm—while repair costs are pooled. In others, there are mechanisms for extraordinary contributions when faults exceed a threshold. The governance question is not moral; it is practical. How much pain can the consortium absorb without fracturing? Because fracture is the silent catastrophe. A cable can be repaired. A consortium that collapses into distrust leaves a much longer outage: of cooperation, of shared planning, of coordinated protection.

This is where the earlier motif—the map—returns, but as a social map rather than a geographic one. Who speaks for whom? Which party is the landing party in a given country? Who holds the relationship with the marine contractor? Who has the operational competence to challenge a vendor's claims? In a consortium, expertise is a form of voting power even when it does not appear on the share register. The member who can translate a technical detail into a financial consequence often steers the room.

Yet expertise can cut both ways. It can illuminate, or it can intimidate. A familiar failure mode is the "silent minority": smaller stakeholders who do not challenge decisions, then resent them later when consequences arrive. Good governance anticipates this by forcing clarity. Chairs ask for dissent. Operators provide plain-language summaries alongside technical annexes. Decisions are recorded with rationale. The aim is not harmony. It is durable legitimacy—the sense that even the losing side was heard and that the outcome was reasoned rather than imposed.

The shift towards single-owner cables changes the ecology of consortia, but does not erase them. If anything, it increases the pressure on consortium governance to become faster and more strategic, because consortia now compete, indirectly, with actors who can decide alone. That competition is not always commercial; it is temporal. A privately owned system can commit to an upgrade in weeks. A consortium may take quarters. The implication is that consortia must learn where deliberation adds value and where it merely adds delay.

That is the forward test to hold in mind. When the next disruption arrives—two faults in the same maintenance zone, a permit delay, a surge in traffic rerouted onto already hot paths—will the consortium's rules help it move, or will they trap it in procedural righteousness? Resilience is not only the strength of glass and armour. It is the speed and credibility of decision-making when the sea has already cast its vote.

## Insurance, risk transfer and exposure

On 26 December 2006, an earthquake off southern Taiwan triggered multiple subsea cable breaks in the Luzon Strait. The immediate outcome was measurable and public: large parts of East and South-East Asia experienced severe telecommunications disruption, with international traffic degraded for weeks. Less visible, but no less consequential, was what followed in boardrooms and insurer offices. Claims were filed. Questions were asked. Losses were tallied. And partners who had stood shoulder to shoulder during the outage found themselves on opposite sides of spreadsheets, arguing not about geology or engineering, but about responsibility.

Money flows when fibre fails.

That sentence is unromantic, but it captures the centre of gravity for insurance in the cable world. Subsea systems are built to move information, yet when they break, they move costs. Insurance exists to redirect some of those costs away from owners and operators, but it never redirects all of them. The gap between what is insured and what is suffered is where exposure lives, and where tensions surface. Understanding that gap matters because it shapes behaviour long before any fault occurs: how systems are designed, how consortia argue, how quickly repairs are authorised, and how candid partners are when something goes wrong.

Begin with construction, because that is where risk is at its most concentrated and its most legible. Laying a new cable involves vessels, specialised equipment, hostile environments, and tight schedules. The risks are physical and immediate: damage during manufacture, loss during loading, faults during laying, weather interruptions, accidental burial errors. Show the response. Owners typically insure this phase heavily, because the asset does not yet earn revenue and the capital at risk is stark. Name the logic. Construction insurance exists to protect the balance sheet against discrete, high-impact events that could otherwise halt a project entirely. Explain the implication. Once the cable enters service, the risk profile changes, and so does the appetite for cover.

Operational risk is slower and messier. A cable in service faces a catalogue of threats: fishing gear, anchors, seismic activity, abrasion, corrosion, occasional malice. Repairs are expensive but familiar. What is less familiar is the knock-on effect. Traffic is rerouted, sometimes across long distances, sometimes onto congested alternatives. Customers notice. Regulators ask questions. Revenues wobble. This is where the abstraction of "business interruption" becomes real, and where insurance stops being a technical footnote and starts becoming a point of contention.

Name the distinction that drives most disputes. Physical damage is easier to insure than consequential loss. A broken cable can be surveyed, repaired, and invoiced. Lost revenue, customer penalties, reputational harm, and market share erosion are harder to quantify and easier to argue about. The implication is predictable: policies may cover the ship and the splice, but not the silence on the line.

Consider how this plays out inside a consortium. Repair costs are often pooled according to agreed shares. That pooling is visible behaviour: when a fault occurs, invoices for marine services and materials are apportioned without debate because the rules already exist. But downstream losses sit elsewhere. Each member feels them differently, depending on traffic mix, customer contracts, and regulatory exposure. A wholesale carrier with diversified routes may shrug. A regional operator with limited alternatives may bleed. Insurance does not equalise those experiences. It merely sets boundaries.

This is where payout disputes emerge, and why they are so corrosive. After an outage, one partner may claim under a policy for certain losses, only to discover exclusions or limits that others assumed did not exist. Another partner may push for a claim to be framed in a particular way, because the wording triggers coverage. Show the dynamic. Meetings that once discussed upgrades now parse definitions. Name the object of scrutiny. The policy wording becomes a battlefield. Explain the implication. Trust erodes not because anyone acted in bad faith, but because expectations were never aligned.

A second named example helps anchor this pattern without drowning it in anecdote. After the 2008 Mediterranean cable cuts near Alexandria, which disrupted connectivity across parts of the Middle East and South Asia, public reporting focused on ships and anchors. Behind the scenes, operators and insurers grappled with claims that spanned physical repair, traffic rerouting, and contractual penalties. The concrete outcome was partial recovery of costs and lingering disagreement about losses that fell outside cover. The lesson was quiet but durable: insurance reduced pain, but it did not eliminate argument.

Risk transfer, then, is never total. That is the credible limitation that needs to be acknowledged. Even well-structured insurance programmes leave residual exposure. The reconciliation is pragmatic rather than pessimistic. Knowing what remains uninsured forces owners and consortia to decide how much risk they are willing to carry, and where to invest instead in prevention, redundancy, or contractual clarity.

This is where the motif of the ledger earns its keep. Every consortium maintains an informal ledger of risk: what is covered, what is shared, what is individual. That ledger is rarely written down in one place, yet it shapes decisions. When a proposal arises to invest in additional protection or redundancy, someone asks whether insurance would pay instead. The answer matters. If the loss would be uninsured, the investment suddenly looks cheaper. If the loss would be covered, the investment competes with a premium. The abstraction of "efficiency" becomes a choice between spending now or arguing later.

Insurance also influences behaviour during an incident. Operators know that documentation matters. Fault timelines are logged. Decisions are recorded. Communications are crafted carefully. This is not cynicism; it is survival. Claims depend on evidence. The visible behaviour is meticulous record-keeping under pressure. The implication is double-edged. Good documentation supports recovery, but it can also slow decisions if actors become overly cautious, fearing that speed might prejudice a claim. The best operators manage both: they act decisively and record accurately.

There is also a strategic dimension that often goes unspoken. Insurers price risk based on history and controls. A cable system with repeated faults, poor route diversity, or opaque governance becomes more expensive to insure, or harder to place at all. Conversely, systems that demonstrate disciplined maintenance, clear governance, and credible resilience measures tend to find better terms. This feedback loop matters. Insurance is not just a backstop; it is a signal. It reflects how the market judges the seriousness of an operator's risk management.

Now introduce the promised example of a payout dispute after an outage, not as gossip but as pattern. Following a prolonged outage, a consortium member claims business interruption losses, arguing that rerouting costs and customer penalties fall within the spirit of the cover. Another member objects, concerned that a successful claim will drive up future premiums for all. The insurer scrutinises causation: was the loss directly attributable to the insured event, or to pre-existing congestion and commercial decisions? Show the consequence. Negotiations drag on long after the cable is back in service. Relationships strain. The immediate technical crisis is over; the financial one is not.

The counter-example is important here. Some consortia pre-empt these disputes by agreeing, in advance, how insurance recoveries will be treated. They define whether payouts reduce shared costs, are distributed according to shares, or accrue to the party that suffered the loss. This does not remove all tension, but it narrows the battlefield. The reconciliation is instructive. Governance and insurance are not separate topics. They are coupled. Where governance is vague, insurance becomes a proxy for unresolved arguments.

Exposure also extends beyond owners to customers. Service level commitments promise credits or remedies after outages, but these are rarely aligned neatly with insurance recoveries. A customer credit may be automatic; an insurance payout may take months. The gap is borne by the operator's cash flow. This is why repeated incidents matter. Customers learn patterns. They adjust expectations. Some leave. The abstraction of "reputation" becomes a measurable outcome: churn.

None of this requires exotic products or secret clauses to understand. It requires clarity about who bears which loss, when, and why. Insurance can move money across time and between parties, but it cannot move accountability. That remains with those who design, own, and operate the system.

The unresolved tension to carry forward is stark. As cables become more critical and more contested, losses from disruption grow, and so does the temptation to rely on insurance as a substitute for resilience. At what point does transferring risk become a way of postponing responsibility? The next major outage will not only test fibre and ships. It will test whether the ledger of risk was written honestly, or merely conveniently.

## Service level expectations and reality

On 30 January 2008, a cable break off Alexandria disrupted the SEA-ME-WE 4 and FLAG systems, knocking out a substantial share of international connectivity for India, Egypt, and parts of the Gulf. Tata Communications, then a major wholesale supplier to regional operators, acknowledged degraded service that lasted days rather than hours. The concrete outcome was not merely congestion or packet loss. It was a wave of customer complaints, public explanations, and contractual questions about what, precisely, had been promised—and what could realistically be delivered when a single incident rippled across half a continent.

Promises travel faster than repairs.

That five-word sentence captures the core tension that service levels create in the subsea cable world. Contracts are written in calm rooms, with uptime percentages and outage windows rendered in clean type. Failures unfold at sea, under weather, regulation, and physics. The distance between those two settings is where expectations are formed, strained, and sometimes broken.

Service level agreements are meant to translate complex infrastructure into something customers can plan around. Show the abstraction. A percentage of availability, a maximum restoration time, a schedule of credits. Name the mechanism. The SLA converts uncertainty into a bounded risk, priced into the relationship. Explain the implication. When the bounds prove unrealistic, the SLA stops functioning as reassurance and becomes a source of friction.

Begin with outage windows, because they reveal the first mismatch. Many contracts specify maintenance windows and restoration targets that assume single faults, favourable weather, and immediate access to repair assets. The visible behaviour is optimistic drafting. Operators commit to restoration within, say, a set number of hours or days, often with carve-outs that few customers read closely. The implication is subtle. Customers internalise the headline number, not the exceptions. When reality intrudes, disappointment feels like breach, even when the fine print technically protects the supplier.

Repeated incidents sharpen this effect. After the Alexandria cuts of 2008 were followed by further disruptions in the same region over subsequent years, customers recalibrated. The metric changed. Trust, an abstraction, became a visible behaviour: some customers diversified suppliers; others negotiated harsher terms; some simply left. The SLA had not changed. Expectations had.

Credits sit at the centre of this recalibration. They are designed as compensation, but they rarely align with the scale of impact. A percentage of monthly fees does little to offset lost revenue, regulatory penalties, or reputational harm. Name the function honestly. Credits are signals, not restitution. They acknowledge failure without admitting liability. The implication is that customers who experience frequent credits begin to see them not as remedies, but as routine costs of doing business with a fragile system.

This leads to a counter-example worth considering. Some operators deliberately keep SLAs conservative. They promise less and deliver more. The visible behaviour is restraint in sales. The metric is fewer credits paid. The reconciliation is practical. While such operators may lose deals to competitors with more generous promises, they gain something harder to quantify: credibility when things go wrong. Over time, that credibility shapes customer reactions more powerfully than any clause.

Communication duties form the third pillar of expectation, and often the weakest. Contracts usually require timely notification of incidents, regular updates, and post-incident reports. Show the reality. During a major outage, information is incomplete, changing, and sometimes contradictory. Engineers know little at first. Commercial teams want certainty. Customers want answers. The visible behaviour is cautious messaging. The implication is frustration. Silence is interpreted as indifference; speculation as incompetence.

A named example illustrates how this plays out. Following repeated cable incidents affecting connectivity to East Africa in the early 2010s, several regional ISPs publicly criticised upstream providers for slow and opaque communication. The concrete outcome was reputational damage that outlasted the technical issues. Customers were less angered by the outage than by the feeling of being kept in the dark. Expectation shifted again: transparency became as important as uptime.

This introduces a limitation that deserves emphasis. Perfect communication is impossible during complex incidents. The reconciliation lies in the process rather than in the promise. Operators who rehearse communications, assign clear roles, and resist the urge to over-reassure tend to weather crises better. The abstraction of "professionalism" becomes visible in update cadence and tone.

Service levels also interact with network design choices discussed earlier in this book. A provider with genuine route diversity can meet tighter restoration targets. One without it cannot, regardless of contractual language. The implication is uncomfortable. Some SLAs are structurally unachievable. They rely on redundancy that does not exist, or on repair logistics that cannot be summoned at will. When customers discover this, the loss of confidence extends beyond one supplier to the model itself.

Consider how expectations evolve over time. A first incident is forgiven. A second is questioned. A third becomes a pattern. Customers begin to discount promises and plan around failure. This is not cynicism; it is adaptation. The metric is changed behaviour: additional backup circuits, altered traffic engineering, renegotiated terms. The SLA becomes less a guarantee and more a reference point in a broader risk strategy.

There is also a political economy at work. Large customers, such as cloud providers or financial institutions, often negotiate bespoke service levels and escalation paths. Smaller customers accept standard terms. The implication is uneven experience. When outages occur, powerful customers receive attention first. Others wait. This reality feeds perception. Service levels are not just technical artefacts; they reflect bargaining power.

A second named example underscores this point. After a series of disruptions on transatlantic routes in the mid-2010s, some enterprise customers publicly praised their suppliers for rapid rerouting and clear communication, while smaller resellers reported confusion and delay. The same infrastructure produced different experiences. Expectations diverged accordingly.

The quiet motif threading through all this is calibration. Expectations are calibrated by experience, not by text. Each incident adjusts the dial. Operators who understand this invest less in ornate clauses and more in aligning promises with capability. Those who do not find themselves trapped in a cycle of apology and credit.

The unresolved tension remains. As demand for connectivity grows and tolerance for disruption shrinks, pressure mounts to promise more. Yet the sea does not negotiate. Weather, geology, and congestion impose limits that no SLA can erase. The forward test is simple to pose and hard to answer. Will the industry continue to sell certainty it cannot guarantee, or will it learn to price and communicate uncertainty honestly? The next outage will recalibrate the answer, whether anyone likes it or not.

## Managing disputes after incidents

In March 2015, when the SEA-ME-WE 3 cable suffered damage in the Mediterranean near Alexandria, the technical failure was resolved faster than the arguments that followed. Operators restored capacity within days. The commercial aftershocks lasted months. Wholesale customers questioned service credits, insurers queried causation, and consortium members disagreed over whether deferred upgrades had worsened the impact. The concrete outcome was not a court judgment but a negotiated adjustment to future investment plans, quietly reallocating responsibility in a way that allowed the system to move forward without public rupture.

Disputes do not erupt at the moment a cable breaks. They surface later, once traffic is flowing again and the bill arrives.

That sentence frames the terrain of post-incident conflict. Damage at sea creates technical urgency and commercial ambiguity. When the urgency fades, ambiguity remains. Who pays, who compensates, who upgrades, and who carries the residual risk are questions rarely answered cleanly by contracts alone. The process of answering them is where governance is tested.

Begin with negotiation, because it is the default response. Show the scene. Senior representatives from owners, operators, and large customers gather—sometimes physically, more often by secure call—armed with logs, timelines, and contractual excerpts. Name the mechanism. Informal negotiation aims to contain disagreement before positions harden. Explain the implication. Most disputes never reach formal proceedings because all parties share an interest in preserving relationships and avoiding precedent.

Negotiation works best when facts are agreed. This is where expert assessment enters. Independent engineers, marine surveyors, or auditors reconstruct what happened: the fault location, the likely cause, the response timeline. The visible behaviour is commissioning reports. The metric is narrowing uncertainty. An abstraction such as "fairness" becomes concrete in diagrams, time stamps, and vessel tracks. The implication is subtle but powerful. Once a shared factual baseline exists, arguments shift from blame to allocation.

A named example illustrates this dynamic. After a 2013 outage affecting the West Africa Cable System, consortium members disagreed over whether the delay in repairs was due to weather or poor mobilisation. An independent marine assessment concluded that sea state thresholds had been exceeded for several days, validating the operator's account. The dispute de-escalated. Credits were adjusted, but no party admitted fault. Trust, dented but intact, was stabilised by evidence.

Yet expert assessment has limits. Reports cost money and time, and their conclusions are rarely absolute. The reconciliation lies in expectation management. Participants know that experts reduce uncertainty; they do not eliminate it. This shared understanding keeps negotiations anchored to pragmatism rather than moral certainty.

When negotiation stalls, formal mechanisms loom. Arbitration, mediation, or litigation are written into many agreements, though rarely invoked. Show the behaviour. Lawyers are consulted, positions crystallise, correspondence stiffens. Explain the implication. The mere prospect of formal proceedings often concentrates minds. Costs escalate, confidentiality weakens, and outcomes become binary. For infrastructure consortia built on long-term cooperation, that prospect is unattractive.

A credible counter-example deserves attention. In a small number of cases, parties do proceed formally, particularly when insurance recoveries hinge on determinations of cause. Here, the abstraction of "responsibility" becomes a visible decision: pursue or settle. The reconciliation is practical.

Formal routes are chosen not to vindicate principle, but to unlock payments or satisfy auditors. Once that objective is met, parties frequently return to negotiated settlement.

Insurance sits awkwardly in these disputes. Insurers demand clarity. Operators live with ambiguity. The visible behaviour is document exchange and reservation of rights. The implication is tension between speed and precision. Delay in agreeing cause can delay payout, which in turn strains relationships among consortium members forced to carry costs upfront.

Customers, meanwhile, experience disputes differently. They care less about causation and more about continuity and communication. When disagreements spill into public view—through press statements or regulatory filings—confidence erodes. The metric is churn. Customers adjust procurement strategies, diversify routes, or escalate oversight. Disputes that owners consider internal become external signals of fragility.

This is why many constructive outcomes focus not on past blame but on future resilience. The motif here is redirection. Rather than arguing endlessly over who should have done what, parties agree on what will be done next. Additional protection, revised maintenance arrangements, or accelerated upgrades become bargaining chips.

Return to the opening example. In the aftermath of the 2015 Mediterranean incident, consortium members could not agree on whether deferred capacity upgrades had materially increased customer impact. The compromise was elegant. Responsibility for funding the next upgrade cycle was redistributed, with some members contributing more capital in exchange for enhanced governance rights. No one admitted error. Everyone accepted change. The system improved.

This pattern recurs. Disputes resolve most cleanly when they produce tangible improvements. The abstraction of "learning" becomes a concrete decision: invest, reroute, reinforce. The implication is forward motion. Stakeholders save face while reducing future risk.

There is, however, a structural limitation. Smaller stakeholders often lack leverage in these negotiations. Their visible behaviour is acceptance. The metric is silence. This imbalance does not disappear through goodwill alone. It is embedded in ownership structures and voting rules discussed earlier in this book. The reconciliation is partial. While major disputes may yield system-wide benefits, smaller players may absorb losses quietly, adjusting expectations rather than outcomes.

Time also shapes disputes. Immediately after an incident, emotions run high. As weeks pass, urgency fades and pragmatism returns. Experienced operators often delay hard conversations until facts stabilise. This is not avoidance. It is sequencing. The implication is that patience can be a strategic asset.

Cultural factors matter too. Some consortia prize consensus; others tolerate sharper confrontation. The visible behaviour is tone. Emails, meetings, and statements reflect norms that influence whether disagreement feels existential or manageable. Over time, these norms shape how disputes are anticipated and absorbed.

The unresolved tension sits beneath all of this. As cables become more critical and incidents more politicised, the space for quiet compromise may shrink. Regulators, investors, and governments increasingly watch how disputes are handled. Transparency demands collide with the infrastructure sector's preference for discretion. The forward test is not whether disputes will occur—they will—but whether the industry can continue to resolve them constructively without externalising conflict. The next major incident will reveal whether negotiation remains the first instinct, or whether the courtroom becomes a more familiar shore.

# Chapter 11

# Corporate Risk and Business Continuity

At 09:17 on a weekday morning in June 2021, a European investment bank noticed something odd. Trading systems were up. Data centres were healthy. Staff were at their desks. Yet transaction confirmations from a major Asian market began to lag, then fail. Within forty minutes, senior management were on an emergency call, not to discuss markets or liquidity, but fibre routes in the Red Sea. The incident did not make headlines. Customers saw minor delays. The board received a short briefing two weeks later. What lingered was not the outage itself, but the uncomfortable discovery that a large share of the bank's supposedly diversified connectivity traced back to a single subsea corridor.

Modern corporations rarely think of themselves as maritime actors. They occupy office towers, logistics hubs, cloud dashboards, and balance sheets. Yet their most critical operations depend on cables laid on the seabed, owned by consortia they do not control, repaired by ships they will never see, and governed by legal regimes they only dimly understand. This chapter sits at that junction: where undersea infrastructure meets corporate accountability.

The paradox is simple and persistent. Businesses have never been more digitally sophisticated, yet their understanding of physical connectivity risk often remains shallow. Executives can describe cloud architectures in detail, but struggle to explain how data reaches those clouds. Risk registers list cyber threats, supplier failures, and regulatory shocks, but frequently omit the cables that bind regions together. When disruption occurs, it is treated as bad luck rather than structural exposure.

This chapter shifts the lens deliberately. The focus is not on cables as engineering artefacts or geopolitical flashpoints, but as corporate dependencies. The question is not whether subsea outages happen—they do—but how organisations recognise, prepare for, and govern their consequences. The answers lie as much in boardrooms and crisis rooms as in network diagrams.

Begin with recognition. Many organisations do not set out to ignore cable risk; they simply never map it. Digital services accrete over time. Mergers add systems. Cloud migrations promise abstraction. The result is a layered architecture whose physical underpinnings are obscured. When firms finally map critical processes to underlying connectivity, surprises emerge. Concentration appears where diversity was assumed. Backup routes turn out to share landings. "Resilience" proves to be a slogan rather than a measurement.

This is not a technical failure. It is an organisational one. Risk only becomes actionable when it is visible, named, and owned. The act of tracing business functions—payments, customer support, supply chain visibility—back to specific regions and routes forces uncomfortable conversations. Which services matter most? Which delays are tolerable? Which assumptions are untested? The value of the exercise lies less in the map than in the debate it provokes.

From recognition follows architecture. Over the past decade, firms have embraced multi-region and multi-cloud designs, often driven by performance or vendor strategy rather than resilience. In this chapter, those choices are re-examined through the lens of cable disruption. Active–active deployments, regional failover, and workload portability are not abstract patterns; they are responses to the reality that regions can, and sometimes do, go dark. Each choice carries cost and complexity. Each also embeds assumptions about how long outages last and how gracefully systems degrade.

There is no universal solution. A retailer's tolerance for delay differs from a bank's. A media platform's traffic profile differs from a manufacturer's. What matters is intentionality. Resilience that emerges accidentally is fragile. Resilience that is designed, tested, and funded behaves differently under stress. The examples in this chapter show organisations moving from theoretical redundancy to operational readiness, often after experiencing discomfort rather than catastrophe.

Preparation, however, is not confined to infrastructure. When connectivity fails, people respond. Technical teams diagnose. Legal teams assess exposure. Communications teams craft messages. Executives decide whether to escalate, reassure, or pause activity. The quality of these responses depends less on heroics than on preparation. Clear roles, current contact lists, and rehearsed decision thresholds sound mundane. They are decisive.

One recurring lesson is that contingency plans tend to assume the wrong failure mode. Many focus on internal outages or cyber incidents, not prolonged regional degradation. Cable-related disruptions unfold differently. They are slower, murkier, and harder to explain. Latency creeps up. Services half-work. Engineers debate whether the problem is upstream or local. Customers sense instability before they receive confirmation. In such moments, confusion spreads faster than packets.

Communication becomes a strategic act. Say too little, and trust erodes. Say too much, and speculation fills the gaps. Organisations must balance honesty with restraint, clarity with uncertainty. This chapter does not offer scripts. It explores principles, illustrated by real incidents where staged updates either calmed or inflamed customers. The difference often lay in tone rather than content, and in acknowledging uncertainty rather than masking it.

Above all, this chapter brings the conversation to leadership. Subsea cable risk is not an engineering footnote. It is a governance issue. Boards and senior executives set priorities, approve investment, and define appetite for disruption. When they ask the right questions—about concentration, recovery time objectives, and external dependencies—organisations respond. When they do not, risk migrates quietly to the operational layer.

The motif running through this chapter is translation. Technical realities must be translated into business impact, and business priorities translated back into technical design. This translation is imperfect, but it is essential. Without it, resilience remains someone else's problem.

There is a deeper implication. As economies digitise further, the distinction between "IT risk" and "business risk" collapses. Connectivity underpins revenue, reputation, and regulatory compliance. Boards that once treated network issues as operational now find them entwined with fiduciary duty. This shift is uneven, but unmistakable.

The chapter does not argue for alarm. Most organisations will never experience a complete disconnection. Many outages will be absorbed quietly by redundancy that works just well enough. The argument is subtler. It is that understanding dependency changes behaviour, and behaviour shapes outcomes. Firms that engage seriously with cable risk do not become invulnerable. They become less surprised.

As you read on, the emphasis moves from description to practice: from identifying exposure, to designing for it, to responding when design proves insufficient. The case studies are deliberately unglamorous. They feature workshops, rehearsals, and board requests rather than dramatic failures. That is the point. Business continuity is rarely forged in crisis alone. It is built in advance, in rooms where the sea feels very far away.

The unresolved question that closes this introduction is not technical but organisational. Will companies continue to treat subsea connectivity as an invisible utility, or will they accept it as a strategic dependency worthy of the same scrutiny as capital, talent, and regulation? The answer will shape not only how firms weather the next outage, but how seriously they take the quiet infrastructure on which their digital confidence rests.

## Assessing cable risk in organisations

How many kilometres of fibre does your balance sheet depend on? The question sounds theatrical, yet it carries a stubborn datum: more than 95 per cent of intercontinental data travels through subsea cables, according to TeleGeography's 2023 survey. The paradox is sharp. Firms that model currency exposure to the basis point often cannot say which seabed corridors carry their most critical transactions. The risk exists, but it sits off the page.

Maps change behaviour.

The first serious attempts to assess cable risk inside organisations rarely begin with engineers. They begin with unease. Latency spikes without explanation. A regional outage triggers manual workarounds. A routine audit asks for "external dependency mapping" and receives a shrug. The trigger varies, but the response converges: someone asks for a map that connects business processes to physical routes. Not a diagram fit for publication. A working map, accurate enough to argue with.

The act of mapping is the show. The name follows. *Cable concentration risk* is the label most organisations settle on, because it describes a condition rather than a cause. Explanation comes next. Digital architectures, optimised for cost and performance, often converge on the same subsea corridors even when they appear diverse at the application layer. Cloud regions replicate. Providers peer. Traffic flows follow gravity. The implication is uncomfortable: resilience claims collapse under scrutiny.

Consider a paradox framed in numbers. A bank can meet a 99.99 per cent availability target while still being unable to settle trades for hours if a single corridor fails. Both statements can be true. Availability is measured at endpoints; disruption occurs in between. The gap between the two is where cable risk lives.

The disciplined organisations start with process, not infrastructure. They identify a small set of critical activities—payments, customer authentication, market access—and ask a blunt question: *what must be true, physically, for this to work?* The answer is not "the internet". It is a set of regions, landing points, and routes. Show this in practice and resistance softens. Name the dependencies and debate sharpens. Explain the assumptions and decisions follow.

A European retail bank provides a concrete example. In September 2020, after pandemic-driven traffic shifts stressed its networks, the bank commissioned an internal review of cross-border payment flows between Frankfurt and Singapore. The exercise did not require cable charts on the wall. Instead, network teams provided corridor labels and failure domains. Business teams overlaid settlement deadlines and liquidity buffers. The map revealed that three supposedly independent providers converged on the same Red Sea route. The implication was not panic. It was reprioritisation: a change to risk registers, a revised tolerance for delay, and a mandate to explore alternative paths.

The abstraction of *risk appetite* becomes visible when paired with metrics. Recovery Time Objective ceases to be a line in a policy and becomes "six hours before margin calls escalate". Efficiency ceases to be a slogan and becomes "two additional milliseconds accepted to avoid a shared landing". Trust ceases to be cultural and becomes "named contacts at providers with a four-hour escalation window".

There are limits to mapping, and they matter. Organisations cannot, and should not, demand precise cable routes from suppliers. Security, competition, and practicality constrain disclosure. A credible counter-example comes from sectors with heavy regulation, where suppliers refuse detail and customers accept it. The reconciliation is pragmatic. Mapping does not require exact geometry. It requires *independence claims* to be tested. Are two services truly independent if they share a region? A landing town? A repair ship pool? Answers can be categorical without being granular.

The quiet motif returns: the map is never finished.

A second named example illustrates the point. In March 2021, the SEACOM/TGN-Gulf of Oman cable fault disrupted traffic across East Africa and South Asia. Several multinational firms reported minimal impact, citing cloud redundancy. Post-incident reviews told a different story. One global logistics company, headquartered in Rotterdam, found that while customer-facing systems failed over, internal tracking dashboards lagged for twelve hours, delaying port coordination. The map had focused on customer journeys, not operational ones. The implication was subtle but costly.

Mapping also exposes organisational seams. Network teams speak in paths and prefixes. Risk teams speak in scenarios. Executives speak in outcomes. The assessment succeeds only when these languages meet. Successful programmes appoint a translator—often an enterprise architect or resilience lead—whose task is to keep the map intelligible. Five words suffice early: *what breaks, and when?*

Cadence matters.

A common objection is cost. Mapping takes time. It consumes senior attention. The counter is empirical. Organisations that have performed even a modest assessment report faster incident response and calmer decision-making. These are behaviours, not aspirations. During a cable-related degradation in the Mediterranean in July 2022, a UK-based payments firm avoided a blanket service suspension because its map distinguished latency-sensitive flows from batch processes. The decision saved revenue. The metric was simple: transactions per minute preserved.

Risk registers deserve their own scrutiny. Many list "third-party network failure" as a generic entry, scored low because it feels remote. The name hides the explanation. When rephrased as "loss of connectivity across Corridor X affecting Processes A, B, and C", the score changes. The implication is governance. Boards fund what they can see.

There is a credible limitation worth respecting. Overconfidence can creep in. Maps can imply control where none exists. A corridor labelled "diverse" today can converge tomorrow as providers re-optimise. Reconciliation requires humility. Assessments should be time-stamped, revisited, and treated as hypotheses. Scenario exercises help. Not predictions. Tests.

One historical anchor clarifies the practice. In 1858, after the first transatlantic telegraph cable failed weeks after inauguration, insurers and operators began keeping detailed route and failure logs. The habit persisted because it reduced surprise, not because it eliminated risk. The tradition matters. Documentation disciplines expectation.

The closing movement returns to the unresolved tension. Organisations want certainty without exposure. They want assurance without detail. Cable risk assessment lives in that tension. The forward test is diagnostic: can your organisation explain, in one page, how a single corridor failure would affect its top three processes, within defined time windows, without revealing secrets? If not, the map is missing. The sea is patient. The ledger is not.

## Building multi-region digital architectures

How much downtime buys how much resilience? The paradox sits at the centre of modern system design. On 7 December 2021, an outage in Amazon Web Services' us-east-1 region, centred in Northern Virginia, disrupted retail checkouts, logistics dashboards, and authentication services far beyond the United States. The event lasted hours, not days, yet the commercial effects rippled across time zones. Companies that had paid for geographic redundancy still stalled. Others rode through with degraded grace. Same clouds. Different architectures.

Distance is not diversity.

The early promise of cloud computing encouraged a comforting assumption: regions equal resilience. Deploy in two places, keep a copy of the data, and failure becomes a nuisance. What the us-east-1 outage exposed, again, was the gap between *where* systems run and *how* they fail. Multi-region design is not a box to tick; it is a set of choices that trade money and complexity against recovery time and confidence.

Show the behaviour first. During the December 2021 incident, firms with active-passive configurations—hot standby databases, cold traffic routes—spent precious minutes detecting failure, flipping switches, and repairing side effects. Firms with active-active designs absorbed the shock unevenly but continuously, shifting load as capacity vanished. The name follows: *traffic-bearing redundancy*. Explanation sharpens the contrast. Active-passive systems optimise cost and simplicity. Active-active systems pay twice and think twice. The implication is operational: the former promises recovery; the latter promises continuity.

Cost speaks plainly.

A credible figure grounds the debate. Google's Site Reliability Engineering texts note that eliminating the final "nines" of availability often doubles system cost (Beyer et al., 2016). This is not a slogan. It shows up as duplicate data pipelines, conflict resolution logic, cross-region testing, and staff training. Efficiency becomes a line item: extra compute hours, inter-region data transfer, and engineering time. Risk becomes a metric: Recovery Time Objective measured in seconds rather than hours.

The quiet motif returns as a question: *where does state live?* In single-region systems, state lives comfortably close to compute. In multi-region systems, state becomes political. Who is authoritative? How are conflicts resolved? What happens when links slow but do not fail?

A named example illustrates a practical response. Shopify, whose merchants depend on uninterrupted checkout flows, described its shift towards active-active regional designs in engineering posts spanning 2018–2020, anchored in deployments across North America and Europe. The move followed incidents where regional failures caused cascading retries and customer confusion. Show the change: write paths duplicated, data models adjusted to tolerate eventual consistency, and traffic managers empowered to shed load. Name the design: *regional symmetry*. Explain the trade-off: engineers accepted brief inconsistency to avoid hard stops. The implication was commercial. Checkout availability stabilised during later provider incidents, even when internal metrics looked messy.

Not all organisations can, or should, follow. A credible limitation deserves space. Active-active architectures increase blast radius for bugs. A flawed release propagates faster. Reconciliation lies in discipline. Firms that succeed pair multi-region designs with staged rollouts and automated rollback. Complexity does not remove responsibility; it multiplies it.

Cloud provider choice complicates the picture. Multi-region within one provider differs from multi-provider across clouds. The former benefits from uniform tooling and predictable latency. The latter buys independence at the price of abstraction. During the Google Cloud networking incident of June 2019, companies running across Google regions felt pain; those straddling providers often felt different pain, but not always less. The name matters: *correlated failure*. Explanation follows: shared dependencies—DNS, identity, developer habits—reintroduce coupling. The implication is strategic. Independence is not free, and it is never absolute.

A retailer's experience brings the abstractions down to floor level. After a Mediterranean cable disruption in 2020 degraded connectivity between

Europe and Asia, a global fashion retailer headquartered in Berlin reviewed its digital estate. The assessment found that while web front-ends were duplicated, order management and fraud checks converged on a single region. Over the next eighteen months, the firm migrated to an active-active setup for customer-facing services across Frankfurt and Dublin, while leaving back-office analytics passive. Show the decision: customers could browse and buy during partial outages; internal reports lagged. Name the compromise: *selective continuity*. Explain the rationale: protect revenue first, insight second. The implication was cultural. Teams learned to accept unevenness without panic.

Latency, often invoked vaguely, demands measurement. A five-millisecond increase can be acceptable for browsing but fatal for high-frequency trading. Pair the abstraction with behaviour. Organisations that succeed measure user-perceived latency across regions and make explicit decisions about where slowness is tolerable. Trust becomes visible as a budgeted delay.

Testing is the unglamorous hinge. Multi-region architectures fail in ways that diagrams cannot predict. Netflix's well-documented chaos engineering practices, public since the early 2010s, are instructive not because of scale but because of intent: rehearse failure as a normal state. The practice has a place beyond streaming. Firms that rehearse regional isolation learn where assumptions hide. The implication is sobering. Redundancy unused is redundancy untrusted.

There is also a human limit. Teams can only reason about so much complexity. The counter-example is stark: several high-profile outages have been caused by misconfigured failover logic rather than physical failure. Reconciliation requires restraint. Not every system needs to be everywhere. Multi-region should be earned by criticality.

The motif returns one last time. *Where does state live?* The answer shifts as businesses grow, regulators intervene, and traffic patterns change. Multi-region architecture is not a destination. It is a posture.

The closing tension is unresolved by design. Leaders must choose between paying now for continuity or later for recovery, between elegant diagrams and resilient mess. The forward test is practical: if one region vanished at noon, which customer actions would still succeed at 12:01, and which would you explain away? The answer defines the architecture, not the other way round.

## Incident response and contingency planning

At 11:39 a.m. Pacific Time on 4 October 2021, engineers at Facebook lost access to their own tools. The company's global services vanished from the public internet, not because of a cyber-attack or physical damage, but because a routine network change withdrew critical routes. For several hours, messaging apps failed, advertising dashboards froze, and internal badge systems reportedly stopped working at offices around Menlo Park, California. The outcome was measurable. Facebook later acknowledged lost revenue and widespread disruption. The more instructive detail lay elsewhere: when connectivity went, coordination went with it.

Plans met reality fast.

The incident is now a touchstone because it exposed a truth that architecture diagrams rarely capture. Connectivity shocks are not purely technical events. They are organisational tests. Systems fail at machine speed; responses move at human speed. The difference determines damage.

The first claim must be shown before it is named. During the Facebook outage, engineers struggled to reach routers because authentication systems depended on the same network paths that were down. Physical access was required. Name the pattern: *tool dependency collapse*. Explain it plainly. Incident response tools often sit inside the same connectivity envelope as the systems they manage. When the envelope tears, visibility and control fall together. The implication is operational. Response time stretches not because people hesitate, but because they cannot see.

Roles matter when clocks run.

Effective contingency planning begins with a simple behaviour: someone must be clearly in charge, and everyone must know who that is. This is not hierarchy for its own sake. It is a decision threshold. In well-rehearsed organisations, the handover from routine operations to incident command happens on objective signals—packet loss above a set percentage, latency beyond a defined window, customer impact crossing a numeric threshold. Trust becomes visible as a metric. When thresholds are vague, authority diffuses. Time leaks.

A second named example grounds the point. Following a major cloud outage in Europe in August 2020, the London Stock Exchange Group published a post-incident review noting delays in escalation between technical teams and business decision-makers. The systems recovered, but communication lagged. Name the behaviour: escalation friction.

Explain why it recurs. Technical teams focus on fixes; commercial teams need forecasts. Without a predefined bridge, each waits for the other. The implication is reputational. Markets forgive disruption faster than silence.

The quiet motif threading this section is mundane by design: *the call list*. It appears trivial. It fails often.

Consider a rehearsal conducted by a large European bank in Frankfurt in March 2019. The scenario was modest: partial loss of international connectivity affecting payment processing. The exercise revealed that while internal roles were well defined, contact details for a key cable operator were outdated. The number rang out. Emails bounced. The bank lost forty minutes before reaching the right network operations centre. Show the outcome. No systems were down in reality, but the rehearsal exposed a single point of organisational failure. Name it: *supplier opacity*. Explain its cause. Contracts change; people move; lists rot. The implication is practical. Contingency planning fails at the edges, not the centre.

Basics decide outcomes.

Communication channels deserve the same scrutiny as routers. During connectivity shocks, primary channels often degrade. Organisations that rely solely on corporate email or internal chat discover their fragility too late. The counter-example is instructive. During the 2018 undersea cable outage affecting parts of West Africa, several regional telecoms operators maintained parallel communication via satellite phones and public messaging platforms. Response coordination continued even as customer services struggled. Reconcile the lesson. Redundancy in communication is not a luxury; it is a precondition for action.

Non-technical teams are not spectators. Legal, communications, procurement, and customer support shape the arc of an incident. Pair the abstraction with behaviour. When customer communications are delayed pending technical certainty, rumours fill the gap. When statements acknowledge uncertainty early, expectations stabilise. During a multi-day connectivity disruption affecting New Zealand in January 2022, one major service provider issued time-stamped updates even when no new facts were available. Complaints still arrived. Panic did not. The metric was simple: update frequency.

Decision thresholds close the loop.

A credible limitation must be faced. Over-rehearsal can breed complacency. Teams that practise the same scenario repeatedly learn the script, not the principle. The reconciliation lies in variation. Exercises that change one variable—supplier unavailability, staff illness, regulatory constraint—force adaptive thinking. The implication is cultural. Contingency planning is a habit, not a checklist.

Documentation is the uncelebrated backbone. Runbooks that exist only as PDFs on internal drives fail when access fails. Organisations that succeed print critical contacts, store them offline, and review them quarterly. This is not nostalgia. It is risk arithmetic.

Metrics anchor judgement. Recovery Time Objective is not a slogan; it is a promise. When boards approve an RTO of four hours, they are funding staffing levels, tooling, and rehearsals consistent with that number. When reality drifts, the gap becomes visible only during crisis. The example of a Scandinavian logistics firm illustrates the point. After repeated near-misses caused by regional network issues in 2021, the firm revised its RTO for order intake from six hours to ninety minutes and funded additional on-call coverage. The change was boring. The effect was not.

The motif returns. *The call list.* Who answers at 03:00? Who has authority to spend? Who speaks publicly? Each unanswered question adds minutes. Minutes compound.

End where the pressure sits. Connectivity shocks will not become rarer. They will become more entangled. The unresolved test is stark: if the network went dark now, could your organisation coordinate for the first hour without improvisation? The answer is not in the diagram. It is in the rehearsal.

## Communicating outages to customers

At 06:12 local time on 13 January 2022, Tonga lost its primary international internet connection when the Hunga Tonga–Hunga Ha'apai volcanic eruption severed the country's sole submarine cable north of Nuku'alofa. Within hours, Digicel Tonga issued a short public statement confirming the break and warning that restoration could take weeks. The factual content was sparse. The tone was restrained. Over the following days, updates arrived at predictable intervals, even when there was little new to report. The outcome was paradoxical. Connectivity collapsed. Public trust largely held.

Silence would have been easier. It would also have been fatal.

The first claim must be shown before it is named. During the initial hours after the eruption, rumours spread rapidly through satellite phones and overseas social media. Some suggested deliberate sabotage. Others promised imminent restoration. Digicel's communications cut across the noise by doing something modest: fixing the timeline. Name the practice. *Temporal anchoring*. Explain it. By stating what was known, what was not, and when the next update would arrive, the operator gave customers a clock to hold on to. The implication was behavioural. Anxiety did not disappear, but it did not spiral.

Timing is the first discipline.

Outage communication fails most often at the start. Organisations wait for certainty that never comes. In cable-related incidents, early facts are incomplete by definition. Ships have not sailed. Faults are not yet located. Weather windows remain forecasts. The abstraction is uncertainty; the behaviour that tames it is early acknowledgement. In March 2020, when a cut to the AAE-1 cable disrupted services across parts of East Africa and the Middle East, several regional operators delayed public statements for more than twelve hours while engineering teams assessed rerouting. When messages finally appeared, customers had already filled the gap with speculation. Complaints surged. Call centres jammed. Name the failure: *acknowledgement lag*. The implication is operational. Support costs rise when communication waits for engineering certainty.

Tone does the next piece of work.

A credible counter-example tempers the argument. Over-disclosure can alarm. During a prolonged outage affecting parts of Pakistan in July 2021, one service provider published detailed technical descriptions of cable routes and failure points. The intention was transparency. The effect was confusion. Customers struggled to interpret diagrams and fixated on worst-case scenarios. Reconcile the tension. Effective tone sits between reassurance and candour. It avoids drama without denying difficulty. The metric is linguistic. Plain sentences outperform precision jargon under stress.

Facts travel better than feelings.

Content matters less for its volume than its structure. The most effective outage updates answer three questions, in order. What is happening. What customers should expect next. When the next update will arrive. Trust becomes visible when this structure repeats. During a multi-day cable repair affecting the Canary Islands in October 2019, Telefónica España issued twice-daily bulletins at fixed times. Early updates admitted uncertainty about repair duration. Later ones narrowed the window as vessels arrived and weather improved. Customers reported frustration with the outage, not with the communication. The distinction matters. One damages revenue. The other damages legitimacy.

The quiet motif threading this section is simple: *the next update time.* It appears mundane. It calms crowds.

Channels shape reach.

Cable-related outages often degrade the very platforms used for communication. Organisations that rely solely on affected channels compound the problem. The behaviour that counters this risk is channel diversification. During the 2018 undersea cable failure affecting Mauritania and Mali, several operators used SMS broadcasts—still functioning on local networks—to direct customers to radio updates. The abstraction is resilience; the visible decision is channel choice. The implication is inclusion. Communication that reaches only the least-affected customers deepens inequality.

Language choices signal control.

Words like "catastrophic" and "unprecedented" travel fast and age badly. They inflate expectations of drama and later provoke backlash when recovery proves slow but ordinary. The countervailing behaviour is calibrated language. In Tonga, Digicel's January 2022 statements avoided emotive descriptors, focusing instead on sequence: assessment, mobilisation, repair. This did not minimise hardship. It framed it. The implication is reputational. Calm language keeps options open when timelines slip.

Staged updates reveal character.

The most instructive examples are multi-day incidents where communication evolves. Consider the cable disruption affecting parts of the Faroe Islands in December 2020 after fishing activity damaged a regional link. Føroya Tele issued an initial acknowledgement within an hour, followed by daily updates. On day two, the company revised its repair estimate from "within 48 hours" to "several days" after weather deteriorated. The revision was explicit. Customers noticed. Complaints rose briefly, then stabilised. Contrast this with a neighbouring operator affected by the same incident that repeated the original estimate until it was obviously false. Trust eroded sharply. Name the contrast: *estimate correction versus estimate denial.* The implication is moral. Admitting error early preserves credibility.

A limitation deserves attention. Not all customers want detail. Enterprise clients seek timelines and contingencies. Residential users want reassurance and practical guidance. The reconciliation lies in layered communication. High-level public statements can coexist with targeted briefings to critical customers. The metric is segmentation, not verbosity.

### Measurement closes the loop

Effective organisations review communication performance after incidents. They measure call volumes, complaint ratios, social media sentiment, and churn in the weeks following restoration. These metrics translate tone into outcomes. After repeated cable disruptions affecting the Caribbean in 2017, one regional ISP adjusted its update cadence from ad hoc posts to fixed four-hour intervals during major incidents. The following year, complaint volumes during outages fell by nearly a third, according to the company's annual report. Numbers make trust legible.

The motif returns. *The next update time.* Miss it once, and confidence wobbles. Miss it twice, and narratives take over.

End with the unresolved test. When the cable breaks and facts are scarce, will your organisation speak early, plainly, and on schedule—or will it wait for certainty that never arrives? The outage will end either way. Reputation will not.

## Lessons for boards and senior leaders

On 30 July 2020, Microsoft confirmed that an outage affecting customers across Western Australia traced back to a cut on an international submarine cable landing near Perth. Cloud services degraded, not because data centres failed, but because traffic could not reach them. Within days, several Australian companies disclosed that their boards had asked a pointed follow-up: *where, exactly, does our connectivity break*? The question landed not in engineering teams but in boardrooms.

It was overdue.

Cable risk rarely announces itself in executive dashboards. It hides behind abstractions such as "network resilience" or "third-party dependency". The first lesson for boards is therefore empirical. Show the failure. In Perth, the visible behaviour was application latency spiking across multiple providers at once. Name the issue. *Route concentration*. Explain it. Redundant cloud regions shared the same physical ingress. The implication is governance. Oversight failed not because technology was weak, but because questions stopped at the logical layer.

Ask better questions.

Boards add value when they translate technical fragility into organisational exposure. The effective chair does not request a schematic. They ask for a map that fits on one page. What critical services depend on which international routes. Where those routes converge. How long recovery typically takes when they fail. The abstraction is risk appetite; the metric is time to restore service. In a 2021 review commissioned by a European retail bank after repeated payment delays, the board asked management to compare two scenarios: a single cable cut versus two cuts in the same corridor. The exercise revealed that both scenarios produced the same outcome after eight hours. Redundancy existed on paper. Not in practice.

Funding follows clarity.

Boards influence outcomes through budget choices. Cable resilience competes with visible growth projects and often loses because its benefits are probabilistic. The behaviour that changes this is comparison. When a North American technology firm led the development of a new trans-Pacific cable route announced in October 2021, its board approved capital on the basis of latency and capacity gains. Less publicised was the secondary effect: independence from congested consortium routes. Name the shift. *Strategic ownership*. Explain it. Control over routing alters failure modes. The implication for leaders elsewhere is uncomfortable. Buying capacity is not the same as owning resilience.

A credible limitation tempers enthusiasm. Ownership brings exposure. State-backed systems and big-tech projects alike assume maintenance and geopolitical risk. Boards must reconcile ambition with accountability. The governance move is not maximalism but balance: diversified access across owners and routes, reviewed annually.

Monitoring is not micromanagement.

Senior leaders often fear that asking technical questions drags them into operations. The opposite is true. Monitoring works when it focuses on outcomes. Effective boards request a small set of indicators: number of independent international routes supporting critical services; proportion of traffic that can reroute within defined time thresholds; results of the last failover exercise. These metrics turn resilience into something observable. In 2019, following a series of outages linked to Mediterranean cable disruptions, a listed logistics firm added a single line to its quarterly risk report: *percentage of revenue exposed to a single international corridor*. The number fell over two years. So did incident severity.

The quiet motif here is the *awkward question*. It appears in every successful intervention.

Translate engineering into governance language

Boards operate through challenge and consent. To be effective, cable risk must be framed in terms they recognise. Not packets, but payments. Not latency, but lost orders. During a resilience review requested by the board of a UK financial services company in February 2022, engineers were asked to present findings without acronyms. The result was stark. A single undersea corridor carried authentication traffic for three regulated services. Recovery time exceeded regulatory tolerance. The board authorised changes within weeks. Language unlocked action.

Counter-examples matter. There are organisations where boards over-react, demanding guarantees that no network can provide. This produces performative investment and brittle architectures. Reconcile the tension by naming uncertainty. Resilience reduces risk. It does not abolish it. Leaders who accept this make better trade-offs.

Oversight extends beyond the enterprise.

Senior leaders also shape expectations with partners and suppliers. Contracts often assume "best efforts" without testing what that means when cables fail. Boards can insist that management reviews service level assumptions against historical outage data. Where commitments exceed reality, risk migrates silently. In 2018, after a prolonged cable repair affected services in parts of West Africa, several multinational customers challenged penalties only to discover exclusions buried in contracts. Boards that later requested independent reviews adjusted sourcing strategies accordingly.

Culture completes the loop.

The final lesson is human. Organisations that handle cable incidents well share a trait: senior leaders are curious before crisis. They sponsor rehearsals. They attend debriefs. They ask why a failover took hours, not minutes. In one widely cited internal case from a Southeast Asian bank in 2020, a board-mandated simulation uncovered that emergency contact details for a key carrier were out of date. The fix cost nothing. The insight was priceless.

Return to the motif. *The awkward question.* When was our last review. What would fail first. Who decides when to spend.

End with the forward test. The next cable cut will arrive without warning. When it does, will your board already have asked the questions that matter—or will it discover its dependencies in real time?

# Chapter 12

# Future Paths For The Seabed Network

In August 2017, a research vessel crossed the Arctic Ocean following a route that, until recently, existed mainly in climate models and speculative maps. The ship was not laying cable, but its voyage sharpened a question that has since migrated from scientific journals into boardrooms and defence ministries alike: if the ice retreats, will the internet follow? The possibility of high-latitude subsea routes, once dismissed as impractical, has become a serious proposition. It promises shorter paths between continents. It also exposes infrastructure to some of the planet's least forgiving conditions.

The paradox is stark. The seabed network that underpins global communication has thrived by avoiding attention, hugging stable routes, and relying on incremental improvement. Now it is being asked to change shape. Climate, geopolitics, energy transition, and technological ambition are all pushing against the quiet logic that has governed cable design for decades. The future will not be a clean break. It will be uneven, contested, and layered over what already exists.

This chapter looks forward without drifting into fantasy. It treats the seabed network not as a single system awaiting reinvention, but as an evolving commons shaped by competing incentives and shared risks. The aim is not prediction, but orientation.

The first pressure comes from geography itself. Traditional cable routes cluster along well-understood corridors: transatlantic paths refined since the nineteenth century, trans-Pacific arcs shaped by depth and tectonics, coastal approaches negotiated with regulators and fishermen. Emerging proposals at higher latitudes challenge this inheritance. Shorter distances between Asia, Europe, and North America are alluring. Reduced latency is measurable. Yet every kilometre gained introduces new variables: ice scour, seasonal accessibility, sparse repair infrastructure, and overlapping sovereignty claims. Opportunity and vulnerability arrive together.

The significance is not confined to polar regions. Route diversification more broadly is entering a new phase. As traffic volumes grow and geopolitical risk concentrates around familiar chokepoints, operators and states are reassessing what counts as acceptable exposure. A proposed high-latitude link announced in the early 2020s illustrates this recalibration. It promised resilience through distance from congested corridors, while simultaneously raising questions about who would guarantee repairs in winter darkness. The visible decision was the route itself. The deeper implication was a willingness to trade one class of risk for another.

Energy adds a second layer. Power cables now share the seabed with fibre in ways that would have seemed exceptional a generation ago. Offshore wind, interconnectors, and data-hungry coastal economies are drawing infrastructure into common corridors. The efficiency gains are obvious: shared surveys, coordinated maintenance windows, political support framed around decarbonisation. Less visible are the coupling effects. When power and data converge physically, failures propagate differently. A damaged corridor can darken homes and silence networks at once. Resilience improves in some dimensions and thins in others.

This convergence forces a reframing of responsibility. Energy regulators, telecoms authorities, and maritime agencies often operate in parallel, not in concert. As combined corridors proliferate, governance lags behind engineering. An example from Northern Europe, where a single seabed route carries both electricity and international data traffic, shows how quickly interdependence outpaces policy. Planning assumptions built for separate systems strain when confronted with shared failure modes.

Satellites re-enter the conversation at this point, not as saviours but as complements. For decades, satellites and cables have been framed as rivals, a false binary sustained by marketing and misunderstanding. The reality has always been asymmetrical. Fibre carries the bulk. Satellites offer reach and flexibility. What changes now is integration. Low Earth orbit constellations reduce latency and increase capacity enough to play meaningful roles in contingency planning. They cannot replace subsea networks. They can buy time.

Hybrid architectures already exist. A multinational enterprise blending terrestrial fibre, subsea routes, and satellite links during a prolonged outage in the late 2010s demonstrated a pragmatic approach. Performance degraded, but services continued. The lesson is not technological triumph. It is design humility. Resilience emerges from diversity, not dominance.

Monitoring and repair form the fourth strand. The tools used to watch the seabed have advanced slowly, constrained by physics and cost. Yet incremental change is underway. Distributed sensing along fibres, autonomous underwater vehicles, and experimental repair concepts are being tested on limited routes. None promises revolution on a timetable that executives would recognise. Each nudges the boundary of what is observable and what is fixable.

The pattern matters. Change arrives unevenly. Well-funded corridors see experimentation first. Peripheral routes wait. This unevenness has implications for global equity and strategic stability. A world where some regions enjoy near-real-time seabed awareness while others rely on delayed fault reports is not neutral. It shapes response times, attribution debates, and trust between states.

All of this leads back to governance. The seabed network has always been international in practice and fragmented in oversight. Future paths magnify this tension. New routes cut across sensitive regions. Combined infrastructure blurs regulatory lines. Monitoring technologies raise questions about surveillance and consent. Satellites complicate jurisdiction. Treating cables as a shared interest does not dissolve rivalry, but it can bound it.

There are modest signs of progress. Regional agreements on infrastructure protection, information sharing, and incident coordination do not resolve deeper conflicts. They do establish norms. A recent accord between neighbouring coastal states, agreeing basic principles for protecting subsea assets without disclosing operational details, illustrates how cooperation can advance quietly. It is not a solution. It is a foundation.

The motif threading through this chapter is choice under constraint. Every future path involves trade-offs that cannot be optimised away. Shorter routes invite harsher environments. Shared corridors save money and create coupling. Satellites add resilience and complexity. New tools promise insight and raise expectations they cannot yet meet. Governance can lag or adapt.

The question is not whether the seabed network will change. It already is. The question is who shapes that change, and on what terms. As the final chapter looks ahead, it invites the reader to hold two ideas at once: that the internet's physical foundation remains stubbornly material, and that its future depends as much on collective restraint as on technical ingenuity.

## New routes and polar passages

In March 2019, the Finnish state-owned company Cinia announced plans for the *Far North Fiber* cable, a proposed subsea link running from Northern Europe to East Asia via the Arctic Ocean. The announcement, made in Helsinki, was modest in tone but radical in implication. By tracing a path along high latitudes rather than established southern corridors, the project promised a shorter route between continents and a measurable reduction in latency. It also forced an uncomfortable question into the open: could the planet's most hostile waters become part of the internet's everyday geography?

The answer, still unresolved, lies in the tension between distance and difficulty. A polar route compresses geography while expanding uncertainty. It offers fewer choke points and less congestion, yet exposes fibre to ice scour, sparse repair capacity, and a geopolitical theatre that has grown more crowded, not less. The Far North Fiber proposal did not fail because of a single flaw. It stalled because each advantage arrived paired with a cost that was hard to price.

That pairing — opportunity and vulnerability bound together — defines the current moment for new subsea routes.

The case for emerging paths begins with arithmetic. A cable running between Northern Europe and Northeast Asia through the Arctic is thousands of kilometres shorter than one looping through the Mediterranean, the Suez, the Indian Ocean, and the South China Sea. Shorter distance means lower latency, a metric that matters to cloud providers, financial traders, and real-time services. It also means fewer jurisdictions to cross and, potentially, fewer congested landing points. These are visible benefits, easily graphed and readily sold.

Yet arithmetic is only the opening move. The seabed is not a blank page. High-latitude routes intersect with environments that behave differently from temperate oceans. Ice does not merely float; it scrapes, anchors, and drags. Seasonal freeze and thaw alter seabed conditions year by year. Survey data ages quickly. A route judged safe one summer may not remain so after a winter of heavy ice movement. The implication is practical: uncertainty migrates from the construction phase into the operating life of the system.

This uncertainty reshapes how resilience is understood. Traditional routes trade distance for familiarity. Their risks are well catalogued: fishing activity, anchors, earthquakes, dense shipping lanes. Polar routes invert that balance. Human interference drops sharply, while environmental variability rises. The abstraction of *risk* becomes a set of decisions about ice class, burial depth, slack management, and the acceptability of longer repair windows. Each choice is legible on a balance sheet, but none removes the underlying exposure.

A second named example illustrates how this calculus has evolved. In 2020, the Russian operator Megafon completed the *Arctic Connect* terrestrial fibre project across Siberia, linking Europe and Asia along a high-latitude land corridor. While not subsea, the project served as a proof of concept for northern connectivity. It demonstrated demand for shorter paths and the willingness of states to invest in infrastructure that reinforces strategic geography. It also underscored a limitation: terrestrial routes concentrate risk in places where political control and physical security become inseparable. The lesson travelled south, informing subsea debates even when the medium differed.

Environmental constraints bleed into technical ones. Repair logistics are the quiet determinant of feasibility. A cable's resilience is not defined by how rarely it fails, but by how quickly it can be fixed. In the Arctic, ports capable of supporting cable ships are few and far between. Seasonal access narrows working windows. Weather delays stretch from days into weeks. The visible behaviour here is not speculative; it is the hard scheduling reality of vessels that cannot sail, crews that cannot work, and permits that cannot be expedited by urgency alone.

These constraints explain why high-latitude proposals often include redundancy within the route itself, such as additional slack or alternative landing points. They also explain why many projects remain proposals. The counter-example is instructive. Several Arctic cable concepts announced in the late 2010s attracted attention and then faded without construction. Their disappearance does not prove the routes were impossible. It shows that, when investors compared latency gains measured in milliseconds against repair delays measured in weeks, the equation often failed to close.

Reconciling ambition with restraint requires a broader view of resilience. New routes are not substitutes for existing ones; they are complements. A polar cable does not replace the trans-Pacific system it undercuts. It adds diversity. That diversity has value only if it is genuine. Two routes that diverge on a map but converge operationally — sharing the same repair assets, the same political dependencies, or the same climatic exposure — offer less protection than their diagrams suggest.

Geopolitics sharpens this point. High-latitude waters sit at the intersection of national interests that are neither settled nor static. Arctic coastal states assert extended continental shelves. Military presence has increased. Scientific research, commercial shipping, and resource extraction overlap. For cable owners, this translates into a regulatory environment that is permissive in principle and unpredictable in practice. Permits may be granted, but expectations can shift as strategic priorities change.

The Far North Fiber proposal made this visible without intending to. Its route planning assumed cooperation across multiple Arctic jurisdictions. The technical design could accommodate ice. The business case could accommodate cost overruns. What proved harder to accommodate was uncertainty about long-term access and protection in a region where signalling matters. The implication is subtle but important: resilience depends not only on engineering margins, but on diplomatic ones.

A quiet motif threads through these discussions: distance. Distance reduces congestion. Distance also stretches response. The same remoteness that shields a polar cable from anchors and trawlers isolates it from help. This duality appears again when environmental arguments enter the frame. Proponents of northern routes sometimes point to reduced shipping traffic and lower anthropogenic disturbance. Critics respond with concerns about fragile ecosystems and the difficulty of monitoring compliance. Both positions are grounded in observable behaviours — fewer vessels, fewer patrols — and neither resolves the trade-off.

It would be a mistake to read these tensions as a verdict against innovation. The history of subsea cables is a history of improbable routes becoming mundane. The first transatlantic cable was dismissed as reckless. It failed repeatedly before it worked. What differs now is scale and interdependence. The modern network is less forgiving of prolonged outages. Its users are less patient. Its failures propagate faster.

This is where a limitation must be acknowledged. New routes, especially polar ones, cannot be evaluated solely through the lens of resilience. They also redistribute risk. A state that hosts a landing station gains influence and responsibility. An operator that pioneers a route absorbs reputational exposure. An industry that normalises high-latitude cables commits itself to maintaining them under conditions that will not soften with time. Climate change opens passages and intensifies extremes simultaneously. That is not a slogan; it is a planning constraint.

The reconciliation lies in sequencing rather than replacement. Incremental deployment, limited capacity, and cautious integration into existing meshes allow learning without overcommitment. Experimental segments tested on less critical traffic provide data. They do not deliver salvation. This approach frustrates those seeking decisive leaps. It aligns with how infrastructure actually matures.

As this section closes, the unresolved tension remains deliberately in view. Shorter routes promise efficiency. Harsher environments demand patience. The diagnostic question is not whether polar passages *can* carry fibre. It is whether the institutions that depend on that fibre are prepared to accept a different rhythm of risk — one measured not just in milliseconds saved, but in days waited, seasons watched, and assumptions revised.

## Integrating power and data cables

In October 2018, National Grid and the Belgian transmission system operator Elia switched on the *Nemo Link*, a 140-kilometre subsea high-voltage direct current interconnector between Richborough in Kent and Zeebrugge in Belgium. The project was framed as an energy milestone, enabling electricity trading across the Channel. Less remarked upon was what followed beneath the surface. Along sections of its route, the power cable ran within a broader seabed corridor already dense with fibre-optic links carrying Europe's digital traffic. Power and data, once planned as distinct systems, had begun to share space, schedules, and risk.

Efficiency seduces quickly.

The logic behind such convergence is straightforward. Offshore wind farms require export cables. Interconnectors require carefully surveyed routes. Fibre cables need access to the same continental shelves and landing points. Aligning these projects promises savings in seabed surveys, permitting, and construction mobilisation. When vessels are scarce and ports congested, sharing effort looks prudent. The Nemo Link did not carry data itself, but it normalised the idea of coordinated corridors where energy and information infrastructure coexist.

That normalisation has spread.

A second example, farther north, illustrates the direction of travel. In 2021, the Danish Energy Agency approved sections of the *Viking Link*, a 765-kilometre HVDC interconnector between Denmark and the United Kingdom, landing at Bicker Fen in Lincolnshire. As with Nemo, the route intersected areas already mapped for telecommunications. Operators coordinated surveys and, in places, burial strategies. The visible behaviour was cooperation between industries that had previously planned in parallel. The implication was deeper interdependence, whether acknowledged or not.

The abstraction usually invoked here is *efficiency*. In practice, efficiency takes the form of fewer seabed disturbances, shorter permitting timelines, and shared mobilisation costs. These are measurable. Surveys cost millions. Installation vessels chartered at daily rates north of £200,000 do not wait idly. Combining projects compresses timelines and reduces duplication. For governments pursuing rapid energy transition while demanding resilient connectivity, the attraction is obvious.

Yet integration also concentrates exposure.

Power cables behave differently from fibre. They generate heat. They impose electromagnetic fields. They demand larger exclusion zones during installation and repair. When a power interconnector faults, response times are dictated by grid stability as much as by marine logistics. If data cables share a corridor, their fate becomes entangled with decisions made for a different system under a different regulatory regime.

This is not theoretical. In August 2020, an outage on the *BritNed* interconnector — another UK–Netherlands power link — removed 1,000 megawatts of capacity from the market. The fault lay within the cable itself. While no major fibre systems were damaged, the incident triggered heightened monitoring across nearby routes. Operators quietly reviewed whether coincident maintenance windows or emergency works could cascade into wider disruption. The episode did not cause a data outage. It caused a reassessment.

Risk, here, is not a single event. It is a coupling.

Coupling becomes visible during repair. Power cable repairs are slower and more intrusive than fibre splices. They require heavier equipment, larger crews, and extended safety zones. If a combined corridor is closed to accommodate a power repair, fibre operators may find themselves unable to access their own assets, even when undamaged. The metric that matters is not failure rate, but mean time to access. Delays measured in days matter to grid operators. Delays measured in weeks matter to digital services.

A credible counter-example tempers this concern. In parts of the North Sea, coordinated corridors have functioned without incident for years. Clear separation within the corridor, agreed protocols for access, and staggered maintenance windows have limited interference. This works best where governance is strong and operators few. It reconciles efficiency with resilience through discipline rather than optimism. The limitation is scale. As corridors grow busier and participants multiply, coordination costs rise faster than savings.

Environmental constraints sharpen the dilemma. Regulators increasingly encourage shared routes to minimise seabed disruption. From an ecological perspective, concentrating impact can be preferable to spreading it. From a resilience perspective, concentration raises stakes. The visible decision — approving a single corridor instead of three — carries different meanings depending on whether one values habitat protection or system redundancy more highly. Neither value is trivial. Neither can be maximised simultaneously.

The motif threading these choices is proximity. Bringing systems closer reduces cost. It also narrows margins. Proximity simplifies planning meetings and complicates incident response. It invites cooperation and amplifies disagreement. This is felt most acutely at landings, where power substations and cable landing stations increasingly neighbour one another. Shared security perimeters save money. They also create attractive targets and single points of access that demand higher assurance.

Ownership patterns complicate matters further. Power interconnectors are often state-backed or regulated monopolies. Fibre cables may be owned by consortia or technology firms. Their priorities diverge. A grid operator may accept a prolonged outage to ensure safety. A cloud provider may not. When assets share geography, whose threshold governs? The answer is rarely written in advance. It emerges under pressure.

The integration of power and data also blurs institutional boundaries. Energy regulators focus on supply security and price stability. Communications regulators focus on competition and consumer protection. Seabed infrastructure sits uneasily between them. The behaviour that reveals this tension is the proliferation of memoranda of understanding between agencies that once ignored one another. Coordination improves awareness. It does not eliminate jurisdictional friction.

Historical perspective helps. Subsea telegraph cables in the nineteenth century often followed shipping routes and, later, power lines on land. Co-location is not new. What is new is the speed and scale at which failure propagates. A delayed telegram mattered. A delayed data packet can halt trading systems, payment rails, or emergency services. The implication is that design tolerances inherited from one domain may be inadequate for the other.

Integration also invites new security questions. Power cables are critical national infrastructure. Their protection involves naval patrols and intelligence assessments. Fibre cables increasingly attract similar attention. When routes coincide, surveillance patterns overlap. This can be efficient. It can also create blind spots if assumptions diverge. A patrol optimised to deter sabotage of a power link may not detect subtle interference with data infrastructure. The decision to treat corridors as unified assets demands unified threat models. Those models are still evolving.

None of this argues for separation at all costs. It argues for intentional design. Where integration occurs, it should be deliberate, governed, and reversible where possible. Technical measures such as increased physical separation within corridors, redundant landing points, and independent access agreements reduce coupling. They do not remove it. They price it.

The final implication concerns narratives of transition. As offshore wind expands and data demand accelerates, the seabed becomes crowded. Integrating infrastructure appears as a rational response to scarcity. It may be. The unresolved tension is whether integration becomes a default rather than a choice. Defaults harden quickly. They outlast the conditions that justified them.

The forward test is simple to state and difficult to answer. When power and data share the same ground, whose resilience defines acceptable risk — and who decides when efficiency has gone far enough?

## Satellites as partial backup

On 26 February 2022, two days after Russian forces crossed into Ukraine, SpaceX activated Starlink terminals across Kyiv and other cities. The request came via a public exchange involving Elon Musk; the outcome was concrete. Connectivity persisted for hospitals, government offices, and emergency responders despite widespread disruption to terrestrial networks. Satellites did not replace Ukraine's fibre backbone. They bridged a gap. The episode fixed a new idea in policy circles: space-based links as a *stopgap*, not a substitute.

That distinction matters.

For three decades, satellites have been cast either as the future of global connectivity or as a relic overtaken by glass. Both caricatures miss the point. Subsea cables carry the overwhelming majority of international data because physics favours fibre: lower latency, higher capacity, predictable costs. Satellites persist because geography and failure do not respect neat hierarchies. When cables fail, satellites are there. The question is not whether satellites can replace cables, but when and how they can *meaningfully back them up*.

Capacity sets the first boundary. A single modern transoceanic cable can carry tens of terabits per second. Low Earth orbit constellations operate at a different scale. Starlink's publicly stated capacity figures have evolved, but even generous estimates place aggregate throughput orders of magnitude below that of major fibre routes. The visible metric here is not ambition but bandwidth delivered per user under load. During crises, satellites prioritise essential services, not bulk traffic. That constraint is not a flaw. It defines the role.

Latency defines the second boundary. LEO systems reduce delay compared with geostationary satellites, making real-time applications feasible. They do not outperform fibre. For resilience planning, the implication is clear: satellites can sustain control planes, voice, and essential data flows. They cannot invisibly absorb the loss of a major cable without users noticing. Expectation management becomes part of architecture.

A second example grounds this reality. In 2021, OneWeb completed its initial LEO constellation phase, with a focus on enterprise and government connectivity rather than mass consumer traffic. Tests conducted with partners in Alaska and northern Canada demonstrated reliable links for remote sites poorly served by fibre. When wildfires disrupted terrestrial routes in parts of Alaska in 2022, satellite links maintained essential connectivity for local authorities. Again, the outcome was continuity, not parity. Fibre carried the bulk when available. Satellites carried what mattered when it was not.

The abstraction often invoked is *resilience*. In practice, resilience is measured by recovery time and service prioritisation. Satellites score well on the first and modestly on the second. They can be activated quickly, rerouted dynamically, and scaled incrementally. They struggle with sustained, high-volume demand. This pairing is precisely why they complement cables rather than compete with them.

Hybrid architectures make this explicit. A pragmatic design blends fibre for steady-state traffic with satellite links reserved for failover and surge. Traffic engineering policies decide what moves where under stress. During normal operations, satellites idle or serve niche markets. During disruption, they light up. The quiet motif here is the *narrow bridge*: satellites span the gap while the main road is repaired. They are not the road.

A concrete illustration comes from the Pacific. Following repeated cable outages affecting island states such as Tonga, regional operators and governments explored hybrid solutions combining new fibre routes with satellite backup agreements. After the January 2022 volcanic eruption severed the sole international cable, satellites restored basic connectivity within days, while repairs took weeks. Subsequent planning did not abandon cables; it added redundancy and pre-arranged satellite capacity. The decision behaviour shifted from improvisation to rehearsal.

There is a counter-example worth confronting. Some advocates argue that rapidly expanding LEO constellations will soon render cables redundant. The limitation is economic as much as technical. Launch costs have fallen, but maintaining thousands of satellites, managing spectrum, and replacing hardware every few years imposes a cost curve unlike fibre's long depreciation cycles. Cables are expensive to build and cheap to operate. Satellites invert that ratio. Reconciling the two means accepting that satellites excel in responsiveness, cables in endurance.

Security considerations complicate the picture. Satellites are exposed to different threats than cables: jamming, cyber intrusion, and space debris rather than anchors and trawls. Diversifying across domains reduces correlated risk. It also multiplies attack surfaces. The visible decision here is governance. Organisations that integrate satellite backup must decide who controls activation, how authentication works, and how reliance is audited. These are not engineering afterthoughts. They are board-level questions.

Regulation lags architecture. Subsea cables operate within established legal frameworks, however imperfect. Satellite services cross borders with lighter touch, relying on spectrum coordination and licensing regimes that vary widely. During emergencies, governments may welcome rapid activation. During normal times, they scrutinise foreign-owned constellations carrying domestic traffic. The implication is political as well as technical. Hybrid resilience requires diplomatic comfort as much as bandwidth.

Environmental considerations add another layer. Fibre lies quietly once installed. Satellites contribute to orbital congestion. Responsible use of space is becoming a shared concern, with debris mitigation guidelines tightening. Resilience planning that leans heavily on satellites must account for sustainability beyond the immediate crisis. This is not a reason to reject satellites. It is a reason to bound their role.

The quiet motif returns when planning moves from theory to contracts. Satellite backup that exists only as a concept fails when needed. The visible metric is pre-committed capacity with defined service levels. Organisations that secured such arrangements before incidents recovered faster than those scrambling afterwards. This mirrors lessons from cable repair planning: preparedness beats heroics.

For national planners, satellites offer strategic optionality. They complicate an adversary's calculus by providing alternative paths. They reassure citizens that connectivity is not brittle. They do not remove vulnerability; they redistribute it. The unresolved tension is allocation. How much investment belongs in space-based backup versus additional fibre routes, better repair capacity, or diplomatic risk reduction?

The forward test is straightforward to pose. When the next major cable disruption occurs, will satellite links be treated as a last resort improvisation, or as a rehearsed, limited, and trusted bridge designed precisely for that moment?

## New monitoring and repair technologies

In October 2020, off the coast of Trondheim, the Norwegian research organisation SINTEF announced the results of a quiet experiment. Working with partners from the offshore energy sector, it had tested autonomous underwater vehicles along a short stretch of seabed infrastructure in the Norwegian Sea. The outcome was modest but concrete: repeated, high-resolution inspections without a crewed vessel hovering above. No cables were repaired that month. Something subtler happened instead. The assumption that humans must always be on site began to loosen.

That shift frames the future of seabed protection more accurately than any dramatic promise. For over a century, cable repair has followed a recognisable rhythm: fault detection from shore, mobilisation of a specialist ship, grappling, lifting, splicing, redeployment. It works. It is also slow, expensive, and unevenly distributed. New technologies are not rewriting this script overnight. They are adding footnotes, marginal gains, and occasional detours. The direction matters precisely because the destination remains uncertain.

Monitoring comes first. Today's baseline relies on indirect signals: traffic loss, power anomalies, acoustic cues, and vessel tracking data. The abstraction is *situational awareness*. The visible behaviour is inference. A break occurs; operators deduce where and why. Emerging sensing technologies aim to narrow that gap between event and understanding. Distributed acoustic sensing, which turns fibre itself into a vibration detector, has been demonstrated on terrestrial networks and, in limited cases, subsea segments. The metric is resolution: the ability to distinguish a trawler from a seismic event, or benign movement from deliberate interference.

A checkable example sits in the North Sea. In 2019, research led by the UK's National Physical Laboratory explored the use of existing subsea cables for environmental and activity monitoring, leveraging laser-based sensing techniques. The experiments showed that cables could register acoustic signatures kilometres away. The implication is tantalising but bounded. Retrofitting legacy systems is complex. Data interpretation requires calibration and trust. Operators must decide whether the benefit justifies the noise.

Autonomous inspection extends the same logic. Remotely operated vehicles already play a role, but they depend on support ships. Autonomous underwater vehicles promise persistence: pre-programmed patrols along critical routes, returning data without continuous human control. In practice, their deployment remains limited to shallow or controlled environments. Battery life, navigation accuracy, and recovery logistics constrain scale. The counter-example is instructive. In deep ocean routes thousands of kilometres long, autonomy solves only part of the problem. It sees more, but not everywhere.

Repair technologies lag further behind. The idea of a robot repairing a live deep-sea cable captures imaginations and funding pitches alike. The reality is incremental. Experimental concepts focus on pre-positioned tools, modular joints, and partial automation of splicing under human supervision. In 2021, Japan's NTT and partners tested robotic assistance for cable handling in controlled conditions. The outcome was improved precision, not independence. Humans still directed the critical steps.

The abstraction here is *speed*. Faster repair reduces economic and political fallout. The visible metric is days offline. New tools may shave hours or days at the margins, particularly in shallow waters and busy corridors. They do not eliminate the need for ships, crews, or weather windows. Reconciling expectation with capability is essential. Overpromising erodes trust.

Uneven adoption defines the landscape. Wealthy regions with dense infrastructure and overlapping industries—energy, telecommunications, research—act as testbeds. Peripheral routes wait. This unevenness mirrors cable deployment itself. Innovation arrives where incentives align. The implication for global resilience is uncomfortable. The routes most vulnerable to disruption are often the least likely to see early technological upgrades.

There is a second example worth naming. In 2022, the EU-backed SMART Cables initiative advanced plans to integrate environmental sensors into new subsea cables linking the Mediterranean. The primary goal was tsunami and earthquake detection. Cable protection was secondary. The dual-use nature of the system illustrates a recurring pattern: monitoring gains traction when it serves multiple constituencies. The implication is strategic. Cable owners rarely fund sensing purely for security; they fund it when it delivers broader value.

Governance follows technology, not the reverse. More sensors generate more data. Who owns it? Who interprets it? When does a vibration become a reportable incident? Underfunded agencies struggle to act even when signals exist. The gap between detection and response remains. New tools tighten one end of the chain. They do not automatically strengthen the rest.

A credible limitation deserves attention. False positives carry cost. Increased sensitivity can lead to alarm fatigue, diverting resources and eroding confidence. The visible decision here is threshold setting. Operators must choose what to ignore. This is not purely technical; it reflects risk appetite and political context. In contested waters, caution competes with escalation anxiety.

The quiet motif threading these developments is *distance*. Technologies aim to reduce the distance between seabed and decision-maker, between event and understanding. They succeed partially. Distance remains. Oceans are vast. Repairs still require steel hulls and skilled hands.

Looking ahead, scenarios rather than forecasts are appropriate. One scenario sees incremental automation clustered around critical choke points, paired with improved data sharing between operators and states. Another sees fragmented adoption, with islands of sophistication amid long stretches of traditional practice. A third imagines crisis-driven acceleration after a high-profile incident exposes existing limits. None eliminate cables' physical vulnerability. All reshape how it is managed.

The unresolved tension sits with investment discipline. How much should be spent on emerging tools that promise marginal gains when proven measures—more repair ships, better coordination, clearer governance—remain underfunded? The forward test is simple to state and hard to answer. When the next break occurs, will new technologies meaningfully change the timeline, or merely explain the delay with greater precision?

## Building a more resilient global commons

In January 2023, representatives of the European Union and NATO stood together in Brussels to issue a joint statement on the protection of critical infrastructure. The document was short, deliberately cautious, and light on technical detail. Its concrete outcome lay elsewhere. Two organisations with different memberships and histories agreed, in public, that undersea cables and pipelines were a shared concern requiring coordination rather than competition. Five words captured the mood. *This is about restraint.*

That moment matters because it cuts against an easy assumption. Subsea cables sit at the intersection of sovereignty and interdependence, a place where rivalry often overwhelms cooperation. They cross borders without stopping. They serve states that mistrust one another. They are owned by consortia whose members may be commercial competitors or geopolitical adversaries. The paradox is clear. How can infrastructure so entangled with national power be treated as a common interest?

The answer, if one exists, lies less in grand bargains than in modest habits. The history of cable protection shows that stability emerges not from universal trust but from shared expectations about behaviour. The question is not whether rivalry disappears. It is whether it can be bounded.

The abstraction is *governance*. The visible behaviour is coordination. States already cooperate over flight safety, maritime distress signals, and disease surveillance. Each system rests on the same logic: information sharing, basic norms, and the acceptance that some risks cannot be managed alone. Subsea cables fit this pattern awkwardly but persistently. They are civilian infrastructure with strategic effects. That duality has always been present. It is now harder to ignore.

One concrete example predates recent tensions. In 2008, following multiple cable breaks in the Mediterranean that disrupted connectivity across North Africa and the Middle East, regional operators and governments began informal coordination on repair access and maritime awareness. No treaty emerged. What changed was practice. Repair vessels received clearer passage. Authorities shared timelines. The metric was downtime. It fell. The implication is instructive. Cooperation does not require consensus on everything. It requires agreement on enough.

Formal law provides only part of the framework. International conventions establish freedoms and obligations, but they say little about day-to-day protection. That gap is filled by guidelines, confidence-building measures, and professional norms. The International Cable Protection Committee, a technical body rather than a political one, exemplifies this approach. It produces recommendations, not rules. States and operators choose to follow them because they work. The visible decision is compliance without coercion.

A second named example sits in Southeast Asia. In September 2022, ASEAN defence ministers endorsed principles on safeguarding critical infrastructure, including undersea cables, during their meeting in Cambodia. The language was careful. No adversary was named. The outcome was modest: a shared reference point. The implication is nonetheless significant. Regional forums can articulate norms even when strategic competition persists among members.

There are limits. A credible counter-example is the reluctance of some states to share incident data, citing national security. The abstraction is *trust*. The visible behaviour is silence. When a cable is damaged under ambiguous circumstances, attribution becomes political. Without information sharing, rumours fill the gap. The reconciliation lies in partial disclosure. States need not reveal capabilities to signal concern. They can share timelines, locations, and repair status. This is not transparency for its own sake. It is stability management.

Ownership complicates the picture. Private companies lay and operate most cables. Governments regulate access and security. Their priorities diverge. Operators measure cost and uptime. States measure risk and control. Effective governance aligns incentives. One visible mechanism is joint exercises involving regulators, navies, and cable owners. These do not rehearse conflict. They rehearse coordination. The metric is response time to benign incidents. The benefit transfers to malign scenarios without explicit rehearsal.

The quiet motif threading this discussion is *the seam*. Cables run along seams: between jurisdictions, between public and private authority, between peace and conflict. Resilience emerges when those seams are reinforced rather than pulled apart. Governance does that work. It is unglamorous. It rarely makes headlines.

Data supports caution. The International Telecommunication Union noted in its 2021 resilience reports that most cable outages still result from accidental damage, not hostile acts. This fact undercuts alarmism while strengthening the case for shared protection. If the majority of risk is non-political, then cooperative mitigation pays dividends regardless of geopolitical climate.

That does not dissolve rivalry. It reframes it. States may compete over routes, standards, and influence. They may still signal strength through patrols and statements. The boundary condition is clear. Deliberate harm to shared infrastructure escalates quickly and unpredictably. The visible decision many states make is restraint. They invest in protection and signalling rather than disruption.

Insurance markets offer a parallel. Insurers price risk based on pooled data. They function because participants accept shared exposure. When disputes arise, they are resolved through established processes. The abstraction is *risk transfer*. The behaviour is claims adjustment. Governance of cables borrows this logic at a larger scale. States absorb some uncertainty to reduce systemic shock.

The final implication concerns leadership. Treating cables as a global commons does not mean declaring them neutral or removing them from politics. It means recognising that some interests overlap even when values do not. The forward test is practical. When the next incident occurs in contested waters, will states default to accusation and silence, or to communication and repair?

The answer will not arrive in a single agreement. It will be assembled from statements, habits, and expectations. From Brussels to Phnom Penh, those pieces exist. The tension remains unresolved. That may be enough.

# About the Author

Dalia Aouni writes at the point where technology, security and everyday life intersect. Her work focuses on the physical foundations of the digital world, from cable routes and landing stations to ship movements and repair logistics. Rather than treating connectivity as an abstract cloud, she is interested in the pipes, fibres and contracts that make it possible, and in how they respond under political and environmental stress. Growing up around port cities that once hosted telegraph lines and early radio stations, she developed a lasting curiosity about how empires and alliances shape communications infrastructure. That historical thread runs through her writing, linking nineteenth-century cables and codebooks to today's debates over national security and data sovereignty. In this book, she sets out to give readers clear language and practical mental models for thinking about seabed networks: who builds them, who relies on them and who might seek to disrupt them. Her aim is not to alarm, but to help readers see an invisible system clearly enough to ask better questions about its future.

9 788199 802636

Printed at Repro India Ltd.